AMERICAN INDIANS, AMERICAN JUSTICE

American Indians, American Justice

Vine Deloria, Jr., and Clifford M. Lytle

 University of Texas Press, Austin

Requests for permission to reproduce material from this work
should be sent to Permissions, University of Texas Press,
Box 7819, Austin, Texas 78712.

LIBRARY OF CONGRESS CATALOGING IN PUBLICATION DATA
Deloria, Vine.
   American Indians, American Justice.
   Bibliography: p.
   Includes indexes.
    1. Indians of North America—Courts. 2. Indians of
North America—Legal status, laws, etc. 3. Courts—
United States. I. Lytle, Clifford M. II. Title.
KF8224.C6D44   1983   347.73′1′08997   83-6975
ISBN 0-292-73833-1   347.307108997
ISBN 0-292-73834-X (pbk.)

TO ROBERT BLAKE,
who almost looked the part

Contents

Introduction   ix

1. American Indians in Historical Perspective   1
   Discovery, Conquest, and Treaty-Making (1532–1828)   2
   Removal and Relocation (1828–1887)   6
   Allotment and Assimilation (1887–1928)   8
   Reorganization and Self-Government (1928–1945)   12
   Termination (1945–1961)   15
   → Self-Determination (1961–Present)   21

2. Federal Responsibility and Power over Indian Affairs   25
   Roots of Federal Responsibility   25
   → The Sources of Federal Power   34

3. Indian Country   58

4. The Evolution of Tribal Governments   80
   Traditional Forms of Tribal Government   82
   Transitional Tribal Governments   89
   → Tribal Government in Modern Perspective   99
   → Tribal Government and Contemporary Problems   105

5. The Indian Judicial System   110
   The Development of the Indian Court System   111
   Tribal Judges   120
   Tribal Courts and the 1968 Indian Civil Rights Act   126
   Federal Review of Tribal Court Decisions   131
   → The Tribal Court System: An Assessment   136

6. The Role of Attorneys, Advocates, and Legal Interest
   Groups in the Indian System of Law   139
   Indian Attorneys and American Society   140
   Attorneys and Advocates in an Indian Setting   148
   Indian Legal Services Attorneys   151
   → Indian Legal Interest Groups   155

7. The Criminal System of Justice in Indian Country   161
    Federal Statutes and Criminal Law   162
    Criminal Jurisdiction: Bringing Order to a Complex Maze   178
    Law Enforcement and Criminal Prosecution   182
    Special Problems in Law Enforcement   187

8. The Civil System of Justice in Indian Country   193
    Traditional Civil Law   194
    The Civil System in Operation   198
    Immunity from State Encroachment   203
    The Indian-State Conflict of Laws   209

9. Public Policy and the Legal Rights of Indians   216
    The Civil Liberties of American Indians   217
    American Indian Religious Freedom   230
    The Right to Basic Governmental Services   239

Bibliographic References   247
Index of Cases   251
Index of Topics   255

Introduction

American Indians seem an enigma to most other Americans. The images portrayed in the movies, whether of noble redman or bloodthirsty savage, recall the stereotypes of western history. Newspaper stories dealing with oil wells, uranium mining, land claims, and the occupation of public buildings and reservation hamlets almost seem to speak of another group altogether and it is difficult to connect the two perceptions of Indians in any single and comprehensible reality. Literature on Indians provides no clues to understanding the present or remembering the past. Much contemporary literature is a thinly disguised romanticism that looks at Indians as the last and best spiritual hope for a society disheartened and disorganized.

Were a serious reader to attempt to understand the complexities of the present Indian situation, particularly in the fields of legal and political rights, he or she would not find much that is helpful. The classic treatise on Indian rights, the *Handbook of Federal Indian Law*, by Felix S. Cohen, has been revised twice and, although the authors and sponsors of the second and third editions cautioned that it must be understood as a reference work rather than an unassailable authority, it is viewed by everyone who uses it as the ultimate expression of Indian law. But the *Handbook of Federal Indian Law* is very specific in its intent: it is designed to be a ready and concise manual for the practicing attorney or judge who, suddenly confronted with an Indian case, can gain immediate understanding of the complexity of the topic while reviewing the major cases and statutes that have established both law and policy in such exotic subjects as Indian treaties, water rights, taxation, civil and criminal jurisdiction, and property.

Cohen's masterpiece is designed to educate the specialists in federal law dealing with Indians, but it does not seek to provide much understanding of the manner in which things happened or how the different subjects came to be regarded as important. The

Handbook will outline the powers of tribal governments without so much as a sketchy discussion of what tribal governments are and how they came to be. Other studies attempting to provide information on legal and political rights of American Indians seem to view Cohen's work as the mountain they must scale in order to view the landscape. Some treatises seek to state the present condition of Indians in legal terminology. Other studies attempt to trace the flow of political power from one sovereign to another without telling the reader what sovereignty means in the modern world. The student is generally as baffled when he or she finishes the work as when the first page was turned, and the historical-cultural dimension of Indian life, its antecedents and its philosophical values, and the practicalities of modern Indian life remain hidden from view.

This study does not purport to be an exhaustive encyclopedia of the legal and political rights of American Indians. Rather, it focuses on a particular institution—the judicial branch of government. Courts—federal, state, and tribal—have become the most important branch of government. More than the legislative arm, which seems generally to frustrate the citizen, or the executive branch, which has recently appeared to be a futile exercise in public relations, the judicial institutions of our country affect most intimately the conduct of our lives. Whether a person views the Constitution as truth written in granite in 1789 or sees it as a flexible document capable of reinterpretation by each generation, few will deny that when a court announces its decision in a case certain things change and perceptions of society are never quite the same again.

In choosing the judicial function of government as the subject of a study, we therefore place ourselves in a position where we can see how law affects people. There are no abstract ideologies and concepts in a court of law although at times it appears that the judges do speak of a different world than that in which we live. Nevertheless, within the courts we find the tools whereby a society adjusts its daily patterns of behavior and where other institutions, both public and private, learn about the boundaries of acceptable behavior and conduct themselves accordingly.

Providing the student and the interested layperson with a study of tribal courts involves a recognition that most people do not understand how non-Indian judicial institutions operate. Thus it is not possible to examine and comment on tribal judicial institutions without referring to the corresponding non-Indian institutions so that where differences exist they will appear as clearly as possible. This study provides both historical and cultural background in American Indian history as well as comparisons with non-Indian institutions and their manner of operation. This format enables us to see how Indian tribes, once completely independent of all external influences, have adapted their institutions, customs, and values to the necessity of living in the modern world. While many Americans yearn for the romantic days of the past when seemingly noble Indian chiefs provided us with memorable aphorisms regarding the meaning of life, American Indians today do not live in that world. Like other Americans they have to adjust to economic trends, respond to changes in political climate and thought, and act responsibly in relation to others. Indians have survived and that means that they have successfully and consistently adapted themselves and their institutions to new situations.

Indian tribes, as we shall see, were once primarily judicial in the sense that the council, whether it was that of a village, a league of tribes, or a simple hunting band, looked to custom and precedent in resolving novel and difficult social questions that arose. Tribes were homogeneous units—linguistically, religiously, economically, and politically. All aspects of life were interwoven so that there were no sharp distinctions between the various aspects of life such as those we see in today's world. Everyone knew and respected the customs and beliefs of the tribal community. The task of the council, when it had a difficult question to resolve, was to appeal to that larger sense of reality shared by the people of the community and to reach a decision that people would see as consonant with the tradition. Few new laws or customs were needed and when these occasions presented themselves the homogeneity of the community made the adoption of the innovation simple. Executive leadership in most tribes depended almost wholly on the prestige and charisma of individuals so that Indian chiefs did not need a program or platform to announce to establish their leadership in the community.

With the coming of the white settlers, Indians faced the problem of adjusting to new realities. Had the tribes abandoned their old ways and wholeheartedly adopted the new institutions of the intruders, we would have no identifiable Indians today. On the other hand, if they had absolutely resisted any changes, we most probably would not have Indians today either. Tribes might have stubbornly held their ground but they would not have been able to withstand many of the overtures and intrusions that contact with Europeans made inevitable and they most probably would have perished in their effort to remain stationary while the world about them changed. Consequently, tribes everywhere adjusted cautiously and did their best to keep what was good in the old culture while adopting those things that helped them deal with new realities and new people.

Indians will be with us for the foreseeable future. After a period of nearly five centuries of almost continuous contact with European culture, Indian tribes do not resemble the pristine and stable societies that existed in the remote past, but they do resemble those societies enough so that, given a choice between Indian society and non-Indian society, most Indians feel comfortable with their own institutions, lands, and traditions. In order to perpetuate themselves, tribes have successfully used many of the institutions of the non-Indian as a defense against further intrusions and erosions. Tribal courts have been one of the most successful institutions in assisting Indians to defend themselves against too rapid change and destruction, although it has not been until recently that tribal courts have received any significant financial support for their operations.

The social legislation of the last two decades sought to help reservations build the proper institutions for local self-government. In addition to locally controlled schools and economic development projects, tribal courts have been the beneficiaries of this new policy of self-determination. Although federal funding has been drastically reduced with the onset of the Reagan administration, there is every indication that tribal judicial systems have become an integral part of Indian life so that they will be able to survive and grow. Such pieces of legislation as the Indian Civil Rights Act and the Indian Child Welfare Act have provided tribal courts with a new basis for exercising their powers, and as the provisions of these acts take hold and become a part of contemporary Indian life tribal courts will also grow and prosper.

This study is designed to provide the reader with a knowledge of the Indian judicial system as it has come to be in our generation. Many cases and statutes are cited here but primarily for the purposes of illumination of the issues and understanding. A great deal of attention has been paid to the historical antecedents of tribal institutions. The sharp cleavages that many students of Indian affairs believe to exist are more abstract and remote than they would like to believe. In the daily lives of people on the reservations certain practical compromises are always in order and we have tried to highlight the practical aspect of life rather than the theoretical.

Those readers who wish to go into great depth concerning a particular legal or political problem can most certainly find the precision and sophistication they seek in the latest revision of the *Handbook of Federal Indian Law*. Our volume, on the other hand, should be particularly useful for the student of Indian affairs, the teacher of social science, the scholar in a related field, and the tribal council person who wishes to find in one place a comprehensive overview of the subject matter. Although future cases may alter somewhat particular interpretations of certain doctrines of law, they will most certainly not alter the manner in which the tribal judicial system has come into being and is recorded here.

As both Indians and non-Indians seek to refine their judicial institutions and make them more suitable for community purposes, we can anticipate institutional and procedural changes. Such new functions and tasks can only be understood in a historical perspective and, once understood as a continuing process of human adjustment to social realities, changes become second nature and are accepted without question. The spectrum of Indian life as we have experienced it in the last two decades indicates that Indian people are increasingly returning to examine their ancient traditions with the intent of adapting them to modern problems. Therefore, it is imperative that people understand the usefulness of tradition in human affairs. With the hope that as future problems arise our framework of interpretation will prove increasingly useful in understanding social and judicial change, we have tried, wherever possible, to give special emphasis to the manner in which Indians use tradition and informal procedures.

The efficacy of law ultimately depends on society's perception of its ability to provide justice. People obey laws they consider just and rebel at laws they see as unjust; but the perception is not rational, it is emotional. Indian people, from the establishment of the reservations, were forced into a situation where they could not always perceive the justness of federal laws. And the federal laws were not always just, nor were they suited to the needs of many tribes. In recent decades the great gulf that once existed between the Indian people's perception of law and its effect on their lives has considerably narrowed. The predictable result of this change is that tribal judicial systems have gained much respect and have become an important part of the everyday lives of people. We hope this study will contribute to further understanding of the judicial process and assist tribal courts in their task of helping Indians govern themselves.

AMERICAN INDIANS, AMERICAN JUSTICE

1. American Indians in Historical Perspective

American Indians are a unique branch of the human family possessing a wide variety of cultural expressions, origins, and traditions. The very diversity of Indian tribes has dampened efforts to treat Indians as a monolithic group although historians have often struggled to bring meaning and understanding to what the non-Indian community views as "the Indians." Almost all generalizations that have been constructed to explain the nature of Indian life have dissolved when the particularities of tribal existence have been noted. Complicating an analysis of Indian history is the fact that it has been written largely from the non-Indian point of view by advocates of that position. The perspective of the non-Indian, generally colored by the uncritical acceptance of cultural evolution as the definitive experience of our species, has rarely coincided with the view from the reservation. Some Indian advocates would argue against cultural evolution, feeling that it is not an accurate characterization of events that their traditions inform them have been most important in shaping their perception of the world.

It is impossible to understand American Indians in their contemporary setting without first gaining some knowledge of their history as it has been formed and shaped by the Indian experience with Western civilization. Many of the customs and traditions of the past persist in the minds and lives of Indians today and have been jealously preserved over several centuries of contact with non-Indians as the last remaining values that distinguish Indians from the people around them. This is particularly true in the case of Indian notions of law and justice. Indian judicial systems call upon a special blending of the past and the present in order to solve intratribal disputes. This blending has not been an easy task. Indians must continually choose to follow the dictates of their traditions or to accept the values of the outsider. History, therefore, cannot be divorced from an analysis of American Indian life. But it must be tempered with a knowledge of the Indian perspective, which provides it with the substance for understanding the cultural conflict it represents.

The following historical examination will be divided into separate periods of federal Indian policy, each phase of which may be characterized by the impact of some kind of federal initiative in resolving the continuing problem of dealing with American Indians. With this tentative outline of policy development in hand, we will be better able to understand the development and operation of the contemporary Indian legal system. We will be able to see its historical roots and note the expedient compromises that both Indians and non-Indians made and must continue to make in order to ensure that the institutions that affect people today continue to grow and to serve people. Division of Indian history into six separate periods, then, is a convenient way of giving us sufficient data for reflection and orientation so that we can transcend mere information and come to our own conclusions about the future of Indian societies as exemplified in their contemporary institutions.

DISCOVERY, CONQUEST, AND TREATY-MAKING (1532–1828)

When the European settlers arrived in America, long before the establishment of the United States government, they were faced with a formidable problem. How were the newly arrived immigrants to deal with the native inhabitants of the land—the American Indians? The laws of discovery and conquest had been applied in different fashions throughout human history. Those who discovered and conquered other lands were entitled to them, their riches, and their spoils. The conquered people could be treated as slaves, banished to other lands, or assimilated into the society and institutions of the conquering people. Indeed, human history had been the story of conquest, assimilation or extinction, and yet more conquest. But the discovery of America was different. New continents had not been conquered before and the richness of the prize inspired the maritime powers of Europe to gain whatever advantages they might in the new hemisphere.

Felix Cohen traced the historical antecedents of Indian legal history back to 1532, when the popularly supported solution to the European dilemma on Indian relations was conceived. At that time the emperor of Spain, a devout Catholic monarch, in order to ensure that his country followed the dictates of the religion it strongly professed, sought the advice of Francisco de Vitoria, a prominent theologian, as to the rights the Spanish should claim in the new world (Cohen, p. 46). Vitoria reached the conclusion that the natives were the true owners of the land. Since the Indians owned the land, the Spanish could not claim title through discovery, for title by discovery could only be justified where property is ownerless (Vitoria, p. 139). Furthermore, in the absence of a just war, which was defined with theological precision and could not be undertaken at a whim, only the voluntary consent of the aborigines could justify the taking of Indian land. "So long as the Indians respected the natural rights of the Spaniards, recognized by the law of nations, to travel in their lands and to sojourn, trade, and defend their rights therein, the Spaniards could not wage a just war against the Indians and therefore could not claim any rights by conquest" (as summarized by Cohen, pp. 46–47).

On this basis, the Europeans decided to adopt much, but certainly not all, of Vitoria's philosophy. The Indian tribes, at least in North America, were recognized as legitimate entities capable of dealing with the European nations by treaty. Since the first settlements were very small, mere outposts in a hostile land, and rarely contained more than a few hundred inhabitants, treaty-making was a feasible method of gaining a foothold on the continent without alarming the natives. Most early settlements in fact needed the protection of larger Indian tribes in order to survive threats made by smaller groups whose lands they invaded. Treating with the Indians, then, brought an air of civility and legitimacy to the white settlers' relations with the Indians and provoked no immediate retaliation by the tribes. Instead of the Indians being subjected to bondage or their lands merely seized through the use of force, which Spain eventually did, civility reigned in North America. Indian land and the rights to live in certain areas were purchased at formal treaty sessions.

The impact of Vitoria's view on European-Indian relations for the next two hundred years was very important because it encouraged respect for the tribes as societies of people. Treaty-making became the basis for defining both the legal and political relationships between the Indians and the European colonists. And when the young colonies finally became the United States, the treaty-making powers that earlier had been exercised by the European nations were assumed by the Americans with their independence. In 1778 the United States government entered into its first treaty with the Indians—the Delaware tribe. In the course of the next century over six hundred treaties and agreements were made with the tribes and nations of North America. Not only were these treaties designed, as was the first treaty, to ensure peaceful relations with the Indians but, even more important, they were also a means of securing an orderly transfer of landownership from the tribes to the United States.

In 1823 in the case of *Johnson v. McIntosh*, 21 U.S. (8 Wheat.) 543 (1823), Chief Justice John Marshall both adopted and amended Vitoria's theory for the domestic law of the United States. He suggested that discovery did indeed give title to the land and that this title was recognized by the other European countries. It was a title that gave exclusive right to extinguish the Indians' title, which became, as a matter of course, something of an equitable title or occupancy. Thus Indian rights, according to Marshall, were not extinguished but merely "impaired" by European assertions. Since the Indians were unaware of the complexity of Marshall's revision and since there was no international forum in which such a claim could be challenged had the Indians known and objected, Marshall's definition in effect traded a vested property right for a recognized political right of quasi sovereignty for the tribes.

This judicial acknowledgment of Indians as recognized political bodies is also affirmed in the *Cherokee Nation Cases* (to be discussed at length in the next chapter). Marshall was again confronted with the necessity of making new law where none had previously existed. He characterized Indian nations as "domestic dependent nations" (*Cherokee Nation v. Georgia*, 30 U.S. (5 Pet.) 1 (1831)). Though subject to the guardianship protection and superior political power of the federal government, Indian nations did possess some degree of sovereignty. Thus, while the tribes did not fall within the category of "foreign nations" that possessed full sovereignty, they did constitute legitimate legal and political entities that could manage their own affairs, govern themselves internally, and engage in legal and political relations with the federal government and its subdivisions. This notion was extended even further in the second of the *Cherokee Nation Cases*, *Worcester v. Georgia*, 31 U.S. (6 Pet.) 515 (1832). Marshall, building on this foundation of domestic dependency, interposed a limited sovereignty enjoyed by the Indian nations to prevent the state of Georgia from extending its power over the Cherokee Nation's lands. Andrew Jackson's refusal to enforce Marshall's decision gave him mute testimony that, if the tribes had legal rights affirmed by the highest court in the land, their political status made it easy to void such rights.

Much of the legal history relating to the problems of Indian tribes was shaped by the events that occurred during this first period of discovery, conquest, and treaty-making. Indian nations negotiated at least partially from a position of strength. As the white settlements moved west it became increasingly difficult to supervise, administer, and protect the Indian tribes that stood in their way, and frequent conflicts arose. The United States quickly learned in the Seminole wars of the 1830s that fighting Indians was a very expensive task, and many treaties were made as an alternative to a prolonged war, which the Indians were certain to lose but which would prove extremely costly and politically unsettling. The treaty-making era came to an end when Congress, through a rider to an appropriation bill in 1871, declared that no Indian nation would henceforth be recognized for the purposes of making treaties. This action was a bit premature since various commissions continued making treaties with the tribes until 1914, when the Ute Mountain Utes signed the last major agreement with the United States. But these treaties, because of the prohibition by Congress, had to be called "agreements" when being presented for ratification.

Although "treaty" seems to imply an equal bargaining position, the Indians were often at a clear disadvantage when negotiating such arrangements. The actual document was always written in English and was generally interpreted by people who had a stake in a successful outcome of the proceedings, so the Indians were not always told the truth during these sessions. Toward the end of the treaty-making period, when extensive debate on ratification became tedious, the Senate would often amend the treaties to change their meaning completely. Most often the term of years for annuities and the articles dealing with social services would be changed since the Senate had to negotiate the appropriation of funds with the House of Representatives whenever it agreed by treaty to provide benefits to the tribes. The amended form of the treaty would then be taken back to the tribe and a few chiefs would be found to "touch the pen," in effect ratifying the amended wording. More than one Indian war began because the wrong group of Indians agreed to altered treaty provisions.

Not all legal authorities on Indian matters agree with the popular notion that the Indians were cheated during the making of treaties. Felix Cohen has argued that, absent a few cases where the military took the land by duress, the price that the whites paid for the land was one that satisfied the Indians (Cohen, pp. 42–43). Cohen reasons that most of the treaties were fairly negotiated. In return for their land, Indians received such goods as knives, axes, cloth, and instruments of a new technology that provided them with capabilities they would not otherwise have had. More important, according to Cohen, Indians received the recognition that they had to be treated on a seller-buyer basis. The foremost authority on Indian affairs did admit that this history was not without its "dark pages," but he concluded that, in these real estate transactions, the whites had been "human, not angelic," and this was as much as could be expected. Subsequent claims against the United States filed by the tribes in the Indian Claims Commission for unconscionable dealings based on treaties gave the tribes more than $600 million, which indicates that Cohen was reflecting the attitude of a government attorney when he made such statements.

REMOVAL AND RELOCATION (1828–1887)

During the early years of American history the white community felt that it could live peacefully with the Indians. People believed that over a period of time the Indians would be assimilated into the white culture and become Christianized in the European tradition. Indeed, the colony of Massachusetts divided its Indian relations into three separate categories: the praying Indians, who had already been converted and were living in towns specifically set aside for them; the Indians on its western frontier, who were virtually helpless and caused troubles but were not yet Christianized; and the stronger groups, such as the Iroquois, who were still a distinct military threat to the colony's existence.

The expectations that the colonists had were naïve and proved to be in error. An atmosphere of hostility developed between the two communities shortly after settlements were established because the cultural gap between the two groups was too wide to inspire confidence and trust. From Jamestown to Plymouth, within a generation after the colonists had landed, brutal wars had decimated the indigenous tribes and a pattern of frontier violence had been established. During the administration of Thomas Jefferson, a preview of future Indian policy was revealed when Jefferson proposed to move the Cherokee Indians out of the land obtained under the Louisiana Purchase. He, like so many others of his generation, rejected the idea that Indians and whites could live peacefully together in the same neighborhood and he saw removal as the most humane way to solve this problem. But it was Andrew Jackson who eventually seized on Jefferson's idea and turned it into an official government program.

Jackson won the election of 1828 and was pledged to support westward expansion. In his first message to Congress, on December 8, 1829, Jackson urged voluntary removal by the Indians as a means of protecting both the tribes and the states. When no voluntary migrations began, Jackson's supporters in Congress, mostly southern and western congressmen, introduced a bill to compel the Indians to move. The Indian Removal Act was passed on May 28, 1830, after vigorous debate in which the eastern senators and representatives deplored the policy as a violation of American honor. It was, nevertheless, immediately put into force when the southern tribes were notified that they must meet U.S. treaty commissioners to begin discussing their removal across the Mississippi.

The 1830s witnessed the massive migration of Indian tribes from the Ohio and Mississippi valleys to the western plains. Nearly sixteen thousand Cherokees walked "silently and resigned" from Georgia to their new homes in what became eastern Oklahoma. This journey has been called the "Trail of Tears" because the Indians were leaving their ancestral lands under the most harsh conditions imaginable. But the Cherokees were not the only Indians who were pushed to western reservations. Pursuant to the treaty of Dancing Rabbit Creek, the Choctaws surrendered all their land east of the Mississippi, more than ten million acres, and moved west. Those Indians who remained behind in Mississippi lost their Choctaw citizenship and fared poorly as state citizens in spite of a federal guarantee that they could reserve a homestead of 640 acres and assimilate into southern society.

The relocation of eastern Indians to reservations in the west did not solve the problem of Indian-white relations; it merely postponed it. From an Indian perspective, life on the reservation was still dominated by white intrusions. The sustenance on many reservations was almost wholly dependent upon some kind of annuity assistance from the federal government. Christian missionaries and teachers flooded the reservations in an attempt to "civilize" and assimilate the Indians. The army was conspicuous in its attempts to provide security, but its efforts were almost always directed at keeping the Indians at peace rather than protecting them.

Removal and relocation as policy were doomed from the beginning. Expansionist forces beyond the government's control inevitably destroyed the effort to keep the Indian and white communities apart. The increasing sophistication of American technology enabled settlement where none was thought possible so that, as the Indians were pushed farther west, they were replaced by a civilization that could not easily be dislodged, a civilization that was intimately linked to eastern industrial society. The coming of the railroads meant the destruction of the great buffalo herds, the discovery of gold and its efficient exploitation meant the coming of industrial corporations to the west, and the general movement of non-Indians to support these activities eventually enclosed the open spaces with boundary lines, roads, and settlements. If a policy of removal and isolation was impossible to bring about, what direction could the government move in order to deal with Indian problems? In the 1880s a radical reversal of thinking occurred: if you can no longer push Indians westward to avoid contact with civilization, and it is inhumane to conduct wars of extermination against them, the only alternative is to assimilate them.

ALLOTMENT AND ASSIMILATION (1887–1928)

Allotments of land were not a new idea in the history of Indian policy. The Pilgrim Fathers in Massachusetts had insisted that the praying Indians each take up a plot of ground and become farmers like their white neighbors. Indeed, farming was somewhat akin to the Christian life with its long hours of hard work and reliance on the rural community that watched over one's moral behavior. In the removal treaties tribal members had been given a choice of moving west or accepting land scripts that entitled them to take allotments within the areas they had ceded and to become state citizens. The 1854 treaty with the Omaha tribe had a provision (article 6) that at some future date the president could survey the reservation and distribute allotments to tribal members. But there was no firm federal policy on dividing up the tribal land estate. Some smaller tribes promised to accept the Omaha formula and the larger tribes who signed the famous 1867–1868 treaties on the plains had a tribal "Land Book" to register tracts of land that individual members might want. Apart from these provisions, which were administered in a haphazard manner, allotments were not a major feature of federal policy because no firm ideology undergirded them.

In 1881 the first indication was given that allotments might become a national policy when President Chester A. Arthur, in delivering his first annual message to Congress, proposed a plan by which Indians would be brought into the mainstream of American life. The solution to the nagging Indian problem, he felt, was simply "to introduce among the Indians the customs and pursuits of civilized life and gradually to absorb them into the mass of our citizens." Considering the times, it was a bold stroke that had a solid humanitarian base. Reconstruction was finished, the Hayes-Tilden deal had been struck and the white southerners were back in control of the South, and the Chinese Exclusion Act was on the horizon. To have suggested that a dark-skinned minority, one that had resisted American overtures for centuries of hostility, might be peacefully assimilated with full citizen rights into the society of that day was a daring if somewhat idealistic move.

Congress responded to President Arthur's Indian policy by proposing the Coke Act of 1883, but it failed to achieve a majority in the Senate and inspired some vigorous debate since it appeared to favor railroads and land speculators rather than the Indians. But allotment was an idea whose time had come. Everyone could agree that the Indians owned too much land and that holding land in tracts of millions of acres unnecessarily impeded the orderly settlement of the western states.

Senator Henry Dawes of Massachusetts assumed leadership of the forces that sought to make allotment and assimilation the national policy and, with the help of such private interest groups as the churches and the newly formed Indian Rights Association, he was able to get a new law passed in 1887. The General Allotment Act, or Dawes Act as it was popularly called (25 U.S.C.A. § 331), authorized the president, whenever in his opinion it was advantageous for the Indians, to allot any reservation according to the following formula:

1. To each head of a family, one-quarter section.
2. To each single person over eighteen years of age, one-eighth section.
3. To each orphan child under eighteen years of age, one-eighth section.
4. To each other single person under eighteen years of age living, or who may be born prior to the date of the order to the president directing allotment of the lands, one-sixteenth section.

It goes without saying that the president generally found it was to the advantage of the Indians to allot their lands. A period of twenty-five years was established during which the Indian owner was expected to learn proper business methods; at the end of this time the land, free of restrictions against sale, was to be delivered to the allottee. With a free and clear title the Indian became a citizen and came under the jurisdiction of the state in which he or she resided. Through this simple formula and rather naïve expectation federal officials believed they could solve the problems of the Indians in one generation. Private property, they believed, had mystical magical qualities about it that led people directly to a "civilized" state.

Underlying the allotment policy was the assumption that Indians wanted to become farmers and had the capacity to do so. This policy assumed that the routine work of agriculture would provide the necessary training in thrifty habits that all "civilized" peoples possessed. In 1888, in anticipation of the change to farming and as part of the treaty annuities, $30,000 was appropriated for seeds and equipment for some 3,568 allotments that had already been given under the treaties. This investment was less than $10 per allotment (Otis, p. 428), which indicated that if the Congress believed in farming it also believed that it could be undertaken with virtually no capital. Not only did the allotment act breach numerous treaty provisions but also Indian agents, under orders from Washington, refused to issue rations and other annuities to Indians unwilling to work their allotments, making the policy exceptionally onerous to the plains tribes, who viewed farming with distaste.

As a consequence of the allotment policy, Indian landholdings were reduced from 138 million acres in 1887 to 48 million in 1934 (Collier, p. 16). Of this 48 million acres, nearly 20 million were desert or semiarid and virtually useless for any kind of annual farming ventures. Not all of this land loss occurred immediately upon the division of the land. In 1891 an amendment was made to the General Allotment Act (26 Stat. 794) that allowed the secretary of the interior to lease the lands of any allottee who, in the secretary's opinion, "by reason of age or other disability" could not "personally and with benefit to himself occupy or improve his allotment or any part thereof." In effect this amendment gave the secretary of the interior almost dictatorial powers over the use of allotments since, if the local agent disagreed with the use to which the lands were being put, he could intervene and lease the land to whomsoever he pleased.

As with all general legislation, difficulties in interpretation arose and each congress following the enactment of the legislation saw various proposals to modify the General Allotment Act so that by the first decade of this century it no longer resembled a national policy but an ad hoc arrangement because of the numerous exceptions and exemptions that had been attached to it. The situation was further complicated because Congress generally confused allotment and citizenship. The Burke Act of May 8, 1906 (34 Stat. 182), gave sole authority to the secretary of the interior to issue a patent in fee (a certificate like a deed vesting legal ownership) well before the expiration of the trust period if, in the secretary's opinion, the Indian allottee was competent and capable of managing his or her own affairs. This act produced rapid alienation of lands when the allottees discovered they could immediately sell their lands. Citizenship thereupon became a function of the patent-in-fee status of land and not an indication that Indians were capable of performing their duties as citizens.

While the allotment policy was designed to bring about rapid assimilation, other laws passed during this period also contributed to this goal. In 1885 Congress passed the Major Crimes Act (18 U.S.C.A. § 1153), which permitted the federal government to assume criminal jurisdiction over major felonies committed in Indian Country. Prior to the Major Crimes Act these offenses fell under the exclusive jurisdiction of the Indian tribes. The act was passed by Congress after the Supreme Court had held that an Indian named Crow Dog, who had killed Spotted Tail, a noted Brûlé Sioux chief, could not be tried by the federal government because the crime had been preserved to the Sioux tribe by treaty (*Ex Parte Crow Dog*, 109 U.S. 556 (1883)). When the Court overturned Crow Dog's conviction, releasing to tribal jurisdiction a "murderer" whom many people felt should have been hanged, the incensed legislators responded by stripping tribes of their right to handle crimes according to traditional customs. Criminal jurisdiction, Congress concluded, was a function too important to leave to the Indians and their "primitive" sense of justice.

Without tediously reviewing all the amendments and statutes that were passed during this period to bring about assimilation, two are important enough to mention specifically. The Indian Citizenship Act was passed in 1924 (8 U.S.C.A. § 1401 (a) (2)). This piece of legislation followed an earlier act of 1919 (41 Stat. 350), which gave citizenship to Indians who had served in the armed forces during the First World War and superseded all the citizenship provisions in treaties that had granted the status in what became a crazy-quilt pattern of qualifications. The Act of July 31, 1882 (22 Stat. 181), authorized the secretary of war to set aside vacant army posts and barracks for use as normal and industrial training schools for "youth from the nomadic tribes having educational treaty claims upon the United States." There had been, of course, other acts for the education of Indian children but this statute can be said to demonstrate a major commitment by the United States to Indian education by taking established federal installations and converting them to schools.

Indian education changed from a sporadic activity restricted to those tribes who had educational provisions in their treaties to a national program that policy-makers hoped would hasten the day of complete Indian independence from the government. The most famous army post to be used as an Indian school was, of course, the army barracks at Carlisle, Pennsylvania, but other posts were also used and by the end of the nineteenth century the Bureau of Indian Affairs had a large number of off-reservation boarding schools and many reservation day schools operating. Church societies also worked in this field at the request of the government and for several years tribal appropriations were used by these groups to carry on their activities. By the mid 1920s, however, boarding schools were being closed and day schools were being consolidated. It was the first indication at the reservation level that the government knew its goal of assimilation had been a miscalculation of major proportions.

REORGANIZATION AND SELF-GOVERNMENT (1928–1945)

The adverse effect that the allotment policy had upon traditional Indian life was readily apparent by the first decade of this century but Congress was slow to admit its failure. As criticism of federal Indian policies mounted during the 1920s efforts were started to assess the conditions existing on Indian reservations. The Institute of Government Research in Washington, D.C., was authorized by Secretary of the Interior Hubert Work in June 1926 to conduct a survey of the social and economic status of Indians. The study, conducted by Lewis Meriam and associates, was published in 1928 under the title *The Problem of Indian Administration* and shocked the administration since it called for radical revisions in almost every phase of Indian affairs, including the appropriation of considerably more funds. The Meriam Report, as it came to be popularly called, was characterized by the American Indian Defense Association, the chief critic of the administration's Indian policy, as the "most important single document in Indian Affairs since Helen Hunt Jackson's *A Century of Dishonor*" (*American Indian Life*, p. 6).

The Meriam Report was an exhaustive examination of Indian life as it then existed, covering such topics as health, education, general economic conditions, family and community life, migrated Indians, legal aspects of the Indian problem, and missionary activities among the Indians. The report confronted the past with a healthy honesty unusual in government-sponsored reports: "The work of the government directed toward the education and advancement of the Indian himself, as distinguished from the control and conservation of his property, is largely ineffective. The chief deficiency in this work lies in the fact that the government has not appropriated enough funds to permit the Indian Service to employ an adequate personnel properly qualified for the task before it" (Meriam, p. 8). Of the allotment policy, the report bluntly noted: "When the government adopted the policy of individual ownership of the land on the reservations, the expectation was that the Indians would become farmers. Part of this plan was to instruct and aid them in agriculture, but this vital part was not pressed with vigor and intelligence. It almost seems as if the government assumed that some magic in individual ownership of property would in itself prove an educational civilizing factor, but unfortunately this policy has for the most part operated in the opposite direction" (p. 7). The report outlined procedures for improving the Indian Service and made specific recommendations for the expenditure of funds for programs that it felt were badly needed. Although some of the recommendations did not become law until decades later, almost all of the Meriam Report's proposals were eventually adopted.

The congressional response to the Meriam Report was not heartening. Outraged senators, certain that the report was slanted in favor of the bureaucratic apparatus of the Department of the Interior, authorized their own investigation of Indian affairs in Senate Resolution 79 (70th Congr. 1st sess. 1929). Crisply noting that "it is claimed that the control by the Bureau of Indian Affairs of the persons and property of Indians is preventing them from accommodating themselves to the conditions and requirements of modern life and from exercising that liberty with respect to their own affairs without which they can not develop into self-reliant, free, and independent citizens," and admitting that "numerous complaints have been made by responsible persons and organizations charging improper and improvident administration of Indian property by the Bureau of Indian Affairs" (*Survey of Conditions of the Indians in the United States*, p. 1), the Senate Indian Committee took upon itself the responsibility of verifying the conclusions of the Meriam Report. Devoting a major portion of their energies to extensive field hearings on specific subjects, the committee members traveled to many reservations and held hearings on many subjects in Washington. The Senate study lasted eight years and reached basically the same conclusions; the conditions of the Indians were believed only when the senators saw for themselves in the field on numerous trips the state of poverty to which Indians had been reduced by the existing policy.

Radical reform came with the election of Franklin D. Roosevelt and the inception of the New Deal in the midst of the Great Depression. John Collier, director of the American Indian Defense Association and the Interior Department's most persistent and energetic critic, was named Indian commissioner, and a superb group of legal minds, including Felix S. Cohen and Nathan Margold, was authorized to begin working on major legislation to solve Indian problems. The result was a four-titled bill presented to Congress early in

1934 that incorporated most of the recommendations of the Meriam Report and featured some of Collier's own ideas on cultural renewal and reorganization.

In order to gather Indian support for his ideas, John Collier organized a series of Indian congresses across the country to which all the major tribal delegations were invited. Although the Indians objected to some of the provisions of the legislation, on the whole there was sufficient Indian support to enable the administration to get an amended version of the legislation passed in June of 1934. This act, the Indian Reorganization Act (IRA), popularly known as the Wheeler-Howard Act after its sponsors in the Senate and House of Representatives (25 U.S.C.A. § 461), formally ended the government's policy of allotment. Section 1 stipulated that "no land of any Indian reservation . . . shall be allotted in severalty to any Indian." The first great experiment in social engineering was now officially disclaimed although the damage it had created remained to be repaired.

The act also prevented the alienation (transfer) of Indian land or shares in tribal corporations other than to the tribe itself. The secretary of the interior, however, was given some discretionary powers to authorize voluntary exchanges of land in order to bring about better consolidation of land resources for economic purposes. One of the most important provisions of the act established a revolving credit fund from which the secretary could make loans to tribally chartered corporations for purposes of economic development.

From the standpoint of government organization, the IRA enabled tribes to organize for their common welfare and to adopt federally approved constitutions and bylaws. It permitted the employment of legal counsel of the tribe's own choice and authorized the tribal councils established under the act to negotiate with federal, state, and local governments. The major thrust of the act was to minimize the enormous discretion and power exercised by the Department of the Interior and the Office of Indian Affairs. The focus of power was to be decentralized and moved from the Indian bureaucracy in Washington to the reservation governments. Formal tribal government was expected to become the rule rather than the exception.

The opportunities made available to the tribes under this act were immense. While the act did not provide them with powers they had not previously possessed, it did recognize these powers as inherent in their status and resurrected them in a form in which they could be used at the discretion of the tribe. This recognition, coupled with the promise of expanded social programs and federal funding of projects, was an exciting prospect. Before the IRA could be made applicable to a tribe, however, the enrolled members had to vote within a two-year period to accept it. Within the time allocated, 358 elections were held in which 181 tribes (129,750 Indians) voted to accept the IRA provisions. Seventy-seven tribes rejected the act (86,365 Indians, including the large Navajo tribe of approximately 45,000 people). Some tribes voted to accept the act and then refused to organize under it, which made their status somewhat nebulous ("Tribal Self-Government and the Reorganization Act of 1934," p. 972).

While a number of opportunities for Indian revitalization were initiated under the IRA, its promise was never fully realized. The era of allotment had taken a heavy toll on the tribes. Many of the old customs and traditions that could have been restored under the IRA climate of cultural concern had vanished during the interim period since the tribes had gone to the reservations. The experience of self-government according to Indian traditions had eroded and, while the new constitutions were akin to the traditions of some tribes, they were completely foreign to others. The new constitutions called for election of council members and were based upon the old "boss farmer" districts, which had been drawn when the allotment policy dictated that the Indians would be taught to farm. Familiar cultural groupings and methods of choosing leadership gave way to the more abstract principles of American democracy, which viewed people as interchangeable and communities as geographical marks on a map.

Although there were some variations, in general the new tribal constitutions and bylaws were standardized and largely followed the Anglo-American system of organizing people. Traditional Indians of almost every tribe strongly objected to this method of organizing and criticized the IRA as simply another means of imposing white institutions on the tribes. In some of the constitutions the traditional Indians were able to protect themselves by insisting that the tribal government derive from the more ancient form of government and be subjected in its operation to the powers that the people had allocated to it. Other tribes rejected the idea of a formal, and small, tribal council governing them and demanded that the tribal council consist of the whole tribe meeting in concert. Experiences proved this approach to have its merits and its shortcomings.

TERMINATION (1945–1961)

The Second World War brought an end to the experiments in Indian regeneration. Domestic budgets were severely reduced in order to support the war effort, many agencies were closed or operated on a minimal basis, and many people left the reservations to work in war industries or to serve in the armed forces. The Indian Bureau itself was moved to Chicago during the war years and acted more as a caretaker over programs until the war was brought to a successful conclusion. In 1945 John Collier, under continuing attack by his critics, who charged him with attempting to institute socialism on the reservations, resigned believing that his personality was now attracting as much opposition as his programs. He had served twelve years, more than any other person in history, and his accomplishments were numerous. He had radically shifted federal policy to an admission that Indian culture and ideas were as integral to the successful operation of programs as any policies promulgated by Congress.

In 1947, with a conservative Republican Congress now in power, the Senate Civil Service Committee, desiring to find ways to reduce federal expenditures and dismantle the New Deal programs in the process, opened hearings on ways that government payrolls could be cut and expenditures curtailed. Acting Indian Commissioner William Zimmerman was asked to testify on the Bureau of Indian Affairs programs. Zimmerman was requested to bring an evaluation of tribal conditions and to list those tribes that could immediately succeed without further federal help, those that could be ready to live on their own within a reasonable time, and those that would need continued federal assistance. Zimmerman produced the lists but cautioned that significant and substantial changes and protections must be instituted before any tribe could successfully stand on its own feet.

In 1948 the Hoover Commission, authorized to review all government programs and recommend cost savings by reorganization of the federal government, made its report on Indian programs. Although the report was accompanied by a strong dissent declaring that the commission was not authorized to make policy recommendations, the majority signing the report recommended that the responsibility for Indians be transferred to the states as soon as it was practicable. By coincidence the National Council of Churches also issued a report recommending that Indians be given full citizenship by eliminating much of the discriminating legislation that bound them to the federal government. This report was deeply tinged with the same philosophical views that had been used to justify the allotment act: economic and religious Darwinism—the survival of the fittest, although phrased in traditional Protestant ethical clothing.

Clearly the tenor of the times was beginning to run against further Indian renaissance. A strange coalition of forces now called for the unilateral termination of federal assistance to Indians: conservatives wanted the federal budgets cut and deeply believed that Indians, once freed from government restrictions, would experience a much more profound reawakening; liberals, now ashamed to realize that some of America's laws were reminiscent of the racial restrictions imposed on minorities by the Axis powers whom they had recently defeated, sought immediate release of America's racial minorities from the onerous burden of discriminatory legislation. In 1948 the Democratic liberals had forced a plank into the national platform advocating a strong civil rights position and, if the Democratic liberals could not immediately assist the blacks in their struggle, they could at least assist the Indians, over whom they had a more direct control.

In 1952, while the Democrats were still in control of the White House, a memo was sent out by Indian Commissioner Dillon Myer to all Bureau of Indian Affairs employees alerting them that the government was preparing to withdraw from its Indian programs. "At this point," Myer wrote, "I want to emphasize that withdrawal program formulation and effectuation is to be a cooperative effort of Indian and community groups affected, side by side, with Bureau personnel. We must lend every encouragement to Indian initiative and leadership. I realize that it will not be possible always to obtain Indian cooperation." The die was cast: "We must proceed," Myer declared, "even though Indian cooperation may be lacking in certain cases" (House Report 2503, p. 3). In December 1952 the House of Representatives issued a massive 1,800-page report on Indian conditions, House Report 2503, compiled as a modern version of the famous English "Domesday Book." Although not touching all aspects of the complicated task of withdrawing federal services to Indians, the report indicated many problem areas that appeared to be capable of resolution by the elimination of federal rules and regulations. The report did somewhat resemble the Domesday Book in that it was the most complete listing of Indian assets, treaties, statutes, and services ever assembled and gave as comprehensive a picture of Indian matters as any comparable federal effort.

The Republicans captured the White House and Congress in 1952 and, like the Democrats two decades before, immediately set about making drastic reforms in federal programs. In June 1953, Representative William Henry Harrison of Wyoming introduced House Concurrent Resolution 108 (67 Stat. B132), which articulated the new policy, declaring that it was "the sense of Congress that, at the earliest possible time, all of the Indian tribes and the individual members thereof located within the States of California, Florida, New York and Texas, should be freed from Federal supervision and control and all disabilities and limitations specifically applicable to Indians." This resolution, fraught with controversial implications, hardly caused a ripple in Congress. There was no opposition and virtually no debate. The resolution passed both houses of Congress and set the stage for the policy of terminating Indians from federal supervision.

House Concurrent Resolution 108 only evidenced a sense of Congress and a rather apathetic sense at that. The resolution did not initiate any specific action. To implement the "sense of Congress," specific proposals had to be taken up by the Congress. Then, as the second session of the Congress began in January 1954, a fire storm of activity arose. The Senate and House Indian subcommittees of the Interior Committees began meeting in joint sessions, an unprecedented change in procedures. Several bills were introduced to terminate the federal relations of a number of tribes, some of whom had been on Zimmerman's original list of tribes deemed capable of conducting their own business, others so obscure that few knew where they were located or when the federal government had assumed responsibility for them.

The leading congressional proponent of termination was conservative Republican Senator Arthur V. Watkins of Utah, who was firmly convinced that if the Indians were freed from federal restrictions they would soon prosper by learning in the school of life those lessons that a cynical federal bureaucracy had not been able to instill in them. Using the joint sessions to eliminate any differences in language between the Senate and House versions of the terminal legislative proposals, Watkins quickly pushed a number of bills into law. Two major tribes, the Klamath of Oregon and the Menominee of Wisconsin, and a number of minor tribal groups fell under the onslaught. Commentators differ on the number of tribes that were actually terminated during this period because some advocates insist on counting the number of antecedent tribes that were represented on some of the West Coast reservations. Thus the Siletz and Grand Ronde reservations in Oregon were terminated; these tribes represented a large number of Indians who derived their ancestry from a bewildering number of small coastal tribes who had all been placed on the reservations during the 1850s. Some small Paiute bands in southern Utah were also terminated and a number of California rancherias, created during the Depression as tracts of land for homeless Indians, were also phased out. On the whole, however, the large tribes with treaty commitments and political sophistication were not touched although they were nearly frightened into submission.

In August of 1953, Congress passed Public Law 280 (67 Stat.

588), another piece of controversial legislation. This statute permitted state governments to assume both civil and criminal jurisdiction over Indian reservations in the states of California, Minnesota, Nebraska, Oregon, Wisconsin, and the then-territory of Alaska. While the Indian tribes and their governments were not terminated, their authority was significantly diminished by stripping the tribal governments of their power to handle civil and criminal problems in Indian Country. Most important, however, hunting and fishing rights, a major concern of the Indians since the treaty days, were preserved to tribal and federal protections and states were not given the right to tax Indian lands or properties even though they were expected to provide funds to support law and order services on reservations over which they had extended their jurisdiction. Because the law was so hastily and vaguely written, it spawned a considerable amount of controversy and produced a record amount of litigation between the state governments and the tribes in a number of states.

Two other developments of note made the termination era one of puzzling contradictions. Indian reservations were made a part of the large federal educational programs created by Congress in 1950. In P.L. 815 (64 Stat. 967), Indians were included in the school construction programs and in P.L. 874 (64 Stat. 1100), Indians became eligible for the impact aid programs. These national programs grew out of the wartime necessity to provide some financial cushion for those school districts that had been severely affected by the increased federal activities the war brought. Funding under the two laws rapidly expanded as school districts continually sought ways of bringing themselves under their comfortable financial umbrella. The same Congress that passed H.C.R. 108 also made Indians eligible for these programs. The result was that by 1958 the federal government was more substantially involved in Indian education than ever. This activity was strange if it wanted to reduce and finally eliminate the federal budget for Indians.

The Act of August 5, 1954 (68 Stat. 674), transferred the hospital and health facilities, property, personnel, and budget funds of the Indian Health Service of the Bureau of Indian Affairs to the U.S. Public Health Service. The transfer was conceived as a first step in the eventual placement of Indian health problems under programs open to the other citizens of the country, but the uniqueness of the Indian situation meant that in solving the immediate problems the Public Health Service made its Indian program a permanent part of its national responsibilities. Alarming statistics in the incidence of trachoma, tuberculosis, and diabetes, the relatively isolated regions in which Indians lived, and the need for cultural understanding all made the Indian programs substantially different from other programs administered by the Public Health Service.

The termination era was brought to a close as abruptly as it had begun. In 1958, after half a decade of controversy and Indian protests, Secretary of the Interior Fred Seaton announced that hereinafter no tribe would be terminated without its consent. This admission of failure, made casually on a Gallup, New Mexico, radio talk-show interview, proved embarrassing to the administration but was a welcome respite to the frightened tribes. H.C.R. 108 continued to be cited by proponents of the policy and during the early 1960s Senate hearings were perfunctory when plans to terminate the Colvilles of Washington state and the Senecas of New York were made. Presidents Kennedy and Johnson never activated the policy but were politically embarrassed when Democratic Senator Henry M. Jackson of Washington, chairman of the Senate Interior Committee, attempted to revitalize it. It was not until 1970 that the philosophy of termination was formally repudiated. President Richard Nixon, well aware that the Republicans had been instrumental in framing this tragic interlude between progressive periods of Indian history, announced in a message to Congress delivered on July 8, 1970: "Because termination is morally and legally unacceptable, because it produces bad practical results, and because the mere threat of termination tends to discourage greater self-sufficiency among Indian groups, I am asking the Congress to pass a new Concurrent Resolution which would expressly renounce, repudiate and repeal the termination policy as expressed in House Concurrent Resolution 108 of the 83rd Congress" (H.R. Doc. No. 363).

The impact of termination upon those tribes affected was unmistakable and significant. If the policy did not completely destroy Indian culture, it encroached substantially upon Indian attempts to remain Indian. Charles F. Wilkinson and Eric R. Biggs have catalogued some of the basic consequences of those terminations (Wilkinson and Biggs, pp. 92–93):

1. There were fundamental changes in land ownership patterns.
2. The trust relationship was ended.
3. State legislative jurisdiction was imposed.
4. State judicial authority was imposed.
5. Exemption from state taxing power was ended.
6. Special federal programs to tribes were discontinued.
7. Special federal programs to individual Indians were discontinued.
8. Tribal sovereignty was effectively ended.

One might also note that both the tribal corporations established as a result of termination and the removal of allotments from their trust status resulted in the imposition of federal taxes on the income of Indians, which proved to be a substantial burden in the task of assimilating Indians into the larger society with any degree of economic confidence and security.

In return for these very significant losses in services and protections, the benefit to individual Indians was small. In those instances where the federal government purchased large tracts of tribal lands, the tribes divided their funds held in the U.S. Treasury on a per capita basis while others received nothing in return. Among the Klamaths, for instance, those who chose cash received $43,000 each in 1961 while the remaining members of the tribe, who kept their shares in a corporate trust until 1975, received approximately $150,000 each. But the price was high. The Klamaths lost all federal recognition and assistance and were considered to be outcasts in the national Indian community. A particularly insightful opinion of the United States Supreme Court may have best summed up many Indian feelings: "It may be hard for us to understand why these Indians cling so tenaciously to their lands and traditional tribal way of life. The record does not leave the impression that the lands are the most fertile, the landscape the most beautiful or their homes the most splendid specimens of architecture. But this is their home—their ancestral home. There they, their children and their forebears were born. They, too, have their memories and their loves. Some things are worth more than money and the costs of a new enterprise" (*Federal Power Commission v. Tuscarora Indian Nation*, 362 U.S. 99 (1960)).

SELF-DETERMINATION (1961–PRESENT)

Although termination was not formally repudiated by a federal official until July 1970 when President Nixon rejected it specifically in his message to Congress, a persistent strain of opposition to termination remained strong throughout the period when it was the official policy of Congress. As we have already seen, the educational benefits to Indians were increased throughout the 1950s and Indian health services were improved during the time when all other efforts seemed to indicate a withdrawal of federal services for Indians. In 1961 the first shift in emphasis occurred when, as Congress was debating the passage of the Area Redevelopment Administration Act (75 Stat. 47), consideration was given to making Indian tribes eligible project sponsors under certain sections of the bill. Section 6 allowed Indian tribes to purchase or develop lands and facilities for industrial or commercial use; section 7, for public facilities. This inclusion signaled, at least in the minds of the executive branch, that Indians would be given a chance to develop their resources rather than sever their relations with the federal government.

With the passage of more socially oriented legislation, Indians became an integral part of the expanding human concern of the New Frontier and Great Society programs. Indians were given special consideration when the Economic Opportunity Act passed and was implemented in 1964, and finally, in 1968, President Johnson, in an address to Congress, proposed "a new goal for our Indian programs; a goal that ends the old debate about termination and stresses self-determination."

Indians participated in almost all of the social welfare programs of the sixties but as one segment of that massive but undefined portion of the American population known as "the poor." The first major piece of legislation dealing specifically with Indian matters was the 1968 Indian Civil Rights Act, which was one title in an Omnibus Housing Act passed that year in response to the King assassination, which marred that election year. Part of this title prohibited states from assuming jurisdiction over Indian Country under Public Law 280 without first securing tribal consent (25 U.S.C.A. § 1326). The Nixon speech of July 8, 1970, cited above, set the tone for a new articulation of federal Indian policy that had been a fait accompli since the early sixties and directed attention to specific legislative proposals that could be of assistance to the Indians.

Three pieces of legislation among the many statutes to be written into law during the 1970s stand out as characteristic of the federal change of direction. The Indian Education Act of 1972 (86 Stat. 334) provided a theoretical and programmatic base for moving more directly into Indian education at the local level. It was, unfortunately, based upon the hearings of nearly half a decade before, conducted by Senator Edward Kennedy's Subcommittee on Indian Education, so that several of the sections of the legislation assumed conditions that no longer existed and attempted to resolve them. The act provided for special educational training programs for teachers of Indian children, for fellowships for Indian students in certain narrowly defined fields, and for basic research in Indian education. Almost all these activities were already being conducted by Indians and educational institutions under programs funded by the Office of Economic Opportunity and its successor agencies. One might argue that the 1972 act formalized procedures and programs that had previously existed at the discretion of funding agencies. However, this informality had more strengths than weaknesses. With the formalizing of educational opportunities came increased bureaucratic involvement, serving at times to debilitate rather than facilitate progress in Indian education.

The Indian Self-Determination and Education Assistance Act of 1975 (25 U.S.C.A. § 450a–450n) directed the secretary of the interior, upon the request of any Indian tribe, to contract with the tribe to "plan, conduct, and administer programs" provided for under the IRA or any other program the secretary was authorized to administer. The act permitted Indian tribes, not the Bureau of Indian Affairs or any other branch of the federal government, to decide if they wished to participate in a given program. Veteran observers of Indian affairs noted that this statute was a thinly disguised version of Collier's original program for the tribes in 1934. It is astounding that in over forty-one years the goals of the IRA had not been realized or even well articulated for the tribes. More astonishing, and perhaps more depressing, hardly anyone realized that the act was merely a rehash of a policy nearly half a century old.

The final piece of legislation passed in the 1970s worthy of mention was the establishment of the American Indian Policy Review Commission, which was authorized by Senate Joint Resolution 4 (P.L. 93-580). This resolution established a two-year commission (popularly called the Abourezk Commission after its sponsor) charged with the responsibility of reviewing existing federal policy and making recommendations for positive change. Unfortunately, the commission was mired in the infighting of national Indian politics from the very beginning and never recovered from these fatal wounds it received while yet in its conception. The commission was composed of six members of Congress and five Indians chosen more or less according to the internal politics of the congressional representatives. The commission itself did not attend any field hearings as did the Senate investigation of 1928–1936 but instead delegated this responsibility to eleven "Task Forces," which were appointed to perform this function.

The Task Forces staggered from one end of the country to the other in search of data and some of them compiled a considerable amount of material in their search for an accurate picture of the conditions facing Indians. Staff work was haphazard and sporadic at best and toward the end of the commission's life, when the critical final report had to be drafted, employees of the Bureau of Indian Affairs were pressed into service to write up the findings that were submitted to Congress. Almost all the recommendations made by Indians at the field hearings were ignored and a very fragmentary and highly political agenda was substituted in their stead. The final report contained some 206 different recommendations, which resembled a bureaucratic shopping list rather than a high-level investigation. No philosophical overview or ideology emerged in spite of a continuous recital of the misdeeds of the federal government and the assertion of the ultimate sovereignty of Indian tribes.

The extravagance of the Abourezk Commission seemed to exhaust the good will of Congress in extending a helping hand to Indians. Little of substance resulted from the commission's work even though the Senate Select Committee on Indian Affairs, established as a result of the commission's recommendations the year following the submission of the report, was filled with former commission members who assured the Indian tribes that their presence on the new committee virtually guaranteed that the commission's recommendations were going to be written into law. With the increasing conservative mood in the Congress and the election of Ronald Reagan, the halcyon days of self-determination ended. Major reductions in appropriations were instituted and experienced observers of Indian affairs likened the times to the retrenchment following the Second World War.

Yet it was clear also that significant changes had been wrought in Indian affairs since the Indian Reorganization Act was instituted. In spite of the brief fling with termination of federal supervision, tribal governments emerged in the closing decades of the twentieth century in a much better position and with higher status than they had entered it. Local institutions that served Indians were in a much stronger position even though they now resembled the local units of government that served other Americans and possessed little that was distinctively Indian. Indians themselves had assimilated to a significant degree from their former condition and thus the contemporary institutions were better suited to their needs than had they been able to return to wholly traditional ways. Unfortunately, the Reagan administration budget cuts short-circuited much of the progress Indians had made during the postwar period. Thus, one cannot determine if Indians would have made a successful transition from the isolated cultural and social condition in which they had lived for most of the century. Nevertheless, there were a sufficient number of sophisticated contemporary cultural expressions to keep alive the idea of independence from external pressures and interference that had proven a stumbling block in other periods of Indian history.

2. Federal Responsibility and Power over Indian Affairs

The lives of American Indians are interwoven with the federal government. Federal ownership of tribal and individual lands, the expansive array of governmental services, the control and investment of tribal funds, the assumption of criminal jurisdiction—lives of few tribal members are untouched by the Washington bureaucracy of the Interior Department. The contemporary surge toward self-government and self-determination has reduced this contact for some tribes, but as a general rule much of Indian life falls under the federal umbrella and is subject to its changes.

How did this comprehensive umbrella of federal responsibility over Indian affairs come about? More important, who is charged with the obligation of carrying out these responsibilities and from where is this power derived? The purpose of this chapter is to explore these areas of concern. Attention will focus first on an examination of the roots and theories of federal responsibility. With this background in mind, we shall then proceed to look at the political institutions charged with carrying out these responsibilities. In particular, the roles of the presidency, the bureaucracy, and the Congress will be reviewed. And while the American judiciary has assumed more of an "arbiter's" function with reference to the exercise of power in Indian affairs, this subject would not be complete without an assessment of the role of the federal courts in the promotion/frustration saga of Indian law and politics.

ROOTS OF FEDERAL RESPONSIBILITY

The turmoil that persisted between Indian and non-Indian communities during the embryonic days of our nation's development demanded that some type of action be taken to minimize if not resolve this conflict. This task was clearly a responsibility to be shouldered by the federal government. The brief and ineffectual flirtation with government under the Articles of Confederation, said to have been patterned after the constitution of the League of the Iroquois, had demonstrated that only a different balance of powers between states and the federal government and the cession of more subjects to exclusive federal control would enable the new country to stabilize itself. Indian affairs was clearly a matter to be given to the federal government. Some political institution or personality, however, had to assume the initiative in defining the relationship between the Indian nations and the fledgling American government. While the wording of the Commerce Clause of the Constitution seemed clear, it had not yet been tested. It was the Supreme Court, rather than the Congress to whom constitutional authority for Indians had been given, that stepped forward to assume this role of clarifying and elaborating on the federal-Indian relationship. The political personality thrust into the limelight was none other than the chief justice of the Supreme Court—John Marshall.

The first serious attempt by the Court to define the federal government's relationship to Indian nations was *Johnson v. McIntosh*, 21 U.S. (8 Wheat.) 543 (1823). As will be recalled from the discussion of the *Johnson* case in the last chapter, Marshall used his opinion in this decision to develop an American interpretation of the doctrine of discovery, and this version stressed a theory of Indian subservience to the federal government. While paying lip service to the European notion of discovery and continued Indian autonomy, Marshall reasoned that conquest gave the white settlers ownership and title to Indian lands. This title, while good against all European rivals, was subject, however, to the continued right of Indian occupancy and use. Thus, while the Indians' interest in their lands was not completely extinguished, it was altered so significantly that it became, for practical purposes, a benign fiction that often gave way to the political realities of the times. Land obviously was and continues to be the Indians' most precious resource. And while the right of occupancy and use was an important interest retained by the Indians, ownership in the hands of the federal government effectively restricted the tribes to the role of mere nuisances on the land and they were so regarded by the public, which understood the federal government's claim to the title of the land but could not and would not recognize the Indian right to use the land.

Johnson v. McIntosh created a landlord-tenant relationship between the government and the Indian tribes. The federal government, as the ultimate landlord, not only possessed the power to terminate the "tenancy" of its Indian occupants but also could materially affect the lives of Indians through its control and regulation of land use. With the exercise of power comes responsibility, and *Johnson* constituted the first instance in which a judicially recognized federal responsibility over Indian affairs was articulated. Indeed, a number of subsequent Supreme Court decisions have alluded to the fact that much of the power that the federal government exercises over Indian affairs emanates from the concept of ultimate federal ownership of Indian land and its sovereignty over it. This notion, as a matter of fact, constituted the basis upon which the Court in the *Cherokee Nation Cases* developed its theory of federal guardianship over Indian affairs. But it is important to note in passing that the problem presented in *Johnson* was tracing a land title between two competing parties of non-Indians, one of whom claimed to have taken his interest from an Indian cession. The theory that Marshall thus articulated in *Johnson* was peripheral to Indian concerns as the tribes would have expressed them. The tribes, as the treaties of those days indicate, were much more concerned with defining the political powers to be exercised on the lands than with elaborate chains of title and ownership.

The first three decades of the nineteenth century were fragile ones in the history of the American government. The national government was far from strong and was continuously faced with recalcitrant states challenging its authority. The federal government's guardianship responsibility over Indian nations was conceived during this period of political turmoil. A number of state governments indignantly denounced the efforts by the federal government to assume jurisdiction and power over enterprises the states had previously controlled. Several states talked in terms of "interposition," that is, imposing their sovereignty against the usurping tendencies of the federal government. In 1832, South Carolina, crystallizing its opposition to the federal tariff, attempted to initiate a nullification movement. The federal government, still in its infancy, was vulnerable to these attacks, and the presidents did not wish to invest their precious political influence in unpopular causes.

During this period of unrest and struggle between the states and the national government, the *Cherokee Nation Cases* arose. The state of Georgia was intent on removing the Creek and Cherokee Indians from the western and northern portions of its lands. State authorities openly flouted the terms of federal treaties and threatened to use force against both the Indians and any federal troops who might be ordered to protect them. The federal government, however, moved with a great deal of caution in attempting to remove the Indians from the state. Many influential eastern senators and congressmen regarded the Indians' claim to the lands, as reaffirmed by the treaties, to be a sacred trust imposed on the United States and they insisted that any removal of these tribes be on a voluntary basis and not as the result of force and duress.

In 1827 the Cherokee Nation adopted a written constitution and proclaimed itself to be "independent." Sequoyah invented an alphabet for the Cherokee language enabling it to be put into a written form, and within a very short time almost the whole tribe could read and write its own language. Inspired with this accomplishment, and relying on the federal treaty promises, the Cherokees had every expectation that their efforts to achieve a "civilized" status would be greeted with applause by their white neighbors. But Andrew Jackson won the election of 1828 and the Georgians knew that he was sympathetic to their cause. In December 1828, less than a month after the presidential election, the Georgia legislature passed an act to add Cherokee territory to a designated number of Georgia counties. The Cherokees protested to their friends in Congress who, by resolution of the Senate, asked Jackson what was happening. Jackson curtly blamed the Cherokees for the trouble and said he would not help them.

In December 1829 the Georgia legislature passed another act containing comprehensive civil and criminal jurisdictional provisions that had the effect of abolishing the Cherokee laws. Again the Cherokees complained, but to no avail. The Indian Removal Act was passed on May 28, 1830, and on June 3, 1830, Governor George G. Gilmer of Georgia announced that gold had been discovered in the Cherokee lands and that it rightfully belonged to the state of Georgia. There was an immediate rush into the Indian lands in search of gold, and the wholesale violation of the Cherokee treaties, coupled with the desire of the state to gain the gold fields for itself, enabled Gilmer to justify the use of additional force in subduing the Cherokees. Finally, their patience at an end, in December 1830 the Cherokees filed a bill with the Supreme Court asking for relief from the oppressions visited upon them by the state of Georgia.

In the interim period the state courts had convicted Corn Tassel, a Cherokee leader, and sentenced him to death. His attorneys appealed to Chief Justice John Marshall, who allowed the appeal and issued an order staying execution to the governor of Georgia. But Gilmer, determined to force the issue of state jurisdiction, called the legislators together to get their opinion whether or not the state was bound to respect an order from the United States Supreme Court. The legislature, as one might easily surmise, decided that the writ issued by Marshall was an unconstitutional interference with Georgia's sovereignty and Gilmer ordered Corn Tassel executed forthwith. On March 5, 1830, the Supreme Court dismissed the Cherokees' case, *Cherokee Nation v. Georgia*, 30 U.S. (5 Pet.) 1 (1831), leaving them no practical forum for relief.

A week later a group of missionaries, led by the Reverend Samuel Worcester, were arrested by a Georgia sheriff for violating state laws. They had been invited to Cherokee country under the provisions of the Cherokee treaties some years before and were generally regarded as working under federal auspices. Governor Gilmer immediately inquired of Secretary of War John H. Eaton if the missionaries were to be regarded as federal officers and Eaton replied that only the Moravian and Baptist missionaries were considered to have a direct federal tie. Worcester and his companions were, unfortunately, Congregationalist missionaries. On July 7, 1831, they were convicted in state court of remaining in Cherokee country and obeying Cherokee laws in violation of a state statute that prohibited non-Cherokees from doing so. Sentencing was announced on September 15, and the missionaries were given four years at hard labor. In October, Worcester filed an appeal to the Supreme Court and in January 1832 the court ruled in his favor.

The rush of events that culminated in the *Cherokee Nation Cases* being brought before the Supreme Court, considering the modes of travel and transportation of those days, must have seemed as swift and traumatic as events of our day appear to us. Thus, while it appears that Chief Justice Marshall had the luxury of years to meditate on the theories he used to write the Cherokee opinions, in fact the tension surrounding them foreclosed any possibility of a leisurely and scholarly discourse. In the first case the Cherokees were unable to get a final judgment from a state court that they could appeal as a matter of course to the Supreme Court; in desperation they filed an original motion under article III, section 2, of the Constitution, which allowed foreign states to bring a cause of action in the Supreme Court.

After careful consideration of the procedural precedent that allowing such a motion would create, the Supreme Court dismissed the Cherokee petition. The Court concluded that an Indian tribe was neither a state nor a foreign nation within the meaning of the Constitution. If it was true, the Court remarked, that the tribe did have a legal grievance to pursue, the Supreme Court was not the appropriate forum in which to prosecute that right. Marshall seized on this occasion not only to clarify the relationship of Indian tribes to the government but also to spell out a basis for the federal government's responsibility over Indian affairs. Whether he succeeded in establishing a workable theory or not remains a topic of intense discussion among legal minds since he offered a dualistic interpretation that can be seen as both pro-Indian and anti-Indian.

Marshall observed that the condition of Indians was unlike that of any other people in existence. Using the superior federal title claim that he had established in *Johnson v. McIntosh*, Marshall noted that, while the Indians possess an unquestionable right to occupy the land, the lands are still within a territory to which the United States asserts a title independent of the Indians' will. He pointed out that an invasion of the Cherokee lands, even though their ownership to them was admitted, would be regarded by the United States as a hostile act by another country. Recognizing, nevertheless, that the Cherokees had sufficient political status to be capable of making formal treaties with the United States, Marshall combined the political and geographical aspects of Cherokee existence to create a status in law that he called a "domestic dependent nation." Indians, he declared, resided in a state of pupilage and their relation to the United States resembled that of a ward to a guardian. "They look to our government for protection; rely upon its kindness and its power; appeal to it for relief to their wants; and address the president as their great father. They and their country are considered by foreign nations, as well as by ourselves, as being so completely under the sovereignty of the United States, that any attempt to acquire their lands, or to form a political connection with them, would be considered by all as an invasion of our territory, and an act of hostility" (30 U.S. (5 Pet.) 1, 16 (1831)).

Marshall's views in this case established the foundation upon which much of the idea of federal responsibility over Indian affairs is built. Unfortunately, only one other justice, John McLean, joined the chief justice in his opinion. Two justices disagreed entirely with Marshall's reasoning. While concluding that Marshall was correct in rejecting jurisdiction in this case, Justices Henry Baldwin and William Johnson argued that Indian nations possessed no sovereignty whatsoever although Justice Johnson, in reaching his conclusion, seemed to suggest an inchoate state of sovereignty that might be realized sometime in the future: "Their condition is something like that of the Israelites, when inhabiting the deserts. Though without land that they can call theirs in the sense of property, their right of personal self-government has never been taken from them; and such a form of government may exist though the land occupied be in fact that of another. The right to expel them may exist in that other, but the alternative of departing and retaining the right of self-government may exist in them. And such they certainly do possess; it has never been questioned, nor any attempt made at subjugating them as a people, or restraining their personal liberty except as to their land and trade" (30 U.S. (5 Pet.) 1, 27 (1831)). Johnson seemed to be saying that removal of the Cherokees would be regarded by the Court as an indication of some kind of political sovereignty insofar as it demonstrated their ability to exercise the right of self-government. But regarding trade and land, the two critical topics under consideration when all the theorizing was finished, the Cherokees had no rights whatsoever that were not subject to intervention and expropriation by the United States.

Justices Smith Thompson and Joseph Story, on the other hand, reasoned in dissenting opinions that the Cherokees did qualify as a state under the Constitution so as to bring a cause of action. They defined a state according to classical political principles as a "body of men united together to procure their mutual safety and advantage by means of their union." Citing the same treaties and examples as did the majority, Thompson and Story pointed out that the Cherokees governed themselves by their own authority and laws. And they noted that it was customary in European political relations for smaller, weaker states to attach themselves to larger states for the purposes of protection without surrendering their sovereign status. Clearly, according to Thompson and Story, the Cherokees qualified under these circumstances.

The Court's decision in the *Cherokee Nation* case is, to say the least, perplexing. The justices split four ways in their views:

Marshall and McLean: tribes are domestic dependent nations.
Thompson and Story: tribes are sovereign nations.
Baldwin: tribes have no sovereignty.
Johnson: tribes have no present sovereignty but possess an inherent political power that, given the circumstances, may mature into sovereignty in another place.

Justice Gabriel Duvall did not participate in the decision. Although the concensus is unclear regarding the actual amount of sovereignty that might be possessed by the Cherokees, at least five justices confronted the issue directly. Interestingly, Justices Thompson and Story had not written their opinion at the time the decision was formally announced. The critical response to the case was so overwhelmingly against the Indians that Chief Justice Marshall persuaded the two justices to pen their thoughts into a separate opinion so as to broaden the base of legal support for the Indian cause. The Cherokees, of course, lost their contention that they possessed a political status equal to that of other nations. But Marshall's willingness to explore the question of what their status might actually be was to prove a benefit to Indians in the future.

Chief Justice Marshall was a consummate politician. He was convinced that, had he ruled in favor of the Indians, President Jackson would have attempted to restrict the powers of the Court, and he thus hoped to avoid a confrontation with Jackson over an issue that he believed could be turned aside on procedural grounds. The following year the confrontation that Marshall hoped to avoid occurred when Samuel Worcester's appeal reached the Supreme Court. The *Worcester* case presented a much different situation than had the case the year before. Although Secretary of War Eaton had disclaimed the missionaries as federally related teachers, it was clear that they were in the Cherokee lands under the federal treaties by permission of the Cherokees and that sustaining their conviction would in effect nullify the federal interest in Indian affairs.

Although he would probably have disclaimed it, what Marshall did in the *Worcester* case was to adopt wholeheartedly Justice Thompson's argument of the previous case. Reviewing the same statutory history he had used to reach his decision in *Cherokee Nation v. Georgia*, Marshall now reached much different conclusions. He emphasized the fact that the Indians had their own political institutions and were engaged in self-government. The British, he noted, had never attempted to interfere with the domestic affairs of the Indians. The colonies had followed a similar approach in dealing with them. In analyzing the Treaty of Hopewell between the United States and the Cherokees, Marshall concluded that the treaty explicitly recognized the national character of the Cherokees and their right to self-government. Nothing in the treaties indicated that the Cherokees had surrendered their national character in spite of some phrases indicating that the Congress would henceforth assume some responsibility for their commercial relations with American citizens. The laws and treaties of the United States, Marshall declared, "contemplate the Indian territory as completely separated from that of the states." All intercourse with the Indians was to be carried on exclusively by the government of the Union. "The Cherokee nation, then, is a distinct community occupying its own territory, with boundaries accurately described, in which the laws of Georgia can have no force, and which the citizens of Georgia have no right to enter, but with the assent of the Cherokees themselves. . . . The whole intercourse between the United States and this nation is, by our constitution and laws, vested in the government of the United States" (31 U.S. (6 Pet.) 515, 561 (1832)).

The *Cherokee Nation Cases* should be considered as one fundamental statement having two basic thrusts on the status of Indian tribes. In the first case Marshall defined the relationship of Indian tribes to the federal government and in the second case he described the relationship of the tribes to the several states. Hence, two aspects of sovereignty emerge: tribes are under the protection of the federal government and in this condition lack sufficient sovereignty to claim political independence; tribes possess, however, sufficient powers of sovereignty to shield themselves from any intrusion by the states and it is the federal government's responsibility to ensure that this sovereignty is preserved.

The Cherokees won the *Worcester* case but Marshall's fears were realized. On hearing of the decision, President Jackson is reported to have remarked, "John Marshall has made his decision: now let him enforce it." Deprived of any real federal protection, the Cherokees reluctantly signed the Treaty of New Echota in 1835 and began their mournful march west on the Trail of Tears. Other tribes, seeing the fate of the Cherokees and recognizing that removal was inevitable, capitulated and also signed treaties promising to move across the Mississippi, hoping in the process to strike the best bargain they could under the circumstances.

We have dwelled upon the *Cherokee Nation Cases* at some length because, to most people working in federal Indian law, they are the classic pronouncements of the theoretical underpinnings upon which federal responsibility for Indians is based. The two fundamental ideas that emerge from these cases are contradictory in the extreme: tribes are domestic dependent nations and the relationship between tribes and the federal government resembles that of a ward to a guardian. More important for our purposes is the fact that both the federal government and the Indians have used the contradictory aspect of these ideas whenever it suited their needs. Tribes have claimed to be both domestic dependent nations and wards of the government to whom the United States owes "the highest fiduciary duty." All branches of the federal government have at one time or another labeled Indians as both wards and nations independent except for certain aspects that have been surrendered to the United States by treaty. Predicting the outcome of litigation, the legislative process, or discretionary administrative actions is therefore perilous since it cannot be predicted which set of interpretive tools will be chosen to characterize and resolve the controversy.

THE SOURCES OF FEDERAL POWER

Although the Supreme Court articulated the responsibility of the federal government for Indians in the early cases that reached it, the ultimate source of federal power is, like that of every other power exercised by the federal government, the Constitution of the United States. In the various articles that have been cited to justify federal involvement with Indians we find the allocation by the framers of this document of different functions to different branches of the national government.

Some constitutional powers are obvious in view of American history. The president, for example, is empowered to negotiate treaties (article II, section 2) and treaties with Indians stand on the same footing as those made with foreign nations. The president must have the approval of the Senate, which must ratify the treaty by a two-thirds vote, and this action has been taken on the 371 Indian treaties that are recognized as legally binding on the United States. As commander-in-chief of the armed forces of the United States, the president is also charged with keeping peace, and during the course of our nation's history presidents have directed the army both to fight Indians and to protect them. These powers of the executive are ordinary powers that have been exercised as a normal function of the office and do not specifically relate to Indians. The federal courts, including the Supreme Court, are directed to perform the judicial function, and as a matter of course cases involving Indians have come before them for decision. Only Congress, in the Commerce Clause, article I, section 8, has been specifically empowered to deal with Indians, and consequently both the executive and judicial branches have become accustomed to allowing Congress to take the lead in determining Indian policy and look to congressional intent in formulating their own ideas about the rights of Indians and the responsibilities of the federal government. In order to gain a firm and precise understanding of these sources of power, we shall proceed to examine each of these political institutions separately.

The President and the Executive Agencies

Historically, the president was a much more important political actor in the field of Indian affairs than he is today. Currently, the chief executive's primary contact with Indian problems and policy is largely ceremonial and symbolic. The president sets the tone of the administration. If the president is perceived as being favorable to Indian causes, as was Lyndon Johnson, then the remainder of the executive branch usually reflects this positive attitude and makes decisions and interpretations in tune with Indian desires. If, on the other hand, the president is somewhat aloof, as was Dwight Eisenhower or more recently Jimmy Carter, or hostile, as is Ronald Reagan, the executive branch and its agencies usually adopt a more stark and callous stance toward Indians and accomplishing anything becomes much more difficult for the Indians.

The president, however, is responsible for overseeing the activities of several important executive agencies that touch directly on Indians: the Justice Department, the Office of Management and Budget, the Interior Department, and departments that have more recently held some program responsibility for Indians, such as Agriculture, Education, and Health and Human Services. As "chief administrator," the president sets the direction of the federal government and demands faithful implementation of his policy by executive personnel although the day-to-day details and decisions regarding this implementation are made by upper-echelon administrators, such as the commissioner of Indian Affairs, the solicitor of the Interior Department, and the various undersecretaries of the departments.

During earlier periods of American political history the president assumed a very important role. When the English colonial administrators negotiated treaties with the tribes, they did so on behalf of the king, and Indians became accustomed to the personification of political power in a figure whom they called, out of politeness, their "Great Father." The recorded proceedings of the treaties made with the Iroquois in the 1700s clearly show that the Indians saw the person of the king as a symbol of English commitment to their agreements, and some treaty records show a haughty reference to both French and English "Fathers" who are unable to defend and protect their Indian "children." With the defeat of England and the establishment of the United States as the superior power to treat with, the Indians naturally looked to the president of the United States to guarantee the enforcement of the treaties. The Iroquois, in signing the Pickering treaty of 1794, wanted the assurance of George Washington himself before they would agree to its terms, believing that a personal pledge from the highest officer in the government was worth more than the reassurances of the minor officials who were sent to treat with them.

The Americans continued the English practice of signing treaties with the Indians, and since the Constitution empowered the president to make treaties on behalf of the United States (article II, section 2), subject to ratification by the Senate by two-thirds vote, the president naturally became deeply involved in Indian affairs. The first treaty negotiated by President Washington was with the Delaware Indians in 1778. Its importance is not only that it was the first treaty but also that it signaled the use of the president's assurance as a means of cementing a legal-political relationship with the Indians. Thereafter and until the present, Indians have ultimately looked to the president for the enforcement of their treaties whether or not he personally had the power, political or otherwise, to uphold the treaties.

Another power bestowed upon the president by the Constitution was the war power, which is implied from the designation of the president as commander-in-chief of the armed forces (article II, section 2) and the president's duty to see that the "laws be faithfully executed" (section 3). The Commander-in-Chief Clause is the more important of the two references. The army obviously played a very important role early in American history. It was charged with keeping the peace on the frontier and in Indian Country both as police inside the reservation and as a military buffer to protect the Indians from the whites who threatened them. The Bureau of Indian Affairs, when it was first created, was a minor office in the War Department and for almost all of the first half of the last century army posts were used to distribute treaty annuities and to provide services to the tribes who lived nearby.

One can see the impact that the president's role as commander-in-chief can have on Indian matters. In the Cherokee situation, for example, had President Jackson taken his duty seriously and enforced John Marshall's decision, it would have required him to use the federal troops in Georgia to protect the Indians. President Eisenhower did such a thing in Little Rock, Arkansas, in 1956 when the governor of that state attempted to use the National Guard to prevent the enrollment of black children in the schools of that city. President Grant, in 1875, made the same effort to keep whites out of the Black Hills since that area was preserved to the Sioux under the 1868 treaty. Unfortunately, Grant, like Jackson, finally took a wholly political course and withdrew the troops in November 1875, but as long as he was able to withstand the political criticism he did use the federal troops to protect the Indians.

In addition to the powers bestowed upon the president by the Constitution, the chief executive also possesses certain administrative powers that derive from his responsibilities to ensure that the laws of the United States are enforced. When the president acts specifically with respect to Indians, his actions are described as fulfilling his fiduciary duties; however, he possesses this power independent of his relationship to Indians. If a president, for example, directs the Justice Department to enter a case primarily for the benefit of the Indians, he is fulfilling his trust responsibility at the same time that he is also ensuring that the laws are faithfully administered and carried out. Almost always in these instances the president relies upon a previous act of Congress for his authority. One might suggest that the initiative in finding new ways of using statutory authority is the president's and that the actual authority is that of Congress.

In the closing decades of the nineteenth century, presidents used their powers to issue executive orders to resolve some Indian problems. The prohibition against further treaty-making left the executive branch without a satisfactory means of dealing with tribes that had not previously made some kind of political agreement with the United States. Rather than attempt to establish treaty or agreement relationships with these groups of Indians, presidents would issue executive orders setting aside tracts of land as reservations for them. An executive order is a formal administratively oriented policy pronouncement by the president. Once promulgated by the president and published in the *Federal Register*, it has practically the same effect as policy as if it had been a law passed by Congress and it serves as a clarification of federal law until withdrawn or superseded by an act of Congress on the subject. President Franklin Roosevelt, for example, issued Executive Order 8802 (6 Fed. Reg. 3109, 1941), which established the president's Committee on Fair Employment to ensure that blacks received fair treatment in federal employment. This executive order later was superseded by congressional actions making this subject a significant part of the federal hiring procedures. Congress thus found constitutional grounds and exercised its constitutional prerogatives in upholding and elaborating on a presidential executive order. No president, however, has used his executive order powers in this specific manner to fulfill his trust responsibilities to Indians.

The "guardianship" basis for exercising power is perhaps best perceived in the activities of the federal executive agencies. While the president as chief administrator is ultimately responsible for the policy and conduct of these agencies, the chief executive must of necessity delegate an enormous amount of authority to government officers of lesser rank in the bureaucracy. Typically, administrative agencies are the result of a joint venture between Congress and the presidency. Congress, through general legislative enactments, delegates broad powers to an agency, such as the Bureau of Indian Affairs or the Department of the Interior. The presidency retains superior authority over the agency in its efforts to carry out the congressional mandate. The agency fills in the policy details and makes up the

rules and regulations under which the policy or program will be conducted. Indeed, the congressional authorization is usually so broad
and general that the real decision-making power rests with the
agency itself. The president may chart the overall direction of the
policy, but it is the agency that particularizes it and puts it into effect.

The Bureau of Indian Affairs, perhaps more than any other
agency, spends a great deal of its time and effort formulating rules
and regulations for the development of programs and the enforcement of laws. While technically under congressional authorization
and presidential supervision, the BIA has been given enormous discretion in the development of policy affecting Indians. Its administrative rules and regulations have shaped much of the course of
Indian history and a complete compilation of them would fill a good-
sized library. Although the contemporary developments in attempting to give tribes more chance at self-determination have eroded
some of the BIA's authority, its exercise of power is still awesome.

TABLE 1. Sources of Presidential Power over Indian Affairs

Constitutional Sources	Guardianship Source

1. Treaty-making powers
2. War powers
	1. Congressional authorizations
	exercised through
	  a. Executive orders
	  b. Administrative regulations

While bureaucratic agencies and departments have been delegated immense power, they have not always exercised it in a manner
beneficial to Indians. Federal agencies, like other institutions, are
hesitant to make changes even when the changes are mandated by
the proper authority. Looking to past practices and previous interpretations of the law, federal agencies generally take a conservative
stance in determining both eligibility and scope of programs and responsibilities. And, like many other institutions, federal agencies
develop a "client" relationship with the people they serve so that
mistakes and misadministration are often excused on the grounds
that efficiency and the image of the agency require such tolerance. In
some instances the federal courts have risen to the occasion and
have held agencies responsible for not living up to their fiduciary
duty to promote the well-being of reservation Indians. The "guardianship" theory of federal responsibility is vividly illustrated in
Seminole Nation of Indians v. United States, 316 U.S. 286 (1942).
The Seminole tribes sued the federal government for mishandling

its trust funds, which were due it under the provisions of an 1856 treaty. Among other things, the tribe alleged that the government had made payments to the previous Seminole tribal government knowing that it was corrupt at the time and knowing that it would not administer the funds properly. The Supreme Court, while sending the case back to the lower court for further determinations, noted that the government assumes a distinctive trust obligation when dealing with "these dependent and sometimes exploited people." It is charged, therefore, with "moral obligations of the highest responsibility and trust." In determining a standard of conduct to which governmental agencies must conform, the Court concluded that governmental action must be judged by the "most exacting fiduciary standards."

Governmental agencies acting in their trust capacity for Indian people are thus held to an exceedingly high level of conduct. If the government fails to maintain this high level of performance, it becomes liable for breach of its fiduciary duty. In the past most of the judgments that tribes have received for an administrative breach of fiduciary duty have been in the form of a monetary compensation. Unfortunately, this compensation comes decades after the original breach, much too late to prevent the damage done, and usually in amounts far less than the original damages. In many instances, however, the Indians would prefer a nonmonetary form of compensation, such as the preservation of a land sanctuary or restoration of lands illegally taken by an erroneous survey. There is probably a trend in the direction of Indian complainants seeking nonmonetary relief. During the Nixon administration several tribes, including the Taos Pueblo, the Yakimas, and the Warm Springs Indians, received lands back instead of money. In *Pyramid Lake Paiute Tribe of Indians v. Morton*, 354 F. Supp. 252 (D.C. 1973), the Paiutes challenged an administrative regulation of the secretary of the interior that would have diverted water from Pyramid Lake, which was located within the tribe's reservation and was its only resource. A federal district court found that the secretary's decision had been arbitrary and was a breach of his fiduciary duty to protect the rights of the Indians. Instead of awarding monetary damages, the court ordered the secretary to submit an amended regulation using criteria that would satisfy the "most exacting fiduciary standards."

While the importance of presidential power over Indian affairs is not as extensive as it once was, the influence of the chief executive is still very much alive, especially in the activities and policies of administrative agencies. A summary of these executive powers may be catalogued as shown in Table 1. As impressive as this array of power is, the influence of the chief executive on Indian affairs is not nearly as great or as comprehensive as that exercised by Congress.

Congress and Its Plenary Power

Like the president, Congress derives its powers over Indian affairs from two basic sources. The first is constitutionally based—the Commerce Clause. Article I, section 8, stipulates that Congress shall have the power to regulate commerce with the Indian tribes. This stipulation, by the way, is the only grant of power in the federal constitution that specifically mentions Indians. It is a reservoir of enormous powers that Congress has exercised over the past two centuries. The second basic source of congressional power, like that of the president, emanates from the "guardianship" theory. Taken together, these sources of power provide Congress with an almost omnipotent control over Indians.

The political influence that Congress wields over Indian affairs has been characterized as plenary, which means complete, absolute, and unqualified, and in practice this has proven to be true. The legislative branch has the power to recognize Indian tribes, to provide or withhold services to them, and even to terminate their very existence—at least insofar as the United States recognizes them as having a political nature. Indians and Indian Country are virtually at the mercy of Congress. Judicial restraints, as we shall discuss shortly, are negligible and political restraints are even less an obstacle to the exercise of congressional power over Indians. When it comes to federal policy formation, Congress possesses the strength to be a true savior or a dreadful villain depending on the occasion and one's disposition to view the substance of the policy.

The origins of legislative control over American Indians can be traced back to the first Congress in 1789. Its very first act was to establish a Department of War, one of the duties of which was to render military needs relative to Indian affairs. Using the Indian reference in the Commerce Clause as an enabling device, the legislature proceeded to pass a series of intercourse acts designed to regulate trade with the Indians. The first of these laws, interestingly enough, was designated the Non-Intercourse Act of 1790 (1 Stat. 137). It was designed to protect the Indians from unscrupulous white traders, who had the habit of exploiting the native Americans. The Non-Intercourse Act made it a misdemeanor to negotiate with the Indians for the purchase of land without first obtaining the permission of the federal government. This prohibition not only protected the Indians from commercial exploitation but also centralized enormous power in the hands of Congress and the federal government.

The act was subsequently renewed several times with additional amendments and an expansion of the prohibitions that had to be respected in the Indian trade.

From this early series of legislative enactments, Congress has expanded its control over the destiny of American Indians with hundreds of additional federal statutes. Indeed, the legislature's power to regulate commerce with the Indians is broader than the general authority that Congress has over interstate commerce per se although the recent expansion of the Commerce Clause has grown nearly as broad as the Indian Commerce Clause. The Indian Commerce Clause is expansive enough to engulf all of Indian life and not merely the narrow fields of trade and commerce although it was originally intended merely to supervise the proper commercial relations between the Indian tribes and the individual American citizens who wished to trade with them. Thus, Congress has assumed criminal jurisdiction in major felony cases, authorized land surveys, regulated liquor consumption, bestowed citizenship, protected political rights, and provided for Indian education—all activities touching upon Indian life can be said to fall within the scope of the plenary power of Congress.

In justifying this extensive exercise of power, the courts have suggested that Congress has, in addition to the Indian Commerce Clause, a "guardianship" function to regulate Indian affairs. As early as 1886, the Supreme Court implied a fiduciary obligation in upholding the constitutionality of the Major Crimes Act. In *United States v. Kagama*, 118 U.S. 375 (1886), Justice Samuel F. Miller relied heavily on the notion that Indian tribes were wards of the nation: they were communities dependent on the government for food, protection, and their political rights. "From their very weakness and helplessness . . . there arises the duty of protection, and with it the power." Congress had not only the right but also the duty to exercise its power as it saw fit to provide for the well-being of its Indian wards. The "guardianship" philosophy proclaimed by John Marshall in the *Cherokee Nation* case, originally simply an analogy that described the relationship that tribes had with the United States, in *Kagama* had matured to a complete and absolute power generated by and justified in the needs of the defenseless Indians. This power, because of the disparity in the position of the tribes vis-à-vis the United States, is not limited to the exercise of power by the president or other officer or employee of the executive agencies but serves as a broad foundation upon which Congress may legitimize its control over Indians and Indian-related matters.

But the weakness in *Kagama* is that the Supreme Court argues from the absence of any firm constitutional authority in Congress to imply a general "guardianship." Marshall's original list of enumerated powers, which included the treaty-making power, the Commerce Clause, and federal proprietary rights in the land, formed the context within which the concept of Indians as "wards" made sense. *Kagama* probably assumes the same doctrinal background but the doctrines are not made a central part of the argument. Indeed, it appears in *Kagama* that social-economic-political weakness of the Indians alone provides a justification for congressional intervention and this line of reasoning is a decided departure from the mainstream of constitutionally enumerated powers of Congress.

The destiny of Indian lives is so firmly grasped by congressional hands that even the courts have been reluctant to challenge this tradition. This same measure of judicial self-restraint has not been true, however, with reference to presidential or bureaucratic actions. If either of these institutions infringes upon the rights of individual Indians or Indian tribes, the courts have not been hesitant to invalidate these encroachments. But the judiciary virtually never tweaks the nose of Congress when it passes legislation touching upon Indian matters. Instead the courts adopt a posture of deference toward the legislature. In fact, the Supreme Court has never declared invalid an act of Congress as being beyond the power of the legislature to control Indian Country. This fact is astonishing when one realizes how active the Court has been in restraining Congress in other fields of endeavor. It should be noted, however, that the Supreme Court did stipulate in 1977 that the legislative power of Congress is not immune from judicial scrutiny (*Delaware Tribal Business Committee v. Weeks*, 430 U.S. 73 (1977)).

While the courts have deferred to Congress in hesitating to declare its legislative enactments invalid, this deference does not mean that the judiciary has not indirectly applied restraints to the legislature. Through its judicial commands, the courts have required Congress to exercise its plenary power in an exacting and precise manner. This legal dictate is manifest in a number of court cases, one of which involved an effort by Congress to avoid making an unpopular political decision between two groups of Indian claimants, the other instances being those involving the problem of treaty abrogation.

The Dawes Commission was charged with the allotment of the lands of the Five Civilized Tribes—the Cherokees, Choctaws, Creeks, Chickasaws, and Seminoles—in Oklahoma during the first decade of this century, and in performing its work it naturally made mistakes in determining those tribal members eligible to receive allotments within the tribe. A group of claimants, sophisticated enough to realize that through proper lobbying effort they could get congressional approval to take their individual cases to the Supreme Court, had their congressmen insert in the appropriations act for the fiscal year 1907 a special section that allowed them to appeal to the Supreme Court and also allowed them to recover their legal expenses from Congress. In *United States v. Muskrat*, 219 U.S. 346 (1911), the Supreme Court dismissed the appeal, noting that this effort was a thinly disguised attempt to use the Supreme Court to give an advisory opinion and that no actual controversy had arisen that needed to be resolved. This decision was as much an admonition to the congressional sponsors of the special section as it was a slap on the hand to Congress itself but the occasion has never arisen again and the representatives seem particularly leery of any similar requests from their constituents.

When the Indian nations treated with the United States government, they undoubtedly assumed that the negotiated agreements would endure "ad infinitum." To their surprise, dismay, and chagrin, the treaties hardly lasted long enough for the ink to dry in most cases. Congress and the sweep of historical events together nullified many of the treaties and the western movement of settlements made it necessary to renegotiate many of the treaties until there was little that the tribes could do except endorse the proposals sent to them by the president or the treaty commission. Congress has formally abrogated only one treaty and that occurred in 1862 as a result of the Minnesota war with the eastern Sioux (12 Stat. 512).

More often the situation has arisen where Congress has passed a statute that comes into conflict with the provisions of an earlier treaty. The Supreme Court, attempting to reconcile this impasse, then has implied that Congress created the conflict knowingly and intended to abrogate a certain part of the treaty. Indians have bitterly complained about this practice since it appears to take a rule of construction that should be only a guideline and use it to rewrite history, in the process depriving them of their legal rights. Such was the situation in the landmark case of *Lone Wolf v. Hitchcock*, 187 U.S. 553 (1903), which remains as the classic judicial statement articulating the doctrine of the plenary powers of Congress over Indian affairs. The federal government in *Lone Wolf* attempted to obtain 2.5 million acres of Kiowa, Comanche, and Kiowa-Apache lands. The Jerome Commission, sent to negotiate with the three tribes, was unable to obtain the approval of three-quarters of the adult males of the tribes as required by an 1867 treaty. The Senate, nevertheless, acting as if it had received the tribe's consent, passed an act that varied considerably from the original agreement made by the tribe.

Lone Wolf sued Ethan A. Hitchcock, then secretary of the interior, seeking to prevent him from implementing the statute because it violated the treaty. When the issue of treaty abrogation reached the Supreme Court, Justice Edward D. White concluded that Congress could, in a pressing national emergency, do whatever was necessary with the Indian lands and that therefore this power could be exercised in the instant case. Justice White was never able to point out the emergency that did exist, and at the end of his decision he lamely pretended that the confiscation of the tribal lands was in effect merely a congressional change in the form of tribal investment and hence not a violation of the treaty at all. The Court went on to note that there is no doubt that Congress is under a moral obligation to act in good faith in accordance with past treaties. But, as in the case of treaties with foreign nations, Congress may pass laws that conflict with, amend substantially, or even abrogate existing treaties. In the eyes of the law, if there is a conflict between a treaty and a federal law, it is the one most recent in time, absent a vested property right, that prevails.

While the Court deferred to the treaty abrogation power of Congress in _Lone Wolf_, it was generally assumed that Congress must clearly and specifically indicate its intention to do so before abrogation of a treaty would be implied. Indeed, the judiciary has proclaimed this doctrine in a number of cases, although the lower courts have not always applied it vigorously. In the _Seneca Nation of Indians Cases_, lower federal courts permitted the Corps of Engineers, supposedly acting as a delegated agent of Congress, to make the determination of abrogation (_Seneca Nation of Indians v. Brucker_, 262 F.2d 27 (D.C. 1959), and _Seneca Nation of Indians v. United States_, 338 F.2d 55 (2d Cir. 1964)). But in a more recent decision, a federal court re-affirmed the general notion that a clear expression of congressional purpose to terminate a treaty must be shown. The Corps of Engineers was without authority to take the tribal lands of the Winnebago tribe in the absence of an indication of this intent (_United States v. Winnebago Tribe of Nebraska_, 542 F.2d 1002 (8th Cir. 1976)). The Court stressed that the intention to abrogate a treaty is not to be lightly imputed to Congress.

In 1980 the Court took another step in suggesting that the plenary power of Congress was less than absolute. Climaxing a long struggle with the Sioux Indians, Congress in 1877 passed a law divesting the Sioux Nation of its rights to the Black Hills. The Sioux argued that this was contrary to the Fort Laramie treaty of 1868, which set aside the Black Hills for the absolute and undisturbed use by the Sioux Nation. After a complex legal battle that endured for generations, the Supreme Court awarded to the Sioux Nation $17.1 million, which represented what experts appraised the area to be worth—in defiance of the recorded testimony of several negotiating sessions in which the Sioux demanded specific sums for leasing the region to the United States for a period of years (*United States v. Sioux Nation of Indians*, 100 S.Ct. 2716 (1980)). The Sioux, of course, were furious with the decision since they wanted the land restored or the fair market value plus land but not simply a government check that represented only pennies on the dollar value without interest on the sum that had been due them for over a century.

While recognizing the enormous power of Congress to deal with Indian affairs, the Court in the *Sioux Nation* case proclaimed that congressional control and management were not unlimited. The legislature undoubtedly had the power to abrogate a treaty by subsequent legislation, but in doing so Congress had to take into account the legal rights of those involved. The Court proceeded to reject the legislative rationalization that it was merely taking the Black Hills as a basis for advancing the interest of the tribe through management of tribal property—a theory at which the Supreme Court had hinted in *Lone Wolf*. Instead, a majority of the justices concluded that the statute was in fact a "taking" of the property. As such the Sioux tribe was entitled to just compensation, a legal obligation the Congress owed to the tribe. In arriving at this decision, the Court was restricting congressional power. Admittedly, the limitation was perhaps less than substantial, but the Court at least acknowledged that some limitations existed.

The scope of congressional power over Indian affairs is still not clear. The sweep of judicial decisions at the very least indicates that Congress in abrogating a treaty must take the necessary steps clearly and precisely to indicate its intention to bring about abrogation. Furthermore, as indicated in *Sioux Nation*, Congress must provide compensation to tribes if there is evidence that compensable rights have been violated. But in the scheme of things, the control that Congress possesses over the lives of Indians remains awesome.

The Supreme Court: Arbiter of Indian Legal Problems

Much of the course of Indian history has been determined by the decisions of the federal courts. From the foundations articulated in the *Cherokee Nation Cases* by Chief Justice John Marshall to the contemporary land and treaty controversies confronting the Burger Court, judicial determination of tribal rights has been indispensable to an understanding of Indian law and politics. Not every social issue touching upon Indian Country finds its way into the federal courts, but those issues that have reached the judiciary have left an indelible mark on Indian life and customs.

Before examining the role that the federal courts have played in exercising power over Indian affairs, it is necessary to note that the courts are practical, political institutions. While the ingredients of a judicial opinion include a sizable portion of a judge's ideology, this orientation is often tempered by political practicalities. The compromises that John Marshall brought to the *Cherokee Nation Cases*, for instance, were a reflection of many factors: Marshall's perspective on Indian problems, commercial interests and their possible conflicts, competitive philosophies of state versus national dominance, the combat of competing political parties, and the practicality of the final decision. One should not, therefore, evaluate judicial decisions by the rigorous standard of whether they provided absolute support for or steadfast opposition to the Indian cause. The role of the courts must be judged within the context of the political climate of the times, the identity of the parties in contention, and the general understanding of Indian matters possessed by the public. Furthermore, judicial decision-making must be seen as the "art of the possible," the result of accommodations. This aspect may prove frustrating to the litigants, but it is the way in which our system works.

Given the "accommodating" nature of our judicial system, an assessment of the role of the federal courts with reference to Indian issues reveals that the judiciary has on the whole been quite supportive. Its power has been exercised in a manner that has generally been beneficial to Indians, albeit generally on minor issues, while not wholly detrimental on the larger more important issues. Certainly there are decisions that cast doubt on the validity of this proposition. Some critics point to the patronizing tone of many court opinions and the apparent rejection of Indian values as important points to consider when reviewing a case. But when viewed as a whole, federal courts have been a friend to the Indians more often than they have been a foe. The validity of this notion can be illustrated by examining two important contributions that have resulted from the exercise of judicial power. The first relates to the creation of rules of judicial construction that have favored Indian rights. The second achievement pertains to the protective shield that the courts have provided Indians as a buffer against state encroachment into tribal affairs.

Rules of Judicial Construction.   One of the major responsibilities of the Supreme Court is its formulation of the rules of construction that will be applied to the law in the cases it will hear. It can liberally interpret a statute or it can view it very narrowly. It can create a presumption in favor of constitutionality or it can balance competitive constitutional interests. By adopting a particular position with respect to the interpretation of a statute or treaty or by presuming a theory to be binding, the Court can affect the outcome of a given case and bolster or reduce the development of any particular legal concept. Over the years, the Supreme Court has developed an elaborate number of judicial interpretations to assist the justices in deciding legal issues: statutes are presumed to be constitutional, the courts will not determine the constitutionality of an issue if the case can be decided on other grounds, and judges will not formulate a rule of constitutional law broader than is required by the precise facts of the case under consideration. The application of these norms of judicial construction have dealt many an aspiring litigant a mortal blow.

The Supreme Court has developed a set of judicial rules to be applied to Indian cases as well. On the whole, these norms have been to the advantage of Indian litigants. The Court's attitude toward Indian problems has been conditioned by the distinct disadvantages the Indians faced when treating with whites in the past. The treaties inevitably were written by whites in English for their own benefit and rarely did the Indians know what was actually written on the parchment laid before them during the negotiations. Tribal leaders were accustomed to making treaties without any written account whatsoever. A simple pledge, obtained by looking directly in the eyes of the other party, and a ceremonial occasion marked by the exchange of presents, with mutual promises sealed by religious commitment and individual integrity, were usually sufficient for most Indians. Thus the chiefs were generally inexperienced in a type of negotiations wherein sharp bargaining was the order of the day conducted in a language they did not understand. The federal court in *United States v. Washington*, 384 F. Supp. 312 (W.D. Wash. 1974), a case involving off-reservation treaty fishing rights, captured the essence of these difficulties well: ["Since . . . the vast majority of Indians at the treaty councils did not speak or understand English, the treaty provisions and the remarks of the treaty commissioners were interpreted by Colonel Shaw to the Indians in the Chinook jargon and then translated into native languages by Indian interpreters. Chinook jargon, a trade medium of limited vocabulary and simple grammar, was inadequate to express precisely the legal effects of the treaties, although the general meaning of the treaty language could be explained. Many of those present, however, did not understand Chinook jargon" (p. 315). Most, but not all, of the negotiations conducted with the tribes occurred under similar circumstances.

In addition to language problems, Indians were often overwhelmed by fraud and political and military aggression. White officials were known to choose an Indian whom they considered friendly, designate him as a chief regardless of his standing within the tribe, and negotiate the treaty with him on behalf of the whole Indian nation. The most blatant example of this practice occurred at the Horse Creek treaty, which is otherwise known as the first Fort Laramie treaty, held in 1851. The United States demanded that the Sioux choose a principal chief who would accept responsibility for all their actions, and the Indians refused. So the United States chose Conquering Bear and stated that it would thereafter consider him the leader of the Sioux Nation. When he was killed by American troops in the Grattan fight at Fort Laramie in 1854, the American policy was discredited since the Sioux could not believe that the United States would deliberately kill the man they had chosen to recognize as the leader of the Indians. Other aspects of the historical record have similar unsavory histories.

The courts recognized that the past exploitation of the Indians could not be sanctioned by the force of law and hence developed a set of judicial rules by which to deal with these problems. Among the more important rules of construction are

1. Ambiguities in treaties are to be constructed in favor of the Indian claimants.
2. Indian treaties are to be interpreted as the Indians would have understood them.
3. Indian treaties are to be liberally construed in favor of the Indians.
4. Treaties reserve to Indians all rights that have not been granted away (reserved rights doctrine).

These rules of judicial interpretation were not forced upon the courts by Congress or the presidency; rather, they were created by the courts themselves as an aid in the settlement of Indian legal disputes. They are aids strongly supportive of the Indian cause and designed to offset the past exploitation of native Americans by government negotiators. To illustrate this point in more detail, let us examine one of these rules of construction, the reserved rights doctrine, to see just how important judicial interpretation can be in a given case.

In 1859, the Yakima Indians entered into a treaty with the United States in which the tribe gave up certain lands and retained others. One of the basic provisions in the treaty related to the exclusive right of taking fish on the reservation. Off-reservation fishing rights were to be guaranteed "at all usual and accustomed places, in common with the citizens of the Territory." In 1896 the federal government instituted an action on behalf of the Yakimas to enjoin members of the white community from obstructing the off-reservation fishing rights of the tribe. The white fishermen operated "fish wheels," which were so efficient that they enabled the whites to harvest almost the whole run of salmon and so large that they preempted the traditional fishing sites of the tribe. Thus the Yakimas were effectively deprived of the right to fish because of the activity of the white commercial fishermen.

The lower federal court held that the Indians under the treaty had acquired no rights broader than those enjoyed by the white inhabitants of the state, which meant that fish wheels such as those used by the commercial fishermen, when licensed by the state, effectively eliminated Indian fishing. On appeal to the Supreme Court, the high bench reversed the lower court and found in favor of the Indians (*United States v. Winans*, 198 U.S. 371 (1905)). The Court concluded that in its treaty with the United States the tribe had reserved a right that was superior to and prior to the rights the citizens of the territory held. In emphasizing the "reserved rights doctrine," the Court noted that a "treaty was not a grant of rights *to* Indians, but a grant of rights *from* them—a reservation of those not granted" (emphasis supplied).

The reserved rights doctrine has been exceedingly important in the field of American Indian law, particularly in the area of water law. Instead of narrowly construing treaties and agreements such that Indian rights would be limited to the literal wording in each treaty, the Court has expanded through judicial interpretation the rights of Indian nations. In the classic water rights case, *Winters v. United States*, 207 U.S. 564 (1908), involving an agreement with the Gros Ventre and Assiniboine tribes, the Court constructed a context in which it could examine the probable expectations that must have been present in the minds of the Indians and the federal officials when making the agreement in order to protect the idea that rights obtained in a treaty are grants not from the United States but from the Indians: "The reservation was a part of a very much larger tract which the Indians had the right to occupy and use and which was adequate for the habits and wants of a nomadic and uncivilized people. It was the policy of the Government, it was the desire of the Indians, to change those habits and to become a pastoral and civilized people. If they should become such the original tract was too extensive, but a smaller tract would be inadequate without a change of conditions. The lands were arid and, without irrigation, were practically valueless" (p. 576). The Indians, the Court then found, were entitled to the water that arose upon or passed through the reservation and the appropriators who had diverted water before it had reached the reservation were prohibited from further taking until the Indian needs were satisfied.

The reserved rights doctrine is thus predicated upon the idea that in the beginning the Indian tribes possessed exclusive control over their lands and affairs. When treating with the United States government, the negotiated treaty provisions contained only those rights and benefits. *All else was retained.* The Court just as easily could have reached a contrary conclusion in either the *Winans* or the *Winters* case. Through its power of judicial construction, the Court effectively makes policy by developing legal doctrines and concepts, and in these cases it could have announced a policy fostering Indian rights or restricting them. In announcing the reserved rights doctrine, the Court formulated a rule of judicial construction expanding the rights of Indian tribes and clarifying the manner in which treaty documents should be read so as to eliminate, insofar as possible, the disparities that history and cultural difference had created.

The rules of judicial interpretation that the Court has developed over the years to protect the Indians have played a large role in American Indian law. But being judicially imposed rules, they can be ignored if a court is so disposed. One of the frustrating circumstances surrounding Indian law is, not infrequently, the existence of one set of rules that apply specifically to Indian issues and a different set of rules that apply to the law in general. One judge may apply the Indian law precedent and rules of construction, while another judge may ignore these and incorporate the traditional rules of construction, and a third judge may cite the developed rules of construction traditionally used in Indian cases and then announce that the facts of the situation or other circumstances taken together make it necessary to depart from these rules in this particular case. The decisions emanating from the use of different rules may be in marked contrast—one might favor Indian claimants while the other could destroy their chance of prevailing. The power of the Court in formulating rules of judicial construction is great. Fortunately, the Court has generally exercised this power in a fashion favorable to Indian tribes and the lower courts have not departed from this example to any substantial degree.

Protection from State Encroachment.   A second area in which the federal courts have played a critical role in the protection of Indian rights is their rigorous distinction between state and federal powers and responsibilities. While the overall problem of tribal-state relations is treated later in the text, it is important to note that the federal courts have developed a protective shield in doctrine against state attempts to encroach upon Indian rights and privileges.

Historically, the notions of the internal sovereignty of Indian tribes and their immunity from state intrusion or co-optation were articulated in *Worcester v. Georgia,* the second of the *Cherokee Nation Cases.* In *Worcester,* as will be recalled, Chief Justice Marshall recognized the Cherokee Nation as a distinct political community, complete with geographical boundaries within which the laws of Georgia could have no force. This internal tribal sovereignty as affirmed by the treaty operated as a shield that frustrated attempts by state officials to exercise authority over Indians and their lands and property. Even Justice Johnson, in his opinion in *Cherokee Nation v. Georgia,* did not deny the ancient nature of Cherokee self-government, and if he did not find that the Cherokees constituted a foreign nation in the sense demanded by the constitutional requirement for standing, neither did he deny the existence of a distinct form of political organization possessed by the tribe. Over the years the "domestic dependent" Indian nations became exempt from state taxation, political regulation, administrative intrusion, and preemption as well as the application of criminal and civil state laws.

The difficulties confronting tribal-state relations over the years have been real and not merely figments of the Indian imagination. The quest for Indian land, the lack of understanding by both whites and Indians of one another's cultural differences, the jealousies among the white population over Indian exemptions from state laws and regulations, the continuing racial discrimination existing outside the reservation borders, and, most especially, the economic competition have all contributed to a troubled relationship between the people on the reservations and the white settlements that have come to surround them. Perhaps as distressing as any single factor has been the perpetual and very strong belief held by most whites that equality before the law means cultural homogeneity; the attitude that this belief has produced has generally been responsible for even the most sympathetic whites believing devoutly that the Indians should be classified as regular citizens under state laws. Separateness breeds ignorance, ignorance breeds fear, and fear breeds conflict. Strange as it seems, the fear of the majority generated by the cultural and behavioral differences of the minority is a more potent force than the fear by the minority of oppression by the majority.

The reason for this disparity is obvious. The majority rarely considers the foundations upon which it exists and any alternative style of life that seems successful raises fundamental questions the majority prefers to resolve by imposed force rather than by reflective thought.

The hostility between Indians and whites is particularly intense when two communities compete economically with one another. This hostility has been a continuing theme in Indian-white relations since the colonial farmers sought Indian hunting lands. State political leaders, executive and legislative, have a tendency to respond to the economic interests within the state, and these powerful groups, although frequently few in numbers, represent the forces that constitute important elements of the society. In a similar manner, state judges tend to reflect the values and philosophy of the community and are inclined to protect its interests and to assume that it represents the "common sense" view of things. Most state judges are elected officials and the needs and interests of their "established" constituents are often manifest in state court opinions. While Indians participate in state elections, their influence and priority in state affairs have always been minimal. Federal judges, on the other hand, being appointed for life, possess greater judicial independence and traditionally have responded to the needs of Indians more favorably than state judges. Indians have always been able to secure greater benefits and protection in the federal arena than in that of the states.

An important part of the federal protection extended to Indian rights is the encompassing nature of the federal relationship. Federal judges are not inclined to view state efforts to extend their powers and jurisdictions favorably because of the direct threat that such expansion poses to the exercise of federal powers. The Indian cases producing the most beneficial results for the Indians are those in which the Indian rights are interwoven with federal responsibilities so that it appears as if the state is directly confronting federal authority in that particular area. Absent a federal statute directly and clearly allocating a function to the states, federal judges are inclined to preserve to the federal government—and the tribal governments under its charge—all those powers and rights they can be said to have possessed historically.

Undoubtedly, the judicial independence enjoyed by federal judges permitted them to keep alive and to nurture the doctrine of "internal tribal sovereignty." For years the judges used this notion as a means of isolating Indians until the Congress made a definitive statement on the final disposition of Indian matters. Thus, while it was apparent to everyone following the allotment act that the intent of Congress was to assimilate Indians into the various local societies of the several states, federal courts zealously protected the remaining federal interest until a clear and unmistakable signal came from Congress of the finality of this effort. The classic case in this respect dealt with three Indian tribes in Kansas early in the period in which the federal government was experimenting with allotments.

Under the removal policy the tribes of the Mississippi and Ohio valleys were moved to the area that now composes the states of Kansas and Oklahoma. The Shawnees, the Weas, and the Miamis had all moved to Kansas and exchanged their eastern lands for large tracts in the eastern part of the territory. Over the years they had ceded parts of their new lands, adopted the whites' agriculture, participated in activities of the local communities, and even sold tribal memberships to their white neighbors. The state, recognizing that the Indians were as assimilated as they could possibly be, sought to tax their lands. The Supreme Court, however, turned aside this challenge remarking: "If the tribal organization of the Shawnees is preserved intact, and recognized by the political department of the government as existing, then they are a 'people distinct from others,' capable of making treaties, separated from the jurisdiction of Kansas, and to be governed exclusively by the government of the Union. If under the control of Congress, from necessity there can be no divided authority. If they have outlived many things, they have not outlived the protection afforded by the Constitution, treaties, and laws of Congress" (*The Kansas Indians*, 5 Wall. 737, 755–756 (1866)). This concept, the continued protection of federal laws absent a clear termination by Congress, has formed the barricade at which state efforts to govern Indians have been turned back.

Recent history has witnessed a drift away from this protective cloak the courts have created for tribal governments because of the extreme complexity of modern conditions. The expansion of federal welfare programs to all citizens and the designation of state governments as administrative agents for the distribution of federal largesse has made it difficult to keep the lines of jurisdiction clear. Passage of Public Law 280 and then its subsequent partial repeal in the 1968 Indian Civil Rights Act have only served to complicate the manner in which both tribes and state governments consider their rights and responsibilities. Several efforts have been made recently in Congress to establish procedures whereby states and tribes can draw up and ratify compacts that would enable them to share jurisdiction and responsibilities in certain areas, but no final action has been taken on any of these proposals because of the confusing state of the law.

The initial erosion of the doctrine of internal sovereignty appeared in 1959 in an important decision, *Williams v. Lee*, 358 U.S. 217 (1959). A superior court in the state of Arizona attempted to exercise civil jurisdiction over a case in which a non-Indian sought to collect an overdue debt for goods he had sold to an Indian couple on the Navajo Reservation. Since the Navajo tribe had its own tribal court system in operation, the Supreme Court held that the state of Arizona could not extend its jurisdiction over the reservation. "There can be no doubt," the Court reasoned, "that to allow the exercise of state jurisdiction here would undermine the authority of the tribal courts over Reservation affairs and hence would infringe on the right of the Indians to govern themselves." The key question here is whether, in the absence of congressional legislation giving the state permission to do so, the state intrusion would infringe upon the right of the tribe to govern itself.

Williams v. Lee was a departure from the *Worcester* and *Kansas Indians* pronouncements on internal sovereignty. Under these precedents the protective buffer was high and almost impregnable. But under *Williams* a new test emerges: if the state intrusion does not infringe upon tribal self-government, the state might be able to extend its jurisdiction onto the reservation. In 1973 the Court went a step further in its erosion of tribal sovereignty in *McClanahan v. Arizona State Tax Commission*, 411 U.S. 164 (1973), by indicating that the clear trend had been away from the idea of Indian sovereignty. The concept of sovereignty, the Court suggested, was to be used only as a "backdrop" against which the applicable treaties and statutes must be read. The Court then proceeded to talk in terms of "federal preemption." The question was not so much that of tribal sovereignty but whether the treaties, statutes, and tribal laws had given rise to a "preemption" of the subject field so as to preclude state intrusions into Indian Country.

Observers of Indian legal development argue whether *McClanahan* is the beginning of a new era of gradual but persistent erosion of tribal sovereign powers or whether it reflects the temper of the times. The militant cry of Indian protest, particularly during the occupation of Wounded Knee, which took place the same year the *McClanahan* decision was handed down, was that of unrestricted tribal sovereignty. Indeed, the American Indian Movement has as one of its avowed goals the removal of the tribal government chartered under the Indian Reorganization Act and its replacement with a council of traditional chiefs. It would have been politically explosive, critics of *McClanahan* argue, for the Supreme Court to have upheld tribal sovereignty directly while several hundred Indian activitists were holding a village by armed force. Consequently, the

Court did uphold tribal sovereignty albeit in an oblique and non-controversial manner since the United States would not have signed treaties with nonsovereign entities nor would it have continued a rigorous protection to a group with no political status whatsoever. The controversy may continue for some time between the two interpretations of *McClanahan* until sufficient case law has developed so that the full implications, if any, of this case can be seen in their historical perspective.

Today it is safe to say that the past doctrine of tribal sovereignty, at least as Indians would prefer to have it articulated, has been relegated to a subordinate position in federal law and has been replaced with a more flexible philosophy of federal pre-emption of Indian matters and an occasional recognition of the congressional delegation of federal powers and responsibilities to tribal government (*United States v. Mazurie*, 419 U.S. 544 (1975)). Pre-emption is determined by the Court's examination of past treaties, statutes, tribal laws, and the path of litigation leading to the instant case under consideration. As a "backdrop," Indian sovereignty assumes a peculiar role in that it shifts the burden of proof initially required by the case to place a heavy burden on those states and their agencies who would assume jurisdiction over Indian matters. Tribal sovereignty in this instance provides the substance within the federal-tribal framework against which everything else is measured in its historical context. Shifts in congressional policy respecting the political status of Indian tribes and their consequent exercise of powers can thus be measured against this backdrop of sovereignty.

Tribal sovereignty, however, took a surprising turn in 1982. In *Merrion v. Jicarilla Apache Tribe*, 102 S.Ct. 894 (1982), the Supreme Court held that the tribe has an inherent power to impose a severance tax on mining activities conducted on the reservations as part of its power to govern and pay for the costs of self-government. The Court held that Congress had not acted to deprive the tribe of the power to levy severance taxes and hence its "inherent powers" could be exercised. Citing the Natural Gas Policy Act of 1978, which included taxes imposed by an Indian tribe in its definition of costs that may be recovered under federal energy pricing regulations, the Court felt that such taxes would not contravene national policies and that tribal authority to levy these kinds of taxes was not divested under this or any preceding acts.

In mid-July hearings were held before the Senate Finance Subcommittee on Taxation on a proposal to give tribal governments the same status as municipal and state governments. The proposal would allow a deduction for contributions to a tribal government or to a candidate for tribal office; it would permit a deduction for taxes paid to the tribe, exempt the tribal government from federal highway and fuel taxes, and provide a tax exemption for interest earned on tribal bonds. Tribal leaders in attendance at the hearings stressed the amount of money that tribes spend each year on governmental functions. The Treasury Department, in seeking and supporting this amendment to the Internal Revenue Code, adopted the argument of *Merrion* that, if Congress had not divested the tribal governments of the powers to raise revenue for purposes of self-government and they did perform such functions, they should be treated the same as other units of government for federal tax purposes. While neither *Merrion* nor the hearings provided a definitive statement on tribal sovereignty, they did indicate that practical problems might lend additional strength to the Indian side of the argument.

Given the Supreme Court's notion that tribal sovereignty should be relegated to a "backdrop" status with primary attention focused on federal pre-emption, is it reasonable to argue that the Court is continuing to function as an institutional support for American Indians today? Some Indian observers believe that anything less than a high profile for the idea of sovereignty cannot help but disadvantage Indian tribes. While this view may seem persuasive, there has actually been less change than might be supposed. More to the point may be the present de-emphasis by the Court of tribal sovereignty in an effort to protect it from frontal assault by its opponents. Under the federal pre-emption approach, the Court has permitted state incursions into reservation affairs in only two cases, *Moe v. Confederated Salish and Kootenai Tribes of the Flathead Indian Reservation*, 425 U.S. 463 (1976), and *Washington v. Confederated Tribes of the Colville Indian Reservation*, 100 S.Ct. 2069 (1980). Both of these cases dealt with state cigarette taxes that were imposed on nontribal purchasers. These decisions hardly constitute a significant departure from the general stance of federal support. They follow, in fact, a very rigorous definition of tribal membership and activities and do not intrude on the rights of tribal members. They merely limit the intercourse between tribal matters and state citizens in much the same manner as the original Commerce Clause thinking must have conceived the problem of such activities.

It may be that future decisions will continue to move somewhat in the direction of restricting the clientele with whom Indians can conduct tax-exempted activities, although the movement would undoubtedly be incremental and deliberate and based upon a tightening of the relationship between federal and state interests rather than an erosion of tribal status. There has not even been a hint that the movement has assumed catastrophic forms. The fact remains that the Supreme Court and the lower federal courts continue to offer tribal governments formidable protection against state intrusions into Indian Country and there is every reason to believe that this disposition will continue into the immediate future.

The Supreme Court as the arbiter of Indian legal problems has not always resolved issues in a manner that has pleased the tribes. Particularly in the appeals it has accepted in claims cases, the Court's performance has been somewhat less than satisfactory and its reluctance to probe deeper into characterizations of historical incidents has left much to be desired by the Indians. The pendulum has swung in a contrary manner on many an occasion but it has generally righted itself before too much damage has been done. On the whole, the Court has been a friend, not a foe, and the last bastion of sympathetic understanding in the American political system available to the tribes. Many of its decisions have been the product of political compromise that looked more to the temper of the times than to enduring and somewhat abstract principles of law and this aspect of the judicial process has undoubtedly concerned many Indians who see justice in more fundamental and enduring terms. But accommodation is part of the American system, and judicial decisions must be assessed with this fact in mind. The Court's development of "rules of judicial construction" supporting Indian claims along with its history of protection against state intrusions into tribal affairs are important contributions that cannot be overemphasized.

3. Indian Country

Any examination of Indians and the judicial process must confront, at the very beginning, certain legal concepts that have taken on a status of primacy in the field of federal Indian law. "Indian Country" is such a concept. Since American Indians once owned and controlled the North American continent, many traditional Indians still regard the continent as being under their spiritual and cultural guidance and control. Yet the concept of Indian Country has been elevated by federal law above other ideas because it transcends mere geographical connotations and represents that sphere of influence in which Indian traditions and federal laws passed specifically to deal with the political relationship of the United States to American Indians have primacy. The term originated in the popular designations of the lands beyond the frontier, as the unknown populated by tribes and bands of Indians who rejected contact with "civilized" populations. That the idea moved from a popular conception to a highly technical legal term is testimony to the ability of the law to incorporate customs within its intellectual framework.

In early colonial days Indian Country was predicated largely upon the de facto situation of the frontier. The Iroquois Confederacy (the Seneca, Cayuga, Onondaga, Mohawk, Oneida, and Tuscarora) controlled large parts of the eastern United States, and the watershed of the Appalachian Mountains was the line of demarcation for nearly a century between lands that the colonists occupied and the lands of the Indians. Early agreements, such as the important Treaty of Lancaster in 1744, saw the Indians and the colonial representatives going to elaborate lengths to properly mark the boundaries of influence that each saw as important to their continued growth and survival. The agreements reached at Lancaster required that, if individuals of either race desired to enter upon lands not claimed by their tribe or colony, they had to obtain permission from the proper political authorities. Simple trespass was not allowed and both the

Indians and the colonists had the right, upon apprehending intruders in their territory, to punish them according to their own laws (Indian Treaty Series, no. 3). This arrangement, between the Iroquois on the one side and Maryland, Virginia, and Pennsylvania on the other, dealt primarily with lands that now constitute the state of West Virginia. Other colonies and other tribes had their own agreements but there was no firm imperial policy on the matter. The king was content at that time to issue proprietary grants to court favorites and to allow them to make their own understandings with the tribes who inhabited the region he had given away.

The defeat of the French in the French and Indian War (1754–1763) radically changed the nature of Indian-colonial relationships. While two great European empires contested for supremacy on the eastern Atlantic seaboard, the Iroquois in the north and the Cherokee and Creek confederacies in the south could play one nation against the other and have both contending for their favors. The elimination of the French as a colonial presence in North America meant that the tribes had to deal with the English king alone. There was an occasional flirtation with the Spanish in the Gulf of Mexico region and an overture to the French to renew their struggle against the English, but the important political relationships after the conclusion of this conflict became those with the king of England. The king, for his part, now attempted to exert considerably more influence over colonial events. Recognizing that much of the English difficulty with the tribes of the interior was generated by settlers on the frontier who unnecessarily intruded on favorite hunting grounds of the more powerful tribes, the king issued a proclamation in 1763 at the end of the war that made the crest of the Appalachian Mountains a formal boundary beyond which settlement was prohibited. Although this boundary was simply a confirmation of the status quo on the frontier, it was critically important to the Indian tribes because it was an imperial boundary, not an informally designated line that a colony could change at will. While Indian Country was a practical reality beyond the Appalachians, it was also, now of necessity, a technical legal term because of its recognition by the English crown.

The American Revolution, like the French and Indian war, made necessary certain adjustments in perception when the political balance in North America again changed radically. At the beginning of the war the rebelling colonists asked only that the Indian tribes on the frontier remain at peace with the most isolated settlement (Grinde, p. 62). The English, on the other hand, wishing to instill a fear of failure in the colonists, eagerly sought Indian allies in their military ventures against the American forces (Grinde, p. 81).

Demanding that the tribes remain loyal to the king and support him against his rebellious children, the English used the full emotional value of their treaty relationships with the Indians to get them to assist in the war. As a result, by 1778 the Americans were forced to fight some tribes and to make treaties with others to relieve the pressures building on the frontier. The first American treaty, made September 17, 1778 (7 Stat. 13), with the Delawares at Fort Pitt in western Pennsylvania, contained a provision to allow the American armies to pass peacefully through the Delaware lands in order to attack the British posts on the Great Lakes. Not only did this treaty recognize the Delaware lands as exclusively under the jurisdiction and control of the tribe but it also offered a seat in Congress to the Delawares and such other tribes as might be induced to join them if independence was successful.

The Treaty of Paris of September 3, 1783, which ended the American Revolution with the admission of the United States to the company of recognized nations, left the Indian tribes in a desperate condition. Throughout the negotiations the English sought to establish an Indian state between the Ohio and the Great Lakes, which would effectively block further American expansion and provide them with an almost impassable barrier against competitive European colonizing for that portion of North America which they retained (Combs, pp. 96–99). Indian allies, such as Joseph Brant, the Mohawk chief who led Indian auxiliaries in some of the battles in upper New York state during the Revolution, urged the British to provide for an international guarantee of the sanctity of the Indian lands, but in the final analysis the British gave in to American demands that all tribes south of the Great Lakes should be considered to be under American influence. Many of the interior tribes continued to feel a close alliance with the English who kept their Great Lakes trading posts and remained the leading participant in the northern fur trade—a fact that proved useful to the British and again disastrous to the Indians in the War of 1812.

The American peace treaties with the tribes on the western frontier required by the Peace of Paris reflected both the relative military strength of the tribe and its previous relationships with the colonies. Apart from the usual provisions for the making of peace and returning of hostages taken in the late war, these treaties had some interesting jurisdictional provisions for the resolution of conflicts on the frontier. Although the treaties acknowledged the sovereignty of the United States in formal language in their preambles, it was evident in their remaining articles that former British provisions for handling criminal activity and preventing conflicts were simply being transposed into this new situation. The treaty with the Cherokees, for example, signed in 1785 at Hopewell (7 Stat. 18), provided that if any citizen of the United States or other person (presumably an immigrant who moved to the frontier while not formally recognized as an American citizen) who attempted to settle on any of the Cherokee lands did not remove from his settlement within six months of the ratification of the treaty "such person shall forfeit the protection of the United States, and the Indians may punish him or not as they please" (article 5).

As a general rule the treaties with the Cherokees, Creeks, and Choctaws contained more liberal provisions regarding the punishment of intruders than did the treaties with the smaller tribes. The Shawnee treaty of 1786 (7 Stat. 26), for example, required that Indian wrongdoers and white citizens wronging the Shawnees both be delivered to the nearest military post for punishment under the laws of the United States—a far cry from allowing the Indians to take the measures they believed just. "Indian Country" at this time was a general concept but it began to be used in a more specific manner in the language used at the treaty of Greenville in 1795 (7 Stat. 49). That treaty involved the Miami Confederacy, which dominated the Indiana-Illinois lands, the Wyandots, Delawares, Shawnees, Ottawas, Chippewas, and Pottawatomis, all of whom had participated in the fierce war with the United States that had seen them defeat one American army under Major General Arthur St. Clair in 1791 and finally lose decisively to Mad Anthony Wayne at Fallen Timbers when they tried to copy the whites' military tactics and fight behind log fortifications. Article III of that treaty describes the territory remaining to these tribes as their "country" and within this tract of land the tribes gave many concessions and ceded important lands at river junctions and harbors for trading and military posts.

The first Trade and Intercourse Act of July 22, 1790 (1 Stat. 137), passed by Congress prior to the Indian war, contained the words "Indian Country" but seemed merely to indicate a general notion of lands on the frontier that were occupied by and under the control of the Indians. Sections 5 and 6 of this act dealt with the crimes and trespasses that might be committed by non-Indians against Indians within the Indian Country. These offenders, if convicted (and convictions by a non-Indian jury for crimes committed against an Indian were few and far between), were to be subject to the same punishment they would have received had they committed the same offenses against another non-Indian within the state or jurisdiction in which they resided. The sections suggested a very complicated situation in that the Indians would have to apprehend the wrongdoers, surrender them to the nearest military post, and then wait to see if the government was going to act. Although these jurisdictional provisions represented a good-faith effort by the Congress to fulfill the treaty promises, they made enforcement nearly impossible.

Succeeding amendments to the original Trade and Intercourse Act began to deal more precisely with the kinds of violations the frontier was actually experiencing. The 1793 amendments, for example, authorized the president to remove unauthorized settlers on Indian lands, provided for punishment of horse thieves and unethical horse traders, and prohibited federal employees dealing with Indians from having "any interest or concern in any trade with the Indians" (1 Stat. 329). The 1796 amendments (1 Stat. 329) gave substance to the idea of Indian Country by fixing the boundaries of it as defined by then-existing treaties. This trend toward a geographical conception of Indian Country required further amendments in 1799 and 1802 to reflect the new boundaries that resulted from treaties signed during the interim. Obviously, Congress could not continue to revise Indian Country with every treaty cession. Pressures were already developing to remove the smaller tribes west in order to open the Ohio and Kentucky country to settlement. Then, too, the 1796 amendments had contained a provision for the punishment of any Indian who crossed into any state or territory and committed any one of various listed offenses (section 14). If it was difficult to hold white settlers within the proper boundaries, it was nearly impossible to communicate to every Indian the new lines of demarcation that separated white from Indian. Federal jurisdiction had become almost wholly a racial phenomenon with this amendment although ostensively geographically determined according to congressional mandate.

The international dimension of Indian Country was emphasized in the Act of January 17, 1800 (2 Stat. 6), which provided for the preservation of peace with the Indian tribes. The first section of that act provided "that if any citizen or other person residing within the United States, or the territory thereof, shall send any talk, speech, message or letter to any Indian nation, tribe, or chief, with an intent to produce a contravention or infraction of any treaty or other law of the United States, or to disturb the peace and tranquility of the United States, he shall forfeit a sum not exceeding two thousand dollars, and be imprisoned not exceeding two years." The next section of this act provided penalties for carrying or delivering messages that might tend to incite the Indians against the United States and its laws, and the third section covered seditious correspondence with foreign nations dealing with Indian affairs. So rigorous was the prohibition that it provided a shield against any criticism of the Indian Service whatsoever: ". . . in case any citizen or other person shall alienate or attempt to alienate the confidence of the Indians from the government of the United States, or from any such person or persons as are, or may be employed and entrusted by the President of the United States, as a commissioner or commissioners, agent or agents, in any capacity whatever, for facilitating or preserving a friendly intercourse with the Indians, or for managing the concerns of the United States with them, he shall forfeit a sum not exceeding one thousand dollars, and be imprisoned not exceeding twelve months." These provisions did not, of course, directly affect the Indians but they did place severe restrictions on the ability of the tribes to seek assistance from another country in place of the United States. Great Britain and Spain were very active on the western frontier in the Indian trade and could be relied upon to exploit any discernible American weakness or Indian discontent. Extending federal laws to cover seditious activities and thoughts by persons passing through or entering into the Indian Country confirmed a national primacy that was later articulated by the Supreme Court in *Cherokee Nation v. Georgia*, 30 U.S. (5 Pet.) 1 (1831).

The War of 1812 settled the matter of the western lands and European intrusions and claims. Victorious, the United States pushed immediately for a redefinition of criminal activities within the lands on the western frontier. The Treaty of Ghent (8 Stat. 218), ending the war, required both the United States and Great Britain to reestablish peace with those tribes who had supported their opponents in the late conflict. Since a majority of the tribes had, unfortunately, given the British assistance, they were forced to come to terms with the United States, and the first provision in treaties made fulfilling the Ghent treaty established the exclusive jurisdiction of the United States. Article 3 of these treaties pointedly stated that the tribes were "under the protection of the United States of America, and of no other nation, power, or sovereign whatsoever."

Congress, no longer hesitant about asserting American claims in the west, passed the Act of March 3, 1817 (3 Stat. 383), which established a new system of criminal justice applicable to both Indians and non-Indians within Indian Country. Again racial considerations played a major role in determining the congressional perception of the jurisdictional problem. The act provided that both Indians and non-Indians committing offenses within Indian Country should be subject to the same punishment that would have been applicable if the offense had been committed in any place under the exclusive jurisdiction of the United States. But section 2 exempted Indian tribes, providing that "nothing in this act shall be so construed as to affect any treaty now in force between the United States and any Indian nation, or to extend to any offence committed by one Indian against another, within any Indian boundary." The self-government of the tribes was preserved but intertribal relations, some of which were provided for in the federal treaties, were not covered. Presumably, violence by a member of one tribe against another would be settled by the tribes concerned even though the United States, in the 1815 and other treaties, had promised to protect the tribal members of the respective tribes from its own citizens, from foreign intervention, and from "other persons," some of whom most certainly might be people from neighboring tribes.

After 1817 the United States found itself entering into a number of treaties in which it sought to bring peaceful conditions to intertribal conflicts. The treaty of 1825 (7 Stat. 272) at Prairie du Chien in Wisconsin brought together the Sioux, the Sac and Fox, the Menominee, the Ottawa, the Chippewa and Pottawatomi, the Iowa, and the Winnebago and required the tribes to forego the bloody intertribal wars that had been raging. Each tribe was required to use its good offices to prevent hostilities and the United States was acknowledged to be the final arbiter of disputes. The effect of such provisions on Indian Country cannot be underestimated. Indian Country was thereafter defined according to the specific relationship that individual tribes might have with the United States and was not understood as encompassing a general territory in which traditional Indian law had effect. Absent the ability of a tribe to conduct successful peace negotiations with another tribe, the United States assumed the responsibility of bringing Indian hostilities to a close. With the interventionist role of the United States now accepted as a matter of course, Indian Country became defined according to its political realities and moved away from both cultural and geographical considerations.

The Indian Removal Act of May 28, 1830 (4 Stat. 411), made concrete a policy that had previously been administered on an ad hoc, expedient basis. The act authorized the president to negotiate with tribes living east of the Mississippi for an exchange of lands across the river and immediate removal of the Indians to their new reservations. Smaller tribes and dissident parties within the larger tribes had already been moving west since the War of 1812 but this policy made removal imperative, and with Andrew Jackson the incumbent president there was no doubt in anyone's mind how the statute would be viewed. Apart from very small Indian communities that posed no threat to white settlement, all the larger tribes and Indian nations were rapidly removed from the southeast and midwest and resettled on large tracts in Kansas and Oklahoma.

Removal of the Indians across the father of waters and establishment of new and clearly marked reservations in the west made it possible for Congress to develop a coherent national Indian policy for the first time since the United States had achieved independence. Not only were foreign intrigues impossible on the rolling western plains but also the land itself was regarded as a great desert where only bands of Indians could survive. All Congress needed to do was to make the Indian Service an efficient system whereby it could fulfill its treaty promises. On July 9, 1832, Congress established the position of commissioner of Indian affairs (4 Stat. 564). Two years later on June 30, 1834, it passed a major Trade and Intercourse Act and an act to provide for the organization of the Department of Indian Affairs. The Trade and Intercourse Act substituted a new definition for Indian Country. Congress had previously adjusted the boundary of Indian Country whenever a change in a tribal-U.S. boundary was made by a treaty. This practice was very accurate but extremely tedious and required some considerable administrative work. The new definition under this act defined Indian Country thereafter as "the part of the United States west of the Mississippi and not within the states of Missouri and Louisiana, or the territory of Arkansas, and, also that part of the United States east of the Mississippi river, and not within any state to which the Indian title has not been extinguished, for the purposes of this act, be taken and deemed to be the Indian Country" (4 Stat. 729).

The *Report of the Committee of Indian Affairs of the House of Representatives* issued in conjunction with the passage of the act left no doubt about the intent of Congress: "This act is intended to apply to the whole Indian country, as defined in the first section. On the west side of the Mississippi its limits can only be changed by a legislative act; on the east side of that river it will continue to embrace only those sections of country not within any State to which the Indian title shall not be extinguished. The effect of the extinguishment of the Indian title to any portion of it, will be the exclusion of such portion from the Indian country. The limits of the Indian country will thus be rendered at all times obvious and certain" (p. 10). "Indian Country" was thus a technical term defined by Congress and was thereafter to be those tracts of land that represented unextinguished Indian title regardless of where located. Future legislative enactments and specific treaty provisions were the only contemplated exceptions to this general rule.

The House report, however, did not claim it was extending

criminal jurisdiction as a matter of right. "It will be seen that we cannot, consistently with the provisions of some of our treaties, and of the territorial act, extend our criminal laws to offences committed by or against Indians, of which the tribes have exclusive jurisdiction; and it is rather *of courtesy than of right* that we undertake to punish crimes committed in that territory by and against our own citizens. And *this provision is retained principally on the ground that it may be unsafe to trust to Indian law in the early stages of their Government"* (p. 13, emphasis added).

A great deal can be said about the intent of Congress with respect to this statute. At the time the House report was issued most Americans regarded the Great Plains as the "great American desert," unfit for habitation by whites and fit primarily for nomadic tribes of Indians. The majority of the tribes with whom the United States had political relations at that time lived in the west or, like the Five Civilized Tribes and the Miamis and other tribes of the Ohio-Wabash valleys, had been recently removed there. Since the House committee regarded the Indian tribes as being "in the early stages of their government," we can suggest that they contemplated the evolution of tribal governments into institutions resembling in large measure the federal government. Whether or not Congress would have maintained Indian Country as a locus of exclusive tribal jurisdiction with the maturing of tribal governments is an entirely different matter. One cannot imagine a reversion to the reciprocal jurisdictional rights that are found in the early treaties. Yet the caveat seems to imply a future time when it might have been possible to entrust the tribes with a more comprehensive jurisdiction in civil and criminal matters.

The 1834 act was the last congressional attempt in the nineteenth century to define Indian Country. Settlement seemed to hesitate on the edge of the Great Plains during the 1830s and 1840s. The discovery of gold, the Mexican War, and the rush to populate the Oregon Territory and claim the Pacific Northwest from the British all made the discussion of a large tract of uninhabitable land controlled by Indians moot. In the great Plains, the Rocky Mountains, and the Great Basin areas there were few whites who could run afoul of treaty provisions or federal statutes on a continuing basis. Law enforcement was a simple matter of retaliation by the injured party. Unless a band of Indians attacked a large party of whites, depradations were accepted as a matter of course and were not regarded as serious violations of the treaty agreements as they had been in the eastern United States, where large concentrations of population in small areas had made trespass and criminal activity serious breaches of the peace. The rapid development of the western lands, the relatively quick settlement of Indian tribes on reservations, and the construction of transcontinental railroads all foreclosed speculative discussion of technical points of law. More often than not the army was summoned to subdue hostile tribes, and Indian agents ruled their agencies with an iron hand, pre-empting any sophisticated attempt by the tribes to have their political rights enforced against the federal government.

The first section of the 1834 act, which gave substance to the idea of Indian Country, was not included when the revised statutes were published in 1875, leading some contemporary Indian legal scholars to argue that it had been repealed. The major doctrines of interpretation adopted by the federal courts, however, have suggested that a statute dealing with Indians or Indian rights cannot be regarded as being repealed by omission or implication. Yet the idea of a distinct territory within the United States preserved to Indians in an absolute jurisdictional sense was too abstract when placed within the context of the closing decades of the nineteenth century. Two significantly different cases illustrate the difficulty courts had in applying the concept of "Indian Country" to incidents on the frontier.

The first case to deal directly with Indian Country as a distinct locus of activity was *Bates v. Clark*, 95 U.S. 204 (1877). The case involved the legality of a seizure of liquor by an army officer in Dakota Territory and the question concerned the location of the seizure. If it was made in Indian Country, the subject matter was properly federal; if made in ceded Indian lands to which no covenant was attached, it came under territorial laws. Justice Miller, speaking for the Court, pointed out that, although immense changes had been made in the western lands since 1834, nevertheless Congress had not taken the trouble to change the definition of Indian Country. "These facts afford the strongest presumption that the Congress of the United States, and the judges who administered those laws, must have found in the definition of Indian country, in the act of 1834, such an adaptability to the altered circumstances of what was then Indian country as to enable them to ascertain what it was at any time since then" (p. 207).

The Court gave strong support to the geographical idea of Indian ownership of the lands that had formed the basis of the 1796 amendments: "It follows from this that all the country described by the act of 1834 as Indian country remains Indian country so long as the Indians retain their original title to the soil, and ceases to be Indian country whenever they lose that title, in the absence of any different provision by treaty or act of Congress" (p. 209). Consequently, Indian lands possessing aboriginal title remained Indian Country until they were ceded to the United States and if the cession excepted the lands from state jurisdiction they might remain Indian Country until later changed by Congress.

The lands in *Bates* were within an organized territory where federal law was supreme so that no conflicts of sovereignty between federal and state governments were considered. Four years later in *United States v. McBratney*, 104 U.S. 621 (1881), the Supreme Court faced this question and added another dimension to the jurisdictional problem. McBratney, a white man, killed Thomas Casey, another white man, within the confines of the Ute Reservation in southern Colorado. McBratney, having been indicted and convicted in the federal circuit court, moved for an arrest of judgment on the grounds that the circuit court had no jurisdiction. The Court agreed with him. Citing the second article of the Ute treaty of 1868, which described the reservation as being set apart for the "absolute and undisturbed use and occupation" of the Indians, and the first section of the Colorado territorial act, which excluded the reservation from being included in any state or territory without the consent of the Indians, to emphasize the "Indian" nature of the lands, the Court then turned to the absence of this language in the succeeding statehood act. Failure to exempt the reservation from state jurisdiction in the statehood act meant, according to the Court, that the reservation was within the limits of the state insofar as its non-Indian citizens were concerned. Federal jurisdiction was found to lie within the reservation but only to the extent that it was necessary to fulfill the obligations of the treaty.

This decision, while citing the 1834 statute in its description of the jurisdiction given to circuit courts, created the same division of sovereignty as did the United States Constitution. That is to say, different sovereigns can exercise different powers in the same territory for different purposes and lands can be jurisdictionally distinguished depending upon the subject matter under consideration. Colorado was not given power to intrude upon the Indians or upon any federal matters pertaining to Indians, but its external boundaries, which included the reservation, were preserved intact and no lands within these boundaries were found to be exempt from state control.

Combining *Bates* and *McBratney* to form a coherent picture of Indian Country meant that the concept was preserved when Indians and Indian matters were the subject of inquiry. Absent a strong showing of the federal responsibilities for Indians, state jurisdiction would prevail over lands that still possessed the aboriginal occupancy title when non-Indians were involved. But a further complication appeared on the horizon.

The General Allotment Act of 1887 (24 Stat. 388) authorized the president to negotiate with the tribes for cession of their surplus lands and, upon securing an agreement, to survey them into allotments, issue trust patents (land deeds held in trust by the federal government) to tribal members, and purchase the remainder to be opened for settlement by whites. The story of the rapid loss of tribal lands as a result of this statute is well known and need not be repeated here. Other provisions dealing with the actual allotments are not so well known and bear comment because of their importance in later years in helping to determine the scope and extent of Indian Country in jurisdictional cases. The effect of allotment, according to the Supreme Court, was the surrender by tribal members of the rights to hold lands in common in exchange for individualized shares of the tribal land estate (and often a per capita share of the income from the sale of surplus lands). Section 6 of the act specifically provided "that upon the completion of said allotments and the patenting of the lands to said allottees, each and every member of the respective bands or tribes of Indians to whom allotments have been made shall have the benefit of and be subject to the laws, both civil and criminal, of the State or Territory in which they may reside." Under the *Bates* interpretation of Indian Country, then, allotment worked to extinguish tribal title and took the transformed allotment and made it subject to state or territorial laws—in effect eliminating its classification as Indian Country.

Although the General Allotment Act seemed to extinguish Indian title, it did provide a period of twenty-five years in which a federal trust was imposed on the allotment. The allottee could not sell or lease the lands, they could not be taxed by state or territorial governments, and the president had discretionary powers to extend the life of the trust indefinitely if he decided such an extension was in the best interest of the Indians. This superior federal servitude became more comprehensive with the 1891 amendments to the General Allotment Act, which gave the secretary of the interior authority to lease the allotments of the aged, infirm, and *non compos mentis* Indians. Allotment was designed to teach the Indians how to manage their own property, yet less than five years later in this amendment it was the secretary of the interior who had to learn the bitter lessons of private property on behalf of his Indian wards. With the secretary now involved in the management of allotments, it was obvious that Indian Country as a useful concept carving out the federal interest in the Indian lands could not be abandoned.

The solution to this dilemma was the advocacy by the Interior Department that, until the Indian allotments finally went out of trust, they constituted Indian Country in the original sense of the 1834 act. This interpretation was acceptable to almost everyone at the beginning of allotments since the surplus lands that the tribes had ceded were more than enough to satisfy the first wave of white settlers. It was when the surplus lands were settled and the allottees wanted to sell their allotments that problems arose. Indiscriminate sales of lands within the remaining reservation boundaries quickly produced a "checkerboard" effect with trust lands and former allotments, now fee simple tracts (land held absolutely or completely by the owner), alternating in crazy-quilt patterns. State governments attempted to resolve this problem by enforcing their laws on fee simple lands and calling on federal officials to enforce federal laws on the trust allotments. But before an arrest could be made, in many instances, a map had to be produced to determine the actual status of the land upon which the arrest was in fact made. This situation was even worse than before allotment and some states, such as South Dakota, suggested that the federal government retain control of law and order until the respective areas had been completely cleared of trust allotments. The act of February 14, 1901 (Sess. Laws S.D. 1901 p. 132, c. 106), relinquished to the United States exclusive jurisdiction to arrest, prosecute, and punish all persons who might commit upon any Indian reservations in the state any offenses that might be prohibited by Congress. Two years later Congress conferred jurisdiction upon the circuit and district courts of the District of South Dakota to try cases dealing with various subjects.

The idea of Indian Country in the abstract gave way in some western states to a willingness to leave jurisdiction with the federal government until such time as states could assume total control of geographical areas within their borders. Yet even in this instance there were complications. The old idea of Indian Country assumed that the lands were once totally under the control of the Indians and gradually and grudgingly came under the control of the states. In the southwestern region, in particular, there was no historical precedent of recognized aboriginal title that could be seen in a state of gradual erosion. Under the Mexican-Spanish domination, the Europeans were content to establish small missions where they settled Indian converts and small settlements that could be relied upon in crises to defend themselves. Domination of the nomadic tribes of the desert was a hopeless task and so long as peace was secured the authorities did not attempt to settle large tracts of lands that were already occupied by the Indians. The result was that there were few documents recognizing Indian claims and with the assumption of political control of the region by the United States it became the practice to set aside by executive order large areas where the tribes could be settled.

Were executive order reservations part of Indian Country or not? Arguments could be validly and sincerely raised on either side of the question. The tribes had no written proof that they claimed or owned the lands on which they resided. Yet it was ridiculous to pretend that they had not been living there for uncounted millennia before the coming of either the Spanish or the Americans.

Cases involving jurisdiction that relied upon the 1834 definition now required sophisticated historical research, research that judges in the lower courts were not always bound to respect, appreciate, or support. A forfeiture suit in 1888 dealing with the question of the existence of the Klamath River Indian Reservation in northern California, for example, in order to justify confiscation of goods under Rev. Stat. § 2133, which prescribed a penalty for unlicensed trading with Indians, resulted in a finding that the reservation did not exist at that time. The United States attorney was outraged at the court's decision and appealed that part of the ruling. It was denied (*United States v. Forty-eight Pounds of Rising Star Tea*, 38 F. 400 (C.C.N.D. Cal. 1889)), and the Justice Department was left smarting under the insult. Two years later, when called upon to render an opinion on the matter, the assistant attorney general went out of his way to emphasize the historical record, which he saw as sufficient evidence of the existence of the reservation and its classification as Indian Country (*Crichton v. Shelton*, 33 I.D. 215 (1891)).

In 1913 the Supreme Court finally had to deal with the question of whether or not an executive order reservation was Indian Country. In *Donnelly v. United States*, 228 U.S. 243 (1913), the Court was asked to determine whether a murder committed on an executive order reservation constituted a crime committed in Indian Country. In resolving this issue the Court concluded that Indian Country was simply composed of all the land officially set aside from the public domain to be used as Indian reservations—a rather simple, narrow, and ultimately confusing definition that seemed to resolve the question of executive order reservations and, if nothing else, to broaden the previous definition, which relied upon Indian title.

While sounding the death knell for the old notion of aboriginal title by focusing on reservation land, the new definition of Indian Country failed to take into account a great deal of Indian land that was not delineated by reservation boundaries. A number of Indian homestead acts (Act of February 28, 1891, 26 Stat. 794, 795, and Act of June 25, 1910, 36 Stat. 855, 863) and a provision in the General Allotment Act itself, section 4, had allowed individual Indians to take allotments on the public domain and in national forests. These tracts, while set aside for Indians, were isolated and not generally linked with federal law enforcement activities. Additionally, since the requirement for taking one of these allotments was the desire to abandon tribal relations, no tribal self-governing apparatus could be expected to function to govern these lands. The question of whether certain lands had actually been ceded by the Indians, not a major factor at the turn of the century but certainly a controversial topic in the 1970s, was not even considered by the Court in the *Donnelly* decision.

The defect in the *Donnelly* decision's definition of Indian Country was partially remedied in *United States v. Sandoval*, 231 U.S. 28 (1913), handed down in the same year as *Donnelly*. In *Sandoval* the Court was faced with the problem of classifying the lands of the Pueblo Indians of New Mexico. The Pueblos were not considered federal Indians under a variety of state laws and territorial court decisions, including one United States Supreme Court decision—*United States v. Joseph*, 94 U.S. 614 (1876). But federal administrative actions had included the Pueblos among the federally supervised Indians and the New Mexico statehood act had placed them under federal responsibility, superceding former territorial provisions. The *Donnelly* rule was of little assistance in resolving this dispute because, according to then-current interpretations of the federal trust responsibility, property followed personality and the federal argument in this instance contended that the Pueblo lands should be regarded as Indian Country if the Pueblos themselves were subject to federal supervision. The Court concluded that the notion of Indian Country should include any lands occupied by "distinctly Indian communities" and "recognized and treated by the Government as 'dependent communities' entitled to [federal] protection" (see Cohen, p. 7). Under this expanded definition, the Pueblo lands easily qualified as part and parcel of Indian Country but the new definition meant that exercise of a previously dormant federal interest could transform a parcel of land under state jurisdiction into Indian Country. (This precise situation occurred later in the state of North Carolina when the Eastern Band of Cherokees were shifted from a state-recognized Indian corporation to a federally recognized Indian tribe.)

Both *Donnelly* and *Sandoval* dealt with the problems of tribal and communal lands and their relationship to Indian Country. Neither case touched the issue of allotments held by individual Indians and in both *Donnelly* and *Sandoval* historical data confirmed the long-standing existence of the tribal community, which made the decision a relatively simple matter. The question of allotments, as we have discussed earlier, was extremely complicated if they had to be worked into the Indian Country formula in the same manner as tribal lands had been. The Supreme Court faced this question the year following the *Donnelly* and *Sandoval* decisions in *United States v. Pelican*, 232 U.S. 442 (1914). Placing the major emphasis upon the 25-year trust period that attached to each allotment when it was issued, the Court characterized individual lands as devoted to "Indian occupancy under the limitations imposed by the federal government" and ruled that they continued to fall within the jurisdiction of Indian Country. This rule was later extended to include "restricted" allotments of the Five Civilized Tribes and the Osage as well as "trust" allotments (*United States v. Ramsey*, 271 U.S. 467 (1926)).

Inclusion of allotments in the Indian Country definition was basically a shift to subject matter jurisdiction because it was the continuing federal trust responsibility that covered the allotments, not their geographical location or previous status as tribal lands. In conjunction with this departure from the geographical definition, we must mention *Perrin v. United States*, 232 U.S. 478 (1914), because it helps us to understand the context in which Indian Country was connected to other and intangible concepts by the Supreme Court during these important years. The case involved the sale of liquor at Dante, South Dakota, on a part of the lands ceded by the Yankton Sioux in the agreement of 1894. As a part of that land cession the chiefs insisted that no liquor could be sold on the lands being ceded. The federal statute ratifying the agreement (28 Stat. 319) provided "that every person who shall sell or give away any intoxicating liquors or other intoxicants upon any of the lands included in the Yankton Sioux Indian Reservation as created by the treaty of April nineteenth, eighteen hundred and fifty-eight, shall be punishable by imprisonment for not more than two years and by a fine of not more than three hundred dollars." The Court upheld this provision by holding that "unless sooner repealed, it will continue in force as long as the presence and status of the Indians sustain it as a Federal regulation" (p. 486). The ceded lands were, in a fundamental sense, Indian Country although the Court did not use the term once in its decision. The presence of Indians, with a peculiar status and a negotiated consideration for the cession of their lands, imposed a unique federal servitude on these lands so that, even though they were now wholly within the jurisdiction of South Dakota insofar as location, private title, and political independence from the federal government, they nevertheless were federal lands for the purposes described and would remain so until an affirmative congressional enactment released them from this servitude.

The federal interest emphasis in the Indian Country definition received a major boost during the Indian Reorganization Act period. Under the provisions of that statute the secretary of the interior could purchase lands for landless Indians and in some states, particularly California, considerable acreage was acquired and several hundred landless Indians were settled on these tracts. Were these lands "Indian Country" in the same sense as the other lands whose status was clearly recognized? The answer involved a surprising inclination of the federal government to deal with minutiae; *United States v. McGowan*, 302 U.S. 535 (1938), began this unusual sequence. The case involved forfeiture of automobiles under 25 U.S.C. § 247, a liquor statute that forbade using automobiles to introduce liquor into Indian Country. The offense occurred in the Reno Indian Colony, which had been purchased for the Indians of Nevada in 1917 and 1926. Justice Hugo L. Black, speaking for the Court, concluded that "it is not reasonably possible to draw any distinction between this Indian 'colony' and 'Indian country.'" The case, therefore, expanded the definition of Indian Country to include tracts of land purchased by the federal government for Indians.

The Interior Department, however, felt impelled to comment on the *McGowan* case the following year when the question arose concerning whether the lands of the Phoenix Indian School in Arizona constituted an Indian reservation within the Indian Country definition. In a memorandum opinion dated July 9, 1940, the acting solicitor made a distinction between lands belonging to the United States for institutional purposes of serving Indians and lands purchased by or belonging to the United States that were occupied by Indians whose occupancy came to be recognized by Congress. Federal Indian school lands would not be included in Indian Country; however, abandoned federal Indian school lands where a group of Indians lived, perhaps openly and notoriously for a period of years, would be included. The permutations and combinations of congressional and administrative intent that could be encompassed within this definition are astronomical.

Taken together, the *Donnelly, Sandoval,* and *Pelican* cases established a solid tradition of interpretation of the 1834 provisions, which needed a contemporary expression. Instead of relying on case law and little-publicized Interior Department opinions, which only suggested legal interpretations in interim periods between major pronouncements of the Supreme Court and the Congress, a revised and streamlined expression of congressional understanding and intent was proposed in 1943. A criminal statute (62 Stat. 757, as amended, 63 Stat. 94) was passed defining Indian Country as including:

(a) all land within the limits of any Indian reservation under the jurisdiction of the United States, notwithstanding the issuance of any patent, and, including rights-of-way running through the reservation.

(b) all dependent Indian communities within the borders of the United States whether within the original or subsequently acquired territory thereof, and whether within or without the limits of a state.

(c) all Indian allotments, the Indian titles to which have not been extinguished, including rights-of-way running through the same.

These three basic provisions are a direct outgrowth of the trilogy of cases handed down earlier by the Supreme Court. Section (a) is a codification of *Donnelly v. United States*; section (b) can be traced directly to *United States v. Sandoval*; and section (c) may be attributed to *United States v. Pelican* and its progeny.

In 1953, under the impetus of the policy to terminate federal supervision over Indians as rapidly as possible, Congress passed Public Law 280, which gave civil and criminal jurisdiction over Indian reservations to several states by name and allowed the other states having reservations to assume jurisdiction by amending their constitutions or making similar legislative provisions. Whether Congress intended this transfer of jurisdiction to the states to extinguish the idea of Indian Country is impossible to determine. The provisions of P.L. 280 that prohibited taxation of lands and regulation of hunting and fishing rights became the two areas of major conflict between tribes and states. Shortly after P.L. 280 became law Washington State attempted to exert jurisdiction over the Yakima Reservation. In *Application of Andy*, 40 Wash. 2d 449, 302 P.2d 963 (1956), and *In Re Colwash*, 57 Wash. 2d 196, 356 P.2d 994 (1960), the state supreme court turned back the state's efforts.

The landmark case involving a determination of Indian Country following P.L. 280 is *Seymour v. Superintendent*, 368 U.S. 351 (1962). Seymour was convicted of attempted burglary in Omak, Washington, a town in the southern half of the Colville Reservation. He appealed his conviction claiming that the southern half of the reservation, which was now composed predominantly of fee simple lands owned by non-Indians, was still Indian Country and that his

crime was in fact a federal and not a state offense. The Court supported his argument and ruled that, although the southern half of
the reservation had been opened by a congressional act, it remained
Indian Country because the reservation was simply "diminished"
but not extinguished. Litigation thereafter began to revolve about
the *intent of Congress* in opening reservations in the first decade of
this century and in ratifying land cession agreements with the tribes
during that same period. In *Beardslee v. United States*, 387 F.2d 280
(8th Cir. 1967), for example, the circuit court of appeals found that
the Rosebud Sioux Reservation in South Dakota consisted of the
smaller remaining tract that survived the land cession rather than
the land within the original reservation boundaries as established
under the agreement of 1889. The court noted that "no part of the
Todd County portion of the reservation has ever been formally
opened. Instead, that portion has remained closed since 1889. The
general geographical situation is thus clear" (p. 285). But this interpretation dealt only with the remaining tract of land, which was self-
evidently Indian Country. It failed to deal adequately with the ceded
lands and whether or not they could be classified as Indian Country.

Clearly, the question of Indian Country had radically changed in
the 1960s. The new concentration focused on whether or not Congress had intended to extinguish the federal character of lands within
original reservation boundaries for certain reservations. By extension, then, the 1948 definition of Indian Country, which seemed to
correspond to the concept developed by previous case law, was now
being expanded to raise questions of congressional intent to eliminate boundary lines. Nowhere was this trend more shockingly evident than in the controversial *City of New Town v. United States*,
454 F.2d 121 (8th Cir. 1972). New Town, North Dakota, was a state-
chartered municipality within the former boundaries of the Fort
Berthold Reservation. It had been routinely arresting members of
the Three Affiliated Tribes for violations of municipal ordinances
when it was challenged. The trial court was asked to determine
whether or not the Act of June 1, 1910 (36 Stat. 455), which opened
the reservation for settlement, had changed the boundaries of the
reservation. Judge George Register decided that the boundaries had
not been diminished and filed a memorandum decision to that
effect. The Eighth Circuit Court of Appeals on January 17, 1972,
affirmed this decision and set forth three principles upon which it
upheld the trial court: "(1) When Congress has once established a
reservation, all tracts included within it remain a reservation until
separated therefrom by Congress . . . (2) The purpose to abrogate
treaty rights of Indians is not to be lightly imputed to Congress . . .

(3) The opening of an Indian reservation for settlement by home-steading is not inconsistent with its continued existence as a res-ervation" (p. 125). This extension of the 1948 act meant that for jurisdictional purposes Indian title was no longer the primary con-sideration in determining the nature of Indian Country. Instead the existence or nonexistence of reservation boundaries had become the determinative factor and this question involved congressional intent with respect to a series of federal statutes and agreements, not all of which were clear regarding the question.

A flurry of cases emerged from the *New Town* decision as tribes began to test various aspects of the reservation-boundary definition. In *Mattz v. Arnett*, 412 U.S. 481 (1973), a fishing rights case in Cal-ifornia, the Supreme Court held that an 1892 act, which had ap-peared to have terminated the Klamath River Reservation, did not do so and the lands were still regarded as Indian Country although hardly any Indians lived in the area and its primary value to the Indi-ans was as a fishing site. The same year the same high court nearly welded together tax law and Indian Country in *McClanahan v. Ari-zona State Tax Commission*, 411 U.S. 164 (1973), when, using tribal sovereignty as a "backdrop" for discussion, the state was admon-ished that it could not tax on the Navajo Reservation without the Indians first waiving their treaty rights if the treaty set aside the res-ervation for the "exclusive use and occupancy" of the Indians. But the Navajo Reservation was not an allotted reservation nor had it been diminished by any acts of Congress following the ratification of the 1868 treaty. On the contrary, it had been expanded many times by executive order as the population of the tribe increased. Conse-quently, in *McClanahan* both tribal sovereignty and Indian Country lurked in the background as concepts related to and protected by fed-eral pre-emption.

Of more critical importance, and in line with the fact situation of *New Town*, were instances where the original reservation had been diminished by the sale or allotment of lands. In *DeCoteau v. District County Court*, 420 U.S. 425 (1975), involving the Sisseton-Wahpeton Sioux Reservation in the northeast corner of South Da-kota, the high court found that Congress had intended to abolish the entire reservation when the lands were sold. Two years later, in *Rosebud Sioux Tribe v. Kneip*, 430 U.S. 584 (1977), which involved a reduction of the Rosebud Sioux Reservation in south central South Dakota, the Court found that Congress had intended to remove the surplus lands from the reservation and consequently an intent to re-duce the reservation was implied.

The boundary cases shared several common characteristics that

serve to distinguish them as a class. First, they involved a considerable amount of very precise historical research. Every bit of information that could shed light on the intent of Congress was mustered
and debate centered on which evidence could be reliably used to determine the state of congressional minds at the time the legislation
was considered. Comparisons of minute phrasing were blown out of
proportion as sets of attorneys vigorously argued about various
shades of meaning that could reasonably be implied in the difference
in statutory wording. The cases also seemed to turn on the demo-
graphics of the present situation rather than Indian understanding of
land cessions and allotments or the probable intent of Congress.
Mattz involved a sparsely populated area while the *DeCoteau* and
Kneip cases dealt with considerably more settled geographical regions. A tax case decided during this period suggested a possible escape from the dilemma of balancing historical suppositions against
present demographic realities. In *Moe v. Confederated Salish and
Kootenai Tribes of the Flathead Indian Reservation*, 425 U.S. 463
(1976), the Supreme Court allowed the state of Montana to tax non-
Indians within the Flathead Indian Reservation and required tribal
members operating cigarette stores to collect state excise taxes.
Tribal members purchasing cigarettes were exempted from paying
state excise taxes. The Flathead Reservation was allotted about the
same time as the Sioux reservations in South Dakota but much of its
land had been lost and the Indians only constituted one-fifth of the
population within the reservation boundaries. *Moe* preserved some
aspect of Indian Country but it did so at the cost of making Indian
matters predominantly a racial and political subject that has been
pre-empted by the federal government.

Indian Country in its original expression has most probably
been overtaken by contemporary events and now exists, like tribal
sovereignty, as a backdrop concept that provides a useful historical
context and serves to bolster arguments that have already been made
regarding federal pre-emption of subject matter. In its original meaning, as a location where Indian jurisdiction and self-government
reign supreme, Indian Country will probably continue to be cited in
those instances where Indian lands and population predominate. As
the situations become less clear and the mixture of Indian and non-
Indian becomes more pronounced, we can look for some version of
the three principles articulated by the *New Town* case to emerge.

In viewing Indian Country in the context of this study we have
tried to emphasize its meaning as Indians would prefer to have it understood. From the Indian point of view more is at stake in this
instance than simply a legal doctrine. Traditional life with its cere-

monial and ritual richness is partially dependent upon the continuation and strengthening of tribal governments since without a protective shield preventing intrusions many Indian communities would not be able to practice their customs on terms satisfactory to them. Hence, many Indians believe that Indian Country should have as many connotations of the old ways as possible, and this atmosphere involves the totality of tribal life.

4. The Evolution
of Tribal Governments

Western judicial institutions and procedures, as we have seen, have been the product of a long development in that tradition extending back as far as the Greek and Roman systems of jurisprudence and perhaps even to the ancient Hebrews and Sumerians. Nation after nation has made its contribution to the cumulative mass that now constitutes American jurisprudence, and the familiarity of both institutions and procedures guarantees to the person raised within that tradition a sense of propriety and justice. So long has this tradition been in place that people raised within the Western tradition automatically judge the behavior of non-Western peoples according to standards and concepts of justice that they have accepted without much critical review.

The whites' inability to understand the problems and behavior of American Indians is not a new phenomenon. Indeed, this difficulty in appreciating and comprehending "foreign" cultures and traditions seems to be the peculiar burden that western European peoples carry into their encounters with peoples of different traditions. This blinded vision has affected all dealings with non-Westerners and has often given rise to the belief that Asians, Africans, and natives of the Western Hemisphere place little value on human life. The contrary is true. Each of these traditions placed a high value on human life but quite often did not express this value in terms of a wrong-doer being in violation of the rules and regulations of external social institutions. Many of these other cultures preferred to conceive legal relations as existing between groups of people rather than between individuals and hence appeared to Europeans as people completely without laws and rules for living—ultimately as people without individual independence. When other cultures are seen within their proper context, the amount of individual freedom and the latitude of moral choices seem equally as free as any guarantees that Western legal and political institutions provide for their citizens.

Given the absence of formally structured institutions within the Indian tribes they encountered, it appeared to the earliest settlers that the tribes existed without any forms of government. The Indians were generally viewed as living almost in a state of anarchy and some early political writers, seeking to conceive a "state of nature" upon which they could build the philosophical framework for their natural law–social contract theories of government, frequently referred to Indians as "children of nature" and applauded their apparent ability to live without the confining and complex rules that had been devised within the European systems of government. Tribal governments of enormous complexity did exist but they differed so radically from the forms used by the Europeans that few non-Indian observers could understand them.

The first observations of Indian tribes made by Europeans were explained by reference to familiar European forms of government, which at the time were best characterized by the theory of the "Divine Right of Kings," which assumed that monarchs governed because God intended them to govern. Of the early thinkers who broke away from this traditional interpretation, John Locke established the idea that, if a direct descendant of Adam were capable of identification, he would certainly be monarch of all the world. Pending that discovery, Locke argued, the best and most rational basis for government was the establishment of a social contract in which free individuals came together for a common purpose. This kind of reasoning, best exemplified by John Locke and Charles de Montesquieu, significantly affected the framers of the Declaration of Independence and the Constitution so that governments were conceived as the conglomeration of free people willingly surrendering their right to arbitrary action to a superior in return for the guarantee of law and order. Indians, of course, did not fit into this philosophical framework because there was no contractual right by individuals against Indian society.

Indian tribes, nevertheless, had highly complicated forms of government that could be traced far back into precontact days and, according to some tribal traditions, back as far as their creation and migration stories told them intelligible life has existed. The primacy of the Creek clans, for example, could be traced back to an early condition of chaos in which humans and animals were lost in an immensely thick fog. In order to save themselves the people and the animals joined hands and wandered for many days. Finally, as the fog was clearing and open skies could be discerned, they agreed that henceforth the clans would rank in the order in which they had emerged from the dreadful fog. Such a tradition clearly ranks with the Exodus and other stories cherished by the Western peoples, extending significantly far into the past, as a revered explanation of the manner in which the Creek Nation organized itself. Many other tribes had similar legends that were for them as sacred and ultimate as anything the Europeans possessed.

It is interesting to note, however, that the first written constitution drafted in North America appeared before Columbus ever embarked on his famous journey. The Gayaneshagowa, or Great Binding Law of the Five Nations, was a written constitution created by the Iroquois and enunciated such democratic ideals and doctrines as initiative, recall, referendum, and equal suffrage. It provided a type of central government that would later be suggested by Benjamin Franklin to the colonies as an institution worthy of emulation (Cohen, p. 128). The Iroquois Constitution was written on the sacred wampum belts made of sea shells and displaying a particular pattern, which, when held in a ceremony and used in the recitation of the Great Law, was acknowledged by all as the instrument of Iroquois nationality.

While the Iroquois Constitution provided a written preview of some of the governmental values later to be adopted by the whites in America, written documents as governmental guidelines were not to be found among most tribes for some time to come. Many tribes preferred to incorporate their political and social precedents in stories and anecdotes that explained proper behavior; they relied upon social pressures, particularly the individual's fear of embarrassing his or her relatives and clan members, as their means of determining the proper social response and penalty for violation of the tribal customs. A brief glimpse at the evolutionary development of tribal government reveals that for several generations there was a measurable difference between the perspectives of government held by most Indian tribes and those held by the newly arrived whites. More important, it also indicates that tribal government served as a forerunner to the tribal court systems of today on many reservations.

TRADITIONAL FORMS OF TRIBAL GOVERNMENT

It is difficult to generalize about traditional forms of tribal government because there was such a great variety of Indian social groupings. Many tribes were loose confederations of hunting groups who spoke the same language and ranged over a broad expanse of territory. Such groups as the Shoshone and the Paiutes, for example, were spread thinly in small groups over what is now the Great Basin area of the western United States. The Sioux, as the French called them, or the Dakota, as the Indians called themselves, once ranged from the area near Wisconsin Dells, Wisconsin, to the Big Horn Mountains of Wyoming, a distance of nearly 1,300 miles in width. By contrast, small fishing villages in the Pacific Northwest were scattered independently along the many rivers of that region and had commercial and trading contacts but little political organization above the village or longhouse level. Some tribes, such as the Creek, were occasionally aggressive and incorporated smaller groups into themselves as a result of marriages or wars and eventually had to evolve a national organization to maintain themselves within their expanding territorial domain.

There were, of course, theocracies, such as the Pueblos of New Mexico and the Hopi of Arizona, who traced their form of government back to ancient times and organized their political and social life around a religious ceremonial year following basically religious rather than secular laws. The persistence of priesthood or influence of medicine men was not particularly significant in many tribes and if they followed theocratic forms it was only in deference to old prophecies that guided them in their migrations around the continent. The place of the religious leader should not be underestimated when speaking of the organization of the Indian tribe because most groups were highly sensitive to the admonitions of their holy people. But in comparison with the established clergy and priesthoods that many societies have experienced, on the whole the tribes of North America were exempt from the absolute exercise of political powers by religious leaders.

It is best when discussing tribal political organizations to give some of the better known examples of Indian institutions and see what function they played in the lives of people. Harold Driver describes the elaborate political structure of the Cheyenne as follows:

> The Cheyenne were governed by a civil council of forty-four chiefs, divided into five priestly chiefs, two doormen, and thirty-seven others. The priestly chiefs, who outranked the others, conducted tribal rituals, including the chief-renewal ritual performed every year when the group assembled. One of the five priestly chiefs presided at the meetings of the council of forty-four chiefs and manipulated the sacred medicines in the chief's medicine bundle; he was called the Prophet, and represented the mythical culture hero. The doormen were sometimes called upon to sum up the essence of the discussion and to render a decision for the group. When one of the five priestly chiefs retired, he chose his successor from the remaining thirty-nine members of the group; if he died so sud-

denly that he could not choose his successor, the surviving four priestly chiefs chose one for him. A priestly chief, on retirement, stepped down only to the rank of the undifferentiated thirty-seven chiefs; he did not have to leave the council. If an undifferentiated chief died without choosing his successor, the entire council chose one for him. Each ordinary chief could serve only ten years, which explains why the rules of succession are so complicated. New chiefs were chosen on the basis of merit, and it was considered bad taste for a man to choose his own son. The personal qualities which constituted merit were control of temper and generosity.

None of the forty-four chiefs ever exerted any force to carry out the will of the civil council. Force was applied by the members of one of the six men's societies which the council selected on two important occasions: moving camp, and the tribal buffalo hunt. Moving camp was a military venture because there was always some danger of encountering an enemy. The tribal buffalo hunt was the most important occasion of the year, and teamwork was necessary to kill the maximum number of buffalo.

The two headmen and the two doormen of each of the men's societies formed a council of twenty-four war chiefs. A man could not be both a civil chief and a war chief. If a war chief was chosen as a civil chief, he must first resign his position of war chief before accepting that of civil chief. The council of war chiefs chose the war leader for each military raid; but, once the campaign ended, his authority terminated. (Driver, pp. 300–301)

This rather formal organization complete with provisions for the replacement of chiefs, resignations, and allocation of functions between war and peace would seem to suggest an institution similar in most respects to those of the Western tradition. As the offices of chief were realized among the Cheyennes, however, they differ dramatically from political offices of Western peoples. The first duty of the chief was that he should care for the widows and orphans and consequently generosity was not simply a peripheral concern of the people when choosing a chief. Almost as important in the functioning of the office was the person's ability to act as a mediator in tribal disputes. A chief would often suffer loss himself as a means of resolving a dispute so that it would not disrupt the camp. Performing the function of a chief, therefore, was hardly the enriching experience that modern politicians enjoy when assuming their office.

Apart from their functions of making war, deciding when and where to move the camp, authorizing the annual buffalo hunt, and ensuring that the annual religious ceremonies were held without incident, the role of the chiefs was to provide for the security and well-being of the people. Although chiefs were each charged with the responsibility of mediating disputes among the people, at times the council itself had to act to settle disputes. This duty was particularly true when a series of disputes had resulted in the killing of a person and the relatives sought revenge or demanded some additional form of compensation above that which had been offered by the slayer's relatives. On these occasions the council of chiefs had to satisfy the people and display the utmost wisdom in ensuring that justice was done and was perceived by everyone as settling the matter. Thus the function of the council was a conciliatory-judicial one rather than an executive function as one might initially perceive.

Many tribes considered the relationship between war and peace as critical to the successful operation of tribal harmony and provided for both war and peace functions. The Creeks, for example, as their confederacy grew larger, made provisions for distinct functions of war and peace. It is estimated that the Creek Confederacy had between fifty and eighty separate towns in the century before white contact; these towns represented the six language groups that composed the nation: Muskogee, Hitchiti, Koasati, Euchee, Natchez, and Shawnee. They divided these towns into red and white towns, red for war and white for peace. The white towns had all the councils, performed the adoption ceremonies, enacted the laws and regulations of the nation, and regulated the internal affairs of the confederation, including intertown relationships. No blood was supposed to be shed in the white towns and it was regarded as a serious offense to do so.

The red towns declared and conducted wars on behalf of the confederacy. They planned the military expeditions and conducted foreign relations on behalf of the nation. To prevent intraconfederacy disputes from fragmenting the tenuous alliance, ball games of some degree of ferocity were initiated matching towns against each other. Traditionally, red towns competed against white towns. To hear some tribal traditions about these ball games one would wonder whether a formal war would not have been more humane since these games made the average professional football game appear mild indeed.

Each town was governed by a head chief called a *micco*. He was appointed by a council of lesser *miccos*, generally from their group, and was given life tenure dependent upon his good behavior. Assisting him was a lesser personage called a *micco apotka*, who acted in the role of an administrative assistant. The town itself was governed by a council of wise men and respected family heads called *miccos* who had basically the same function as the council of forty-four chiefs of the Cheyennes. When men became too old to serve in the council of *miccos* they were given the title of "beloved men" and acted as a very senior advisory group occupying places of honor at all councils and ceremonial occasions.

The warriors of each town were organized in a similar fashion with one acknowledged leader, called the *thlocco*, occupying the role of a war chief. The warriors were organized according to several particular ranks: the highest grade of warriors, who would be people well seasoned in the arts of war, were called *tastanagalgi*; of lesser rank were the *imala lakalgi*, who were less experienced; and the young men and relatively inexperienced warriors were called *imala labotskalgi*. The *thlocco* was the absolute leader of the nation during times of military emergency but his powers ended with the war and he reverted to town citizen until his office was needed again. In addition to these offices, the entire nation was divided into red and white clans and each clan was designated as a war or peace clan. By allocating these functions and allowing a certain amount of passage between offices as people matured, the Creeks produced some outstanding statesmen. Since the general posture of the nation, until it became involved with colonial intrigues of the European powers, was peaceful, the system tended to produce a stable and generally happy society.

The colonists had difficulty understanding the Creek system of government. They could not conceive why they had to make war against one well-known chief and trade peacefully or make peace with another. The European treaty commissioners always insisted on dealing with the "head" chief of the Creek Confederacy and, rather than learn the complicated system the Creeks used to allocate the functions of war and peace, began to insist on signing their treaties with the most influential *miccos* of the upper and lower towns of the Creek Confederacy. After a time these offices seemed to appear as a means of dealing with the Europeans and eventually the Creeks organized a council of kings who were the *miccos* of the respective towns presided over by the *miccos* of the most important towns of the upper and lower halves of the nation. The Creeks thus evolved toward the European style of political organization because it was simpler to do so and because the preservation of the peace with the European powers made it necessary.

The Choctaws, another member group of the Five Civilized

Tribes, so named because of their adaptability in developing institutions comparable in many respects to the European models, organized themselves along similar lines. Angie Debo has described the council process of the Choctaw Republic, which bears a striking similarity to both the Creek and the Cheyenne manner of organizing the tribe:

> Councils of the district were called by its Head Chief, and Councils of the entire Nation by the Head Chiefs acting in concert. Runners carrying bundles of sticks to reckon the time of meeting were sent to summon all the town chiefs to the assembly. Apparently only these officials were admitted to participate in the Council, but the common people also came to listen to the speeches and to join in the inevitable feasting, games, and dances. The Councils were distinguished by the decorum with which they were conducted, and by the wild eloquence of the native orators. The members were greatly influenced by the judgment of the Head Chiefs and guided by their recommendations, but the decision was democratic and in accord with the wishes of the assembly.
>
> The Council usually dealt with such matters of public policy as peace, war, or foreign relations, but apparently it sometimes exercised certain judicial power. It was not a legislative body, for the Choctaws like other primitive people thought of law as a universal custom rather than a legislative enactment. (Debo, p. 21)

In addition to the democratic nature of the Choctaw decision-making process, two other important features may be discerned from Debo's description. The first pertains to the seemingly limited role played by the Head Chief, who appears to be a ceremonial leader rather than an executive; the second relates to the nonlegislative quasi-judicial nature of the tribal councils' functions. Both these observations are important because they testify to the fact that traditional tribal councils were charged with the responsibility of ensuring domestic tranquility. They did not enforce a set of laws, or even legislate them, but they did act in a mediation, taking on a problem-solving role on behalf of the community, and they acted as an intercessor for those people who sought public resolution of wrongs they had suffered.

The most highly developed tribal government, as we have already mentioned, was that of the Iroquois who formed a five-nation alliance symbolized by the Great Binding Law and the White Roots of Peace from the great Tree of the Law, which symbolically represented peace to all who would believe. The founding of the league of the Iroquois goes far back into the past and basically involves the bringing of the Great Binding Law by Dekanawideh and his spokesman, Hiawatha. Through subtle diplomacy these two heroes convinced five separate groups to gather together as one nation and to stand united against their foes, who at the time were pressing them severely. The Five Nations, now called the Six Nations with the admittance of the Tuscaroras in the middle of the eighteenth century, continues today as a significant political force in contemporary Indian affairs. The constitution that binds these groups together, however, is a most involved and complicated document that provides for many contingencies and demonstrates a finely balanced appreciation of the fierce pride the Indian nations have traditionally demonstrated.

The central decision-making body of the Iroquois Confederacy is a council, which has fifty seats filled by *rodiyaners* and presided over by the Atotarho, who is always an Onondaga. The council is divided into three separate bodies: the older brothers, who are the Mohawks and Senecas; the younger brothers, who are the Cayugas and Oneidas; and the keepers of the fire, who are the Onondagas. Certain accommodations were made at the founding of the league to ensure the participation of the respective tribes. The Onondagas received 14 seats at the great council, the Mohawks 9, the Senecas 8, the Oneidas 9, and the Cayugas 10. The tribes, however, when voting, each cast but one vote. Drawing upon the immediate disputes that had led these tribes to quarreling with each other, the constitution provided that no meeting would be considered legal unless the Mohawks were in attendance. The Senecas, who received only 8 seats at the council (and then shared these few with the Tuscaroras when they were admitted), were named the keepers of the western door and the war-making powers were vested in them.

The tribes are seated around a central fire during their deliberations, which must be held at least once in every year. The chiefs are further subdivided and they hold open discussions among these lesser groups so that all can hear the arguments and reasoning. In a highly complicated manner the subject under consideration is discussed by each of the tribes until it finally reaches the Onondagas, who have a final vote of "yes" or "no." The genius of this process is that the Onondagas, after having heard the subject analyzed from every possible standpoint, are then able to discern the general sense of the meeting and in effect place their imprimatur on a decision already basically the voice of the assembled people.

The constitution provides for various offices in the league; it establishes the clans that extend across the five nations and bind individual members together in a blood–extended family relationship; and it places ownership of the seats on the council, the *rodiyaners*, in the clan mothers so that women have a powerful voice in selecting the chiefs who sit as representatives of the people. Clan mothers can choose and can recall the chiefs and consequently direct the affairs of the Six Nations in a fundamental way. The constitution also provides for adoption, emigration, rights of foreign nations, rights and powers of war, a definition of treason, protection of religious ceremonies, protection of the house, and funeral addresses. The Iroquois system of government is worthy of study and emulation because it protects the very things—human personality and the home—that many modern non-Indian constitutions seem unable to protect adequately. Of fundamental importance is the recognition that, even in this complicated political framework, the mediating-reconciling function of the chief is not lost but instead is heavily emphasized. Indian chiefs were truly the servants of the people.

This important mediating function of the chief and the council provides a second interesting insight to be gained from an examination of the traditional forms of tribal governments: the primary thrust of traditional government was more judicial than legislative in nature. As characterized by the National American Indian Court Judges Association (*Justice and the American Indians*, p. 18), the system of private settlement of individual criminal offenses was nearly universal among Indian tribes. Unless an offense endangered the well-being of the tribe, the issue was to be settled privately among those affected. The process involved bargaining with a gift or some other form of propitiation or restitution serving as the basis for the settlement. Sometimes the aggrieved family or clan would insist that the wrongdoer join their group to replace the slain member, and the murderer was duty bound to respect their wishes. When the bargaining and negotiations failed, the chief would mediate and make every effort to preserve the peace. He provided the cement that held the tribe together peacefully. This adjudicatory nature of traditional tribal government stands in sharp contrast to the legislative orientation that the European influence would later introduce into Indian Country.

TRANSITIONAL TRIBAL GOVERNMENTS

Contact with the settlers, and the need for a formal organization to deal with the increasing complexity of commercial and political relationships that ensued from these encounters, forced many tribes to adapt their forms of government within several decades of European contact. The small groups of Indians in Massachusetts, for example, began to organize themselves according to the political system of that colony into small towns, which stood for many decades on the same status as other local municipalities. These towns were called "praying towns" because the Indians had by and large adopted the whites' religion and were beginning to participate in the activities of the colony. Several present-day tribes, such as the Mashpees and the Wampanoags, can trace their ancestry back to the establishment of these praying towns.

In the Ohio Valley, tribes encountering the settlers tightened their traditional forms of government considerably in an effort to preserve their lands and independence. The great Miami Confederacy dominated the interior region of Indiana, western Ohio, and eastern Illinois for over a generation by centralizing many of their activities in the villages along the Wabash. With the removal policy and the propensity of the United States to sign treaties with the southernmost villages, the political organization of the Miamis was finally broken and the various Miami villages were moved west or removed from federal protection. Finally only small family units that were engaged in farming and commercial ventures in Indiana remained; some of the families became first citizens of the new state of Indiana and played a substantial role in the development of that society. Today a few families living near Indianapolis are all that remain of the once-extensive Miami Confederacy.

The most creative adaptations of tribal government were made in the south. The Five Civilized Tribes—the Cherokee, Choctaw, Creek, Chickasaw, and Seminole—had intermarried with Scotch-Irish traders as early as the beginning decades of the eighteenth century and by the 1830s possessed a significant mixed-blood element that controlled the political affairs of the nations. These mixed-bloods were generally loyal to the tribe but had acquired sufficient knowledge of the workings of the white world to be successful in both cultures. By the mid 1820s only the Seminoles had not adopted formal political institutions modeled after the European style of government. The Cherokees and Choctaws each had formal constitutions with tripartite forms of government that closely followed the American style of checks and balances in allocating powers. The Creeks modified their traditional form of government slightly to create a House of Kings and a House of Warriors, taking the old positions of *micco* and *thlocco* and making them formal offices which, depending on the village, could be either elective or hereditary.

The Five Civilized Tribes, after removal to Oklahoma, substantially renovated their tribal governments, modeling their new reservations according to the old districts and villages that had existed in their ancient homelands in the south. The Creeks even preserved the distinction between the upper and lower towns, although through a geographical quirk in resettlement in Oklahoma the upper towns were now further south than the lower towns. The Choctaws and Chickasaws lived under one constitution for several years, but finally the Chickasaws seceded from the Choctaw Nation and adopted their own constitution. The Creeks and Seminoles also began life in Oklahoma as one political entity and then gradually saw a need for independent existence and split into two distinct tribes. By the time of the Civil War the Five Civilized Tribes had created smoothly functioning governments that did their business in a very professional manner. The tribes adopted annual budgets; allocated funds for education, police, and social services, including orphans and widows; and had their own judiciaries. A measure of the respect accorded these tribal governments by the national government is a statute passed on June 15, 1860, which directed that the Choctaw, Cherokee, and Chickasaw nations "be furnished by the Secretary of the Interior with such copies or volumes of the laws of the United States, Journals of Congress, and documents printed by order of Congress as are supplied to the States and Territories of the United States" (12 Stat. 116).

At the beginning of the Civil War, there was considerable consternation among the members of the Five Civilized Tribes. They had major treaties with the federal government, negotiated during the imposition of the Removal Act on them, which recognized their title to lands in the west in fee simple and further promised never to enclose their lands within the boundaries of a state without their consent. Risking abrogation of these fundamental political and property rights by siding with the south was a very serious matter and a majority of the people opposed such a move. Yet the influential families of these tribes had generally accommodated themselves to the southern social and economic milieu and felt more in sympathy with the rebels than with the federal government, which represented continual intervention in their lives. When the federal government refused the first overtures of the Five Civilized Tribes to raise troops to assist in the war, the southern sympathizers felt free to make independent agreements with the Confederate states.

With the surrender of the south in 1865, the national government was determined to punish the Five Civilized Tribes for supporting the southern efforts even though only a portion of the tribes had given aid and comfort to the rebels. The treaties of 1866, made to restore the political relationship with the United States that was severed by participation in the Civil War, were extremely punitive and required the Five Civilized Tribes to recognize their former slaves as tribal citizens and to admit the members of other tribes who might wish to join their tribe. These treaties also required the tribal governments to attend a conference for the purpose of developing a territorial government with the eventual goal of becoming a state.

In the post–Civil War decades the Five Civilized Tribes ably protected their own interests against congressional intrusions. They received exemptions from the General Allotment Act and the Seven Major Crimes Act because of their 1866 treaties. When Congress finally turned its attention to them it was because land speculators demanded that their lands be opened for settlement. Under a series of acts their tribal governments were stripped of almost all their governing powers. They were forced to conclude agreements with the United States in 1897 and 1898 that allotted their lands and declared the surplus open for settlement. By 1906 their tribal governments had no function other than to supervise the disposal of tribal property. They were continued by congressional resolution (J. Res. No. 7, 34 Stat. 822) with officers to be appointed by the president of the United States. Eventually a special act of Congress in 1970 (P.L. 91-495) allowed these tribes to elect their own officers again.

Many people believe that tribes, particularly western ones, had little or no government from 1871 when the treaty-making period ended until 1934 when the Indian Reorganization Act was enacted and the reservations were allowed to organize under approved constitutions and by-laws. This view has developed over the years because of the propensity of scholars to summarize events between the Allotment Act and the New Deal. This view is history from a white, not an Indian, perspective. A surprising number of tribes preserved their traditional forms of government for a number of years after they had entered upon the new life on the reservations. The agents assigned to them frequently attempted to break down the communal relationships of the people and to downgrade the chiefs and headmen so that they could manipulate the people more easily. The allotment of the reservations, particularly in the northern plains and Great Lakes areas, also contributed substantially to the erosion of traditional forms of authority. But research indicates that by and large the tribes maintained their traditional forms of government almost until the passage of the Indian Reorganization Act.

The emergence of the Red Lake Chippewa band as a distinct political entity exemplifies the manner in which tribal governments

made the transition from the traditional Indian customs to the beginnings of the modern council system. The Red Lake people were
one of a number of bands that signed treaties with the United States.
Under an 1889 law establishing the upper Minnesota Chippewa reservations, a general tribal council was recognized. The major functions of this council were to hold annual meetings; to allocate, from
the treaty annuity funds held for the Chippewas in the federal treasury, a per capita payment to tribal members; and to spend such
other funds as might have accumulated during the year. The Chippewas agreed to allotment of their reservation lands, except the Red
Lake band, who preferred to keep their lands in common. Following
allotment of Leech Lake, White Earth, Mille Lacs, Fond du Lac, and
Grand Portage, a large number of Chippewas sold their lands to the
timber interests and became landless. In 1916 the other Chippewa
bands proposed to allot the Red Lake reservation to provide allotments for the now-homeless tribal members.

The Red Lake band balked at this proposal arguing that they had
not been foolish in the management of their lands and they saw no
reason for them to now divide their patrimony with those members
of the tribe who had wasted their inheritance. Two years later, in
1918, the Red Lake band seceded from the Chippewa general council
and established its own government under seven chiefs. The general
council of the Chippewas of the Mississippi and Lake Superior sued
the Red Lake band for $10 million, which they argued had been their
loss because of the Red Lake departure. The case lingered in the federal courts until 1933 when the Supreme Court refused to accept a
writ of certiorari from the Chippewa general council, in effect af-
firming the right of the Red Lake band to its political independence.
Finally, in 1956, the Red Lake band adopted a constitution that included the traditional seven chiefs and a new elective council, making their form of government a complicated but cohesive version of a
traditional government modified to meet the exigencies of the day
(Taylor, pp. 54–55).

The experience of most of the western tribes can be best characterized as a government-sponsored transformation of traditional
forms into a more workable version of an informal council, which
could be called upon by the agent whenever it became impossible for
him to work without some form of approval from the people concerned. The Indian agent would gather together the most influential
leaders of the bands or communities living on the reservation and
ask them to form an ongoing council to assist him in whatever functions he felt could be delegated to them. Generally this council reflected the original political subdivisions of the tribal past but also

incorporated the democratic principles in which the agent believed, which usually meant one person/one vote in contrast to the traditional method of choosing leaders. The agent for the Blackfeet Reservation in Montana, in his annual report for 1875, gives a memorable account of the manner in which some early reservation councils were organized:

> My first object was to call the Indians together, nearly all of whom were scattered at long distances from here. After considerable exertion I had the satisfaction of seeing them coming in little by little, until I had over five thousand, embracing bands belonging to the different tribes. I immediately commenced counseling them to organize, elect head-chiefs, and pass laws for their government.
>
> I urged and talked about the matter for several days, pointed out the evils of their condition, the curse of intemperance, which had destroyed their head-chiefs and so many of their kindred, over one hundred and thirty having fallen victims to whiskey the previous year: pointed to the growing white settlements, and told them they must change their course of life or they would become extinct in a few years, as the buffalo would become very scarce after a few more snows. Five days were passed in preliminary talks between the different bands, at the end of which I had the pleasure of convening them in council for the purpose of electing three head-chiefs and passing a code of laws.
>
> Little Plume, White Calf, and Generous Woman were the chiefs elected, and a code of laws was adopted, a copy of which was forwarded to your office April last, abolishing polygamy, traffic in women, punishment for theft, and assault or brutal conduct, and establishing the death-penalty for murder. Everything was fully deliberated upon during the three days' council, and the entire proceedings proclaimed and universally understood through the camp. (AR-CIA, 1875, p. 300)

One might suggest that the code of laws adopted by the newly formed Blackfeet council reflected the teachings of the agent and most probably the Catholic missionaries who worked with the bands, the wisdom of the head-chiefs themselves at recognizing the conditions under which they lived, and the gentle prodding of the agent in attempting to help the Indians devise a system whereby the major responsibilities for maintaining law and order would rest with the natural groupings of the bands and not particularly with the agent and whatever Indians he could get to assist him. In some instances the agent simply chose the leaders of the tribe from among contending and contentious influential chiefs and made them assist him in governing the reservation. Such was the situation as reported by the agent to the Osage in 1877:

> The Osages in many respects differ from other Indians of the Indian Territory. They are more jealous of each other, and of those who have care of them. Each chief seems jealous lest some other chief should outrank him, and hence the difficulty of governing the tribe through the chiefs, and in some instances the chief fails to control his own immediate band. Another year's experience proves the wisdom of the course adopted on taking charge of the agency, in the selection of an executive committee, consisting of governor, chief counselor, and business committee of five, making seven persons selected from among the leading men of all the different factions. These seven men, regardless of character, are recognized as the representative men of the tribe, and through them its business with the agent and Government is transacted. (AR-CIA, 1877, p. 92)

In the initiative of the agents in selecting leaders to compose a reservation council we see the beginnings of the political division between the traditional and assimilated Indians that plagues tribal councils today. Not all such appointments were well regarded by the people, as we can see from the following excerpts from the agent to the Yankton Sioux in his report of 1885:

> From the eight bands of Indians, two from each were selected by me last winter, constituting what is known as a board of advisors. The object was to keep the agent advised of all irregularities, violations of the rules of the agency disposing of issue goods and stock, or plural marriages, crimes, and offenses, and to aid in bringing in children to school, and more especially assist the agent by advising him of persons who were needy and deserving in the distribution of such stock, farming implements, and property as might be furnished for the Indians. . . . I regret to say that the existence of this board has of late evoked serious opposition from some of the "heathen" Indians, mainly because of jealousy, and a foolish apprehension that the prerogatives of some of the old chiefs are jeopardized. (AR-CIA, 1885, p. 60)

Some tribal councils during this transitional period seem to have originated from the agent's efforts to institute a "Court of Indian Offenses" on the reservations. We will discuss these courts in a later chapter but it is important to note how the transition from a wholly traditional tribal government, which basically performed a quasi-judicial function, to the modern tribal council, which performs predominantly executive and legislative functions, varied from tribe to tribe. In discussing the failure of the government to provide funds for the payment of judges for the Court of Indian Offenses, which a large reservation needed, the agent at Pine Ridge, home of the Oglala Sioux, who were among the most independent of the Sioux bands, reported that the newly organized reservation council performed this function:

> In the absence of the above court the agency board of councilmen is doing good service, composed, as it is, of about one hundred delegates from our more progressive Indians, with a duly elected president, vice-president, clerk, advocate, and other officers. This board does not meet the approval of many of our superannuated chiefs, but is, nevertheless, doing good work in trying and punishing offenders, and it is to be hoped that they may be here long sustained and encouraged in their efforts toward civilization by receiving the recognition and approval of the Department. (AR-CIA, 1885, p. 37)

The board of councilmen was organized at Pine Ridge primarily to undercut the tremendous influence that Red Cloud, Bad Wound, and other noted chiefs had on the people. James Olson's *Red Cloud and the Sioux Problem* provides an excellent in-depth study of how strenuous this process of replacing the traditional chiefs proved to be in the case of the Oglalas. On the Yakima Reservation in the Pacific Northwest, the agent was able to deal with a much stronger hand and his report indicates that he forcibly imposed a judicial organization in place of the traditional chiefs.

> Soon after taking charge of this agency I discontinued the ancient barbaric system of rude government by chiefs, divided this reservation into five districts, and had the Indians to elect a justice of the peace in each district; carefully instructed, commissioned and swore into office, taking the territorial statutes as a general guide in these matters. The Indian policeman in each district performs the duties of constable for the justice of the peace of the district. I instituted a reservation court of three judges with original jurisdiction in higher criminal and civil cases and appellate jurisdiction in appeals from justices of the peace; reserving to myself the duties of a supreme court. I appointed the three reservation judges during the first two years; but at a general election last fall, three reservation

judges together with three reservation commissioners (to perform the duties of the boards of county commissioners), were elected. (AR-CIA, 1885, p. 204)

All of the above examples, of course, are the reports of Indian agents on the various reservations and reflect their belief that they were bringing a modicum of self-government to the Indians. We cannot know how the respective tribes viewed the organization of foreign and unfamiliar institutions or how they responded to the agent's expectations of them. Certainly many tribes made an effort to continue their traditional customs and methods of selecting leaders and viewed those tribal members who cooperated with the government with a good deal of suspicion. We know, from various reports, that when a prestigious chief lived on a reservation and represented his people a stronger form of traditional government survived longer. Red Cloud at Pine Ridge, Chief Joseph at the Colville Reservation in Washington state, Washakie on the Wind River Reservation in Wyoming, and Ouray on the Uintah and Ouray Reservation in Utah all presented a formidable barrier to the imposition of new forms of government over the people of those reservations. While agents might make every effort to reduce the power of such a chief, traditional ways of governing, on the whole, remained strong until well after the chief's passing.

Some generalizations about these critical decades can be made. It is first important to note that, with the exception of the Iroquois, Cherokee, Creeks, and perhaps Choctaw-Chickasaws, few tribes attempted to form a large encompassing form of government. Indeed, tribes in the plains, like New England townspeople of the seventeenth century, would have abhorred the idea of governing more than a few hundred people. Confinement to the reservations usually meant that several bands, in some cases several tribes, now had to live within a severely restricted geographical area where the density of population and the total dependence on the largesse of the government created a number of severe social problems that had not been known in their earlier days of unlimited freedom. The reservation boards and councils to which the agents refer represent the gathering of many bands of Indians who would normally govern themselves separately. Hence the reservation council in a real sense represents a *national* rather than a local government for many of these people. Their easy access to the chiefs and leaders of their traditional bands has now been eliminated, breaking the family or clan tie, and in its place has been substituted a form of representation modeled after the American democratic system, which regards the winner of an election as the truly representative political figure.

The major concern for many of the agents seems to have been finding a means whereby the influential leaders of the local communities could take some measure of responsibility for domestic relations, and in this sense these early reservation governments continue, albeit in the whites' institutional clothes, the traditional concern of the chiefs for families, persons, and domestic tranquility. This function of Indian leadership can particularly be seen in those instances where courts and judges were the first devices used to govern the people, with a formal council following years later as the need arose to make decisions concerning the use of resources or the filing of claims against the government. We have emphasized this important transitional period in the life of tribal governments because the available evidence suggests that no tribe simply adopted the forms of government suggested by the federal government. The people of the reservation always made adaptations that suited their needs. No tribe, for example, has ever had the rigid separation of legislative, executive, and judiciary that one would expect from governments modeled after the national government. Even the Indian Reorganization Act governments represented a modification of political institutions to meet specific Indian needs. There was hardly any separation between the legislative and executive arms of the tribal governments, and the tribal courts were created by the council and were not provided for in the tribal constitutions. Without a distinct separation of powers there should not have been any expectations that tribal courts would automatically develop in the same manner as did the courts in England or in this country once political freedoms began to be realized.

By the turn of the century a good number of tribes had adopted formal constitutions. An early Pima constitution adopted by the people at the Gila River Reservation provides:

> The executive power of the Reservation shall be vested in a Chief who shall be elected by the people; such election shall be subject to approval by the U.S. Indian Agent at Sacaton, Arizona. . . .

> The legislative power of the said Reservation shall be vested in the Chief and the Council, the latter to consist of eight Councilmen, two Assistant Chiefs, and the Head Chief. . . .

> It shall be the duty of the Council of the Santan Reservation to discuss and decide all general questions relating to the Reservation.

> They shall try all cases or suits referred to them from the Head Chief. (Russell, p. 222)

These constitutions can be viewed as the first effort, by the Indian people themselves, to establish a government that could represent their needs. Many of these constitutions fail to mention a tribal court system and deal more specifically with representation than with other functions. Therefore they do not conflict with the "Courts of Indian Offenses" established under the supervision of the Bureau of Indian Affairs during the early reservation days. The Klamath constitution of 1929, for example, does not have any provisions for a tribal judicial system (*Survey of Conditions of the Indians in the United States*, parts 11–13, 1931, pp. 5268–5270), whereas the agent's report of 1884 (AR-CIA, 1884, p. 143) indicates that the Indian police and the Court of Indian Offenses were the first institutions established on that reservation.

TRIBAL GOVERNMENT IN MODERN PERSPECTIVE

Modern tribal government can trace its inception, although not its fruition, back to the New Deal administration of Franklin Delano Roosevelt. When the federal government finally awakened to the fact that the Indian allotment policy had been a failure, resulting in the loss of a substantial portion of the Indian land estate and the impoverishment of the people, Congress, at the urging of the president and the secretary of the interior, Harold Ickes, initiated a new Indian policy by enacting the Indian Reorganization Act of 1934 (IRA, 48 Stat. 984). Part of the catalytic force behind this measure was the 1928 Meriam Report, which described the failure of the federal government to provide for Indians. The report mentioned the destructive impact that allotment had had on Indian life and culture and recommended major renovations in the federal bureaucracy. It was followed by various suggestions for even more radical reform, including a proposal advanced by John Collier and Nathan Margold in 1932—described as an "Indian Tribal Councils Bill"—to allow self-government by the tribes. The Collier proposal did not pass but did indicate the direction that reform efforts would take with a change of national administrations.

The Indian Reorganization Act became important because it directed national policy from a deliberate effort to extinguish tribal governments and customs to a goal of establishing self-government and providing it with sufficient authority and powers to represent the reservation population in a variety of political and economic ventures. The act did not enumerate the powers of the new governments established under its provisions. Indeed, Felix S. Cohen noted that "the act of June 18, 1934 had little or no effect upon the substantive powers of tribal self-government . . . [It] did bring about the regularization of procedures of tribal government and a modification of the relations of the Interior Department to the activities of tribal government" (Cohen, pp. 129–130).

The IRA, then, signaled an attitudinal change toward Indians and tribal governments. It provided an opportunity to revitalize tribal governments that had been submerged by the failure of either the legislative or the executive branches of the federal government to articulate the proper relationship that in fact existed between the Department of the Interior and the Bureau of Indian Affairs in their trustee capacity and the tribal governments, which, for better or for worse, were the successors to the gatherings of chiefs and headmen who had signed the treaties on behalf of their nations three-quarters of a century before. In addition to terminating the destructive allotment system, the IRA afforded tribes an opportunity to organize for their common welfare and to adopt written constitutions that would be formally approved by the secretary of the interior and that granted them status as federally chartered corporations.

The tribes who agreed to accept the provisions of this act could employ their own legal counsel (with the approval of the secretary of the interior) and even issue charters of incorporation for business purposes. More important, the act established a special fund from which the secretary of the interior could make loans to tribally chartered corporations for economic development purposes. Tribal members were extended the opportunity to vote on whether or not they wanted to participate in the benefits and accept the responsibilities of the IRA, but this vote was to be a one-time opportunity. If a majority of the tribe voted against participation, it could not reconsider this decision at a later date. Tribes had two years to accept or reject the IRA. Within that period 258 elections were held; 181 tribes accepted the terms of the act while 77 tribes registered a negative vote ("Tribal Self-Government and the Indian Reorganization Act of 1934," p. 977). Even these provisions were significantly vague. The act read that the Indians on every reservation could vote on this opportunity and in some cases, indeed a substantial number of cases, there was more than one tribe living on the reservation in question. Consequently, we derive the new "consolidated" or "confederated" tribal names from the elections held under this act and these bodies then assumed the political status their predecessor entities once possessed. Thus, out of these IRA elections we find the Three Affiliated Tribes of the Fort Berthold Reservation who formerly were the Mandans, Gros Ventres, and Arickaras; the Confederated Salish and Kootenai of the Flathead Reservation; and the Confederated Colville tribe, which was formerly a large number of Indian bands occupying that reservation.

Another difficulty involved with the act concerned the sequence in which the elections were to be held. The secretary of the interior was authorized under the IRA to transfer federal surplus and submarginal lands to the use of Indians who were landless. Once these lands were transferred, and this case occurred with some frequency in California, an election could be held by those Indians who moved onto the land to adopt the provisions of the IRA and to approve a constitution. The question subsequently arose whether a tribe had to have land before it could adopt a constitution or whether a constitution could be approved with the idea of receiving a transfer of land. While these questions did not seem pressing at the time, over the years, as new groups were considered for recognition by the Interior Department, they became major barriers for small groups of Indians achieving federal status and joining in the benefits conferred by the act. Some Indian scholars believe that this question has never been satisfactorily handled in the decades since the IRA became a reality.

When the Indian Reorganization Act was passed in 1934, the first impression was that it would bring about a monumental change in Indian affairs. While there was little new substantively in the act that could not be found in miscellaneous solicitor's opinions or memos of the Interior Department rulings, the act did lay the foundation for a resurrection of tribal government and power. The bureaucratic stranglehold and paternalistic orientation of the BIA were substantially modified. Administrative centralization was replaced by decentralized power in tribal governments. Once these initial positive changes had become institutionalized, however, continuing efforts to reform the bureaucratic stance of the government toward the tribes declined and a mass of additional, sometimes conflicting, opinions and memos accumulated to handicap the tribes in their further development efforts.

The political damage that had been inflicted upon tribal governments for so many decades in the past could not be undone overnight. The traditional forms of tribal government had been dormant for too long and much of the religious undergirding of the informal customs had been badly eroded. The format that emerged under the 1934 act was almost a carbon copy of the structured, legalistic European form of government. Since tribal governments were floundering, the Bureau of Indian Affairs seized the initiative and drafted a model constitution that could be used by tribes as a starting point for their written documents. This model constitution in most instances became the final product, which should not be surprising since Congress in passing the IRA required that all constitutions be approved by the secretary of the interior before becoming operational (25 U.S.C. 476) and homogeneity rather than usefulness consequently became the virtue.

Secretarial approval of constitutions, by-laws, selection of legal counsel, and most tribal resolutions proposing land use and civil and criminal codes was in effect a veto power on the activities of the newly formed tribal governments. In some instances these restrictions were necessary. It was difficult if not impossible, for example, for reservation Indians to check the credentials of attorneys seeking to be the legal counsel of the tribe. In most instances the secretarial veto proved helpful in directing the tribes toward adequate legal representation, but in some cases the integrity of the attorney in opposing the policies of the lower-level bureaucrats was sufficient evidence to delay or disapprove his or her contract. It can certainly be argued that, given the inexperience and impotency of tribal governments during these formative years, BIA assistance to the tribes was needed. But the agency utilized this secretarial approval requirement along with other powers as a basis for maintaining control over tribal affairs. In fact, processes and problems that had formerly been handled by community consensus were now formalized and required tribal resolutions and secretarial approval.

The effort to revitalize tribal governments continued with limited success throughout the 1930s and 1940s. Although the exercise of power by tribal governments took on the appearance of increasing sophistication, these developments came at the expense of certain tribal traditions and informal customs that had served the communities well for nearly three-quarters of a century. Indians, consciously or not, were adopting the whites' legalistic perspective on government. The 1950s, however, posed a significant threat in tribal development. The Eisenhower administration initiated a policy of "termination," initially discussed during the final years of the Truman administration, designed to eliminate the reservations and assimilate the Indians into the mainstream of the white social and economic systems. Termination was a contemporary version of allotment since it divided the tribal assets on a per capita basis and then required the individual tribal members to forfeit their federal rights to services and supervision. The Bureau of Indian Affairs, as it had during the allotment days, played a major role in terminating the tribes and selling off the tribal land estates.

In the overall scheme of things, however, the Eisenhower "termination" policy was but a momentary, though totally destructive, digression from the continuing resurgence of tribal government development. In the two decades following the Eisenhower years, tribes were once again placed in a position to seize the initiative that had begun in the 1930s to exercise self-governing powers. The social programs of the 1960s, the New Frontier and the Great Society social welfare legislation, enabled the tribal governments to be sponsors of federally funded programs, and tribal governments rapidly expanded to take advantage of these opportunities. Soon each tribe had developed its own massive bureaucracy to deal with the multitude of programs for which it was eligible. Although the IRA had enabled tribes to charter organizations for the purposes of economic development, few tribes had any experience in operating complicated subsidiaries. The first thought of many tribes during the 1960s was to designate the tribal council as the housing authority, the economic development corporation, and even sometimes the school board. But it was quickly apparent to both tribes and the federal funding agencies alike that this kind of institutional response was fraught with complications. Consequently, HUD, EDA, and other federal agencies required the tribal councils to charter separate housing authorities and nonprofit development corporations. One of the major problems to arise in these efforts to develop subsidiary institutions was the fact that many programs needed to provide in-kind matching grants and materials and the tribal council had control of and responsibility for tribal property and income. In order to make certain that their people derived every possible service and program for which they were eligible, tribal governments were burdened with responsibilities far in excess of anything conceived during the IRA's formative years.

The Self-Determination and Education Assistance Act of 1975 (25 U.S.C. 4502-450n) created a statutory climate for a real reawakening of tribal efforts. Among other things, this act authorized agencies of the federal government to contract with and make grants directly to Indian tribal governments for the delivery of federal services. The philosophy underlying this concept of tribal self-determination revolved around the vesting of both management and control of governmental service programs in the tribal governments on the theory that tribes knew best their own problems and could therefore allocate their resources and energies in the proper direction. This ideology assumed a sophistication that did not exist and generated tremendous expectations in Congress that the tribes would suddenly respond to new opportunities with the expertise of a modern corporation. When the tribes became bogged down in complicated management problems, some opponents of the policy in the

Bureau of Indian Affairs were quick to emphasize their inability to function in the white world. The experience of self-determination was therefore both good and bad. It allowed tribes to make some decisions without the pressure from bureaucrats to conform to preexisting ideas but it also had pejorative effects when a project failed, further undermining the Indians' confidence in themselves.

During the years when tribal governments were weak, or even nonexistent, the BIA assumed almost total control and management of federal programs. Today the picture has changed significantly. Tribal governments, for the most part, have developed to the extent that they can now undertake these management functions. The loosely knit organization that performed largely quasi-judicial peace-making tasks among tribal members has now taken on all the trappings of the Anglo-American form of local government. Structurally, many tribal governments are composed of representative councils that perform legislative functions, professional bureaucrats charged with managing the administrative business of the tribe, tribal courts that handle the adjudicatory matters of a criminal and civil nature, and even special business councils that conduct the economic development activities on behalf of the reservation.

One of the bolder tribal reorganizations was achieved by the Zuni Pueblo of New Mexico. The main thrust of the "Zuni Plan" was to wrestle control of federal programs away from the Bureau of Indian Affairs and to decentralize their authority so that the key decision-making was lodged at the community level. Prior to this period of self-determination, any abrupt break with the BIA meant termination of federal services. The dual goal under the "Zuni Plan," then, was to preserve tribal access to the variety of federal programs while at the same time cutting the administrative umbilical cord that tied tribal affairs to BIA control. Federal officials were replaced by elected tribal officers and employees. And BIA personnel, who had been located off the Zuni Pueblo lands, moved into the Indian community so that there would be closer interaction between the tribe and the retained BIA employees. Supervision of the BIA employees working in the pueblo would come from the tribe, not from Washington.

The "Zuni Plan" accomplished its two major objectives—greater tribal independence from the BIA and a continuation of federal services—and this accomplishment clearly strengthened tribal self-government. One commentary characterized the changing relationship between tribal governments and the BIA in noting that the Indian agency had "moved from a manager and provider of services toward a granting and contracting agency. The tribes would manage their own land and deliver services to their own people with the Bureau auditing tribal performances" (Getches, Rosenfelt, Wilkinson, p. 121).

The metamorphosis that tribal government has experienced in the past decade from a latent governmental entity to a dynamic political force is not simply the result of such statutes as the Self-Determination Act. During the past decade other active elements on the reservations have worked to produce this change. Several decades ago the reservations were barren of attorneys. The infusion of poverty program OEO attorneys on the reservations provided greater access to the courts and opened up an additional avenue to bring about needed procedural and substantive changes in Indian policy.

In 1970, a legal interest group, the Native American Rights Fund, was established to carry the case of the Indians into the state and federal courts. Whereas the black community had embarked on its legal revolution in the 1930s and had seen its successful culmination in *Brown* and succeeding cases in the 1950s and 1960s, the Indian movement began its litigation activities during the 1970s. The use of the legal system as a pathway to strengthened tribal government and to press for the restoration of Indian rights added an extra and important dimension to the politics of Indian Country that heretofore had been dormant.

TRIBAL GOVERNMENT AND CONTEMPORARY PROBLEMS

While the relationship between tribal governments and the BIA undoubtedly has changed over the past few years, it would be foolish to discount the agency as a constant visible entity in Indian political affairs. The BIA remains a formidable actor in the governmental process and one with which the tribes must continually reckon. Even in the age of self-determination the deep-seated belief held by federal employees that they must be involved in every activity undertaken by the tribes inevitably leads to a continuing irritation that cannot be easily resolved. In addition, the access of tribal officers to other federal agencies with a less rigid view of Indian matters and more willingness to become involved in difficult development projects has led to a sense of futility within the Bureau of Indian Affairs that often manifests itself in overzealous enforcement of rules and regulations. Consequently, both tribal governments and the BIA, and ultimately the federal relationship itself, are in a state of rapid and unpredictable change.

The historical relationship between tribal governments and the BIA resulted in a lack of trust in the federal government by tribal leaders. The Indian agency that was charged with the responsibility of advocating Indian interests is still viewed as an elitist organ of government possessing a cavalier attitude toward Indian rights and resources. This residue of distrust is not simply an atavistic belief but is well founded in fact. In the late 1960s, for instance, the Pala and Rincon Indians brought suit to challenge the authority of the BIA to spend funds appropriated for Indian irrigation laterals on non-Indian lands. While the amount of money involved was only $800, repeated requests for construction funds and repairs of laterals owned by Indians consistently had been denied by the BIA. Indeed, the former Indian owners of the land involved had to sell the property because their trees had died for lack of water. Their requests, like those of the other Indians, also had been denied by the BIA. The only approved request granted by the BIA was to the new white landowners. While the court in *Scholder v. United States,* 428 F.2d 1123 (9th Cir. 1970), concluded that the doctrine of sovereign immunity precluded judicial scrutiny of this issue (and therefore dismissed the challenge), the judges noted that the bureau's conduct in the case "borders on the shocking." "At best," the court continued, "it reflects gross insensitivity." This type of bureaucratic behavior by the BIA hardly contributed to dispelling the distrust Indians have held toward the agency for years.

Some of the difficulties that continue to plague the tribal–federal governmental relationship are of a structural nature. Many of the legal problems that tribes need to resolve are directed to the Solicitor's Office in the Department of the Interior, and the associate solicitor for Indian affairs assumes a prominent role in settling these legal issues. The solicitor, like the Bureau of Indian Affairs, should theoretically be an advocate for the tribal governments. But the Indian tribes are his or her particular clients only with respect to issues involving parties outside the Department of the Interior; with respect to issues between agencies of the department, the solicitor theoretically has the department as his or her client and must determine a course of action that will produce internal satisfaction. Thus, the solicitor can become an advocate in the first discussion of the issues involving Indians. Not infrequently, Indian tribal governments and/or the BIA come into conflict with other agencies housed within Interior, such as the Bureau of Reclamation and the Bureau of Land Management. The solicitor thus may represent multiple clients who frequently possess antagonistic interests. In private practice this representation would give rise to an unethical situation in which the attorney's license would be jeopardized. But instead of facing up to the ethical dilemma, at times the Solicitor's Office will simply attempt to bring about an accommodation of the conflicting interests and quite often this accommodation will be purchased at the cost of enforcing Indian rights.

Reid Chambers conducted a study of legal problems, such as this conflict of interest, for the Senate Judiciary Committee in 1971 and portrayed several apparent conflicts of interests (Chambers, 1971). One of the illustrations involved a land dispute on the Colorado River in which the Bureau of Land Management advised the secretary of the interior that the property should be leased to Yuma County, Arizona, for an airport and park facilities. The Quechan tribe claimed that the land belonged to them as part of the Fort Yuma Reservation. The Solicitor's Office resolved the issue in favor of the non-Indian position, which was pressed by the BLM. By his opinion, Chambers noted, the solicitor was really "arbitrating" the dispute between his two clients, the Bureau of Land Management and the BIA who had resisted the lease on behalf of the Quechan tribe. In reading an organizational manual, the Quechan Indians might have expected the solicitor to have acted as their advocate on this legal issue or they might have expected him to represent the BLM. Instead, administrative and structural practicalities projected the solicitor out of his "advocacy" role into that of an "arbitrator" of intradepartmental disputes.

The administrative apparatus within which tribal governments must operate in Washington, D.C., then, can pose major problems. In the Colorado River case, it resulted in the loss of legal advocacy on behalf of the tribe. One might argue, however, that this institutional problem extends to all agencies within the Department of the Interior. While this is certainly true, it still leaves tribal governments in a disadvantageous position. The BIA is one of the least prestigious and less powerful agencies within Interior. And when it must do battle with more powerful divisions within the department, such as the Bureau of Land Management, the Indians find themselves in a less than competitive political position.

The problems that continue to burden tribal governments are not restricted to their relations with bureaucratic agencies. Many of them are inherent in the tribal institutions themselves. Being relatively new organizations, tribal governments are vulnerable in many ways. The elected leaders often lack experience and are insecure in their offices. Difficulties may arise between the new democratically elected leaders and the old traditional leaders, and the elected officials generally lack the security and sense of authority that tribal customs authenticate. The traditionalists, often slow to accept new ideas and procedures, have occasionally viewed elections as a product of the whites' institutions that have been forced upon the tribe, and they have refused to participate. And the ever growing conflict between the "traditional" way of life and the ideas of the new educated generation, vigorously pushing for economic and commercial development on or near the reservations, has widened the gap considerably. Those supporting commercial development often find themselves working closely with the white community and advocating policies their elders find discordant with traditional Indian values.

It must be remembered that the Indian experience with modern-day forms of government is new. Indeed, for most tribes it spans a period of less than a half a century. Like all contemporary political organizations, tribal councils must constantly struggle with too many untrained employees, function under organizational flow charts that look fine on paper but leave much to be desired in operation, and cope with intra-agency personnel problems of jealousy and ideological conflict.

Any attempt to analyze contemporary tribal governments must of necessity be flawed. The variety of governmental institutions and processes are many, running the length of the administrative spectrum. In 1974 the National American Indian Court Judges Association noted that most tribal governments today fall into one of the following categories:

> *Representative*: Here the tribe elects a governing body that operates under a constitution which the tribal members have approved (Ute., Jicarilla Apache).
>
> *Representative/Traditional Combination*: Under this system, governmental officials are elected by tribal members, but some governmental positions are reserved for traditional leaders by virtue of their traditional lineage. The officials operate under a written constitution voted on by the tribal members (Red Lake Band of Chippewa and the Warm Springs Tribes of Oregon).
>
> *General Council*: The tribal membership adopts by-laws which govern and control the tribal officers, but these tribal officials have no substantive authority. When a substantive issue arises, officers call a General Council meeting of the tribe and the members vote on the issue (Crow Tribe of Montana).
>
> *Theocracy*: Both the civil leaders and officers of the tribe are selected by the religious leaders. This is the most traditional

form of tribal government (guaranteed to the Pueblos by the Treaty of Guadalupe Hidalgo).

Added to this list, of course, must be the traditional government of the Iroquois and the town corporation form of organization enjoyed by some of the eastern Indian tribes who are under state rather than federal supervision.

As complicated as this variety of tribal governments seems to be, there are two important changes that time has brought on the form and nature of tribal governments. First, whereas the traditional form of tribal organization functioned primarily as an adjudicatory body settling disputes within the tribes, today tribal bodies have become legislative in their outlook and bureaucratic in their operations. Policy-making and governmental administration constitute the sinews of their activities. Second, tribal governments have taken on the cloak of Anglo-American institutional forms. The structures, the functions, the technologies, the politics, and even the goals of the white community are in many ways displacing the traditional ways of the Indians. The unanswered question that remains is how much of the traditional Indian culture and values can survive if tribal government continues to develop along these lines.

5. The Indian Judicial System

American Indian law is very complicated. If limited only to the written documents that could be used as a basis for finding "the" law, one would have to cover nearly 400 ratified treaties and agreements, 5,000 federal statutes, 2,000 federal court opinions, and over 250 tribal constitutions and charters (U.S. Civil Rights Commission, *1961 Annual Report*, p. 125). Add to this massive accumulation the traditions and customs of 500 or more individual tribes and the task becomes formidable indeed. But these are simply basic documents. American Indian law also includes state opinions and state statutes (some of which originated before the Constitution of the United States), congressional hearings of legislation, reports of a series of investigative commissions, and field surveys of Indian conditions, many of which are themselves a massive compilation of data. Finally, American Indian law includes solicitor's opinions and memorandum opinions of the Department of the Interior and, more recently, other federal departments that have come to serve Indians in a variety of ways.

The difficulty one faces in searching for substantive Indian law is not made easier by the jurisdictional setting in which Indian law operates. Some issues are handled directly by tribal courts and, since many of these courts have not been until very recent times courts of record where the cases are actually recorded, one must look in vain for the laws and precedents that govern day-to-day life on the reservations. Other cases, however, both civil and criminal, must be sent through the federal court system. Still others are handled by state courts. To clarify this jurisdictional maze is at the very least a challenge, but it must be understood if students are to gain a comprehensive perspective of the Indian legal system. While a discussion of the types of cases that each of these respective courts may entertain appears later in the text, it is important at this point to obtain a visual glimpse of the basic organizational structure of the American court system as it relates to American Indian law. Figure 1 gives the basic set of relationships that link together the federal, state, and tribal judicial systems. It should be remembered that cases involving Indian individuals can be heard in any of these courts, that cases involving Indian tribes can be heard in any of these courts, and that cases involving an interpretation of Indian law, although not involving Indian plaintiffs and defendants, can be heard in any of these courts. American Indian law is consequently one of the most complicated subjects in the entire legal area.

THE DEVELOPMENT OF THE INDIAN COURT SYSTEM

The nucleus of the Indian judicial system revolves around three legal institutions: traditional courts, Courts of Indian Offenses (better known as CFR courts), and tribal courts. While there are only a handful of traditional and CFR courts remaining in existence today, each of these judicial bodies assumed an important role in the historical development of the Indian judicial system and hence requires individual consideration.

The Traditional Courts

In discussing the functions of early tribal governments in the last chapter, it was noted that one of the most important powers exercised by tribal governments involved the resolution of disputes among tribal members. The mechanism charged with performing this was not always a body of appointed or elected judges as we use today; rather, it often fell within the authority of the tribal chief, the council of elders or chiefs, the council of the warrior society leaders, or the religious leaders. Whatever the mechanism used by the tribe, the adjudicatory function was somewhat different from that to which we are most accustomed. The primary goal was simply to mediate the case to everyone's satisfaction. It was not to ascertain guilt and then bestow punishment upon the offender. Under Anglo-American notions of criminal jurisprudence, the objectives are to establish fault or guilt and then to punish. The sentencing goals of retribution, revenge, and deterrence and isolation of the offender are extremely important (though the system often pays much lip service to the concept of rehabilitation as well). Under the traditional Indian system the major objective was more to ensure restitution and compensation than retribution. The idea, therefore, that tribal laws involved some Old Testament eye-for-an-eye mechanism that worked independently of human personality stems merely from inadequate

FIGURE 1. The American Judicial System and Indian Law

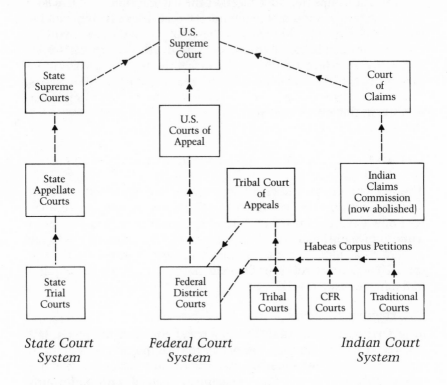

observations of what really occurred in tribal societies. In most instances the system attempted to compensate the victim and his or
her family and to solve the problem in such a manner that all could
forgive and forget and continue to live within the tribal society in
harmony with one another.

Under the traditional tribal system of justice, the ultimate decision was seldom made by a judge. Rather, the job of the mediator
or reconciling chief was to create an atmosphere for participant
decision-making. The two conflicting parties would call upon a
chief, elder, medicine man, or religious leader more for his assistance in keeping the situation within the bounds of tribal customs than for his decision as to who was "right" and who was
"wrong" in a given situation. The role of this tribal figure was to
help the parties discuss the problem until a satisfactory compromise
or solution could be agreed upon. Each of the parties recognized that
a proper settlement required some restitution to the injured party,

but restitution that permitted the offending party to continue to live within the tribal community. Banishment was extremely rare in most tribes and represented a very serious breach of the fundamental folkways that bound the tribe together.

There were occasions when punishment had to be meted out. Whatever mechanism was adopted by the traditional forms of tribal government, religious custom and traditions were the prevailing characteristics that shaped Indian justice. A surprising number of times the mediating chief or elder, in order to ensure that everyone would abide by the decision that was reached, offered compensation himself to the injured party out of his own goods so that no one would continue to brood on his or her loss. Self-help was prevalent in many tribes and the specter of a continuing blood feud between powerful families, with its subsequent disruption of community life, was sufficiently distasteful to prevent family revenge from getting out of hand. Of the traditional courts that can be said to remain today, the Peacemakers' Court of the Iroquois and the religious courts of the Pueblos are the most representative institutions. Since the practices of these courts are held in unusual secrecy by the traditional people, it is not proper to comment extensively on them.

Courts of Indian Offenses

During the early part of the nineteenth century when Indians were being pushed westward to the reservations, law and order in Indian Country was controlled by the military. At this time, the Bureau of Indian Affairs was a part of the Department of War. In 1849, with the creation of the Interior Department, the Bureau of Indian Affairs was transferred to this new department and Indian affairs were placed under civilian control. The military still continued to exercise some police functions on the isolated frontiers, but, in general, law and order was a responsibility of the Indian agents. Since many tribes had preserved law and order to themselves under their treaties, the duty of the agent was to intervene in cases in which whites and Indians were involved and to ensure that the government made some effort to punish whites who had violated the treaties. The ordinary domestic law of the tribes generally continued until well into the allotment period. State and territorial courts, unless the conditions called for swift vengeance, usually deferred to the federal courts and often would not try cases involving two Indians even if they had appealed to the state courts for assistance. Only in New Mexico, where an early Supreme Court ruling (*United States v. Joseph*, 94 U.S. 614 (1876)) seemed to distinguish the Pueblos as ordinary citizens because of their residence in towns under the former Spanish and Mexican rule, did the territorial courts play an active role in deciding cases involving Indians.

Courts of Indian Offenses most probably began with the appeal by disputing chiefs to the agent as arbiter of problems that could not be resolved in the traditional tribal manner. We have already discussed, in the last chapter, how agents handled some of the political problems that reservation life entailed and how their conception of their job, predicated upon the need to keep an orderly community and to prevent intrusions by whites, gave a quasi-judicial aspect to early reservation institutions. On some reservations the early councils were both judicial and legislative and exercised, after the influence of the chiefs had declined, executive powers also. Courts of Indian Offenses mark the first evolution away from one body holding all three political powers in its hands to the tripartite arrangement we see on many reservations today.

The development of the Indian police also played a critical role in this movement toward independent institutions. Unable to rely upon the traditional chiefs to carry out their instructions, many of which were anathema to the old people, the agents early began to enroll Indians as agency policemen. This new group enabled the agent to control the Indians without having to rely upon the presence of federal troops, which in many cases might have created an unpleasant incident or a war. Although the rise of Courts of Indian Offenses certainly indicated the increasing application of the white laws over the Indians, they were not wholly without respect among the Indians. Manuelito, one of the most respected and beloved of the Navajo war chiefs, served for a time as an Indian policeman and performed duties in a Court of Indian Offenses.

The allotment policy considerably increased the need for the Courts of Indian Offenses. In order to break up the traditional family groupings on many reservations, allotments were deliberately mixed so that family members might have their lands scattered all over the reservations. The idea behind this bureaucratic hodgepodge was to encourage the younger generation to move away from the elders and to begin farming on their own. The result of the application of the idea was that it became difficult if not impossible for communities that were dependent on tribal customs to conduct some of their ceremonies because the clan or family was so dispersed. The Courts of Indian Offenses then served to provide them with some forum in which a modicum of justice could be realized. Subsequent sale of allotments and the settling of white purchasers within the reservation borders made it virtually impossible to do anything except rely on these courts for redress.

In 1883 the Courts of Indian Offenses were made a regular part of the Bureau of Indian Affairs activities on the reservations. The status of these courts was never very clear since Congress frequently did not appropriate sufficient funds to make them effective, and they were described, in the only case to deal directly with their legality, *United States v. Clapox*, 35 Fed. 575 (D.C. Ore. 1888), as "mere educational and disciplinary instrumentalities by which the Government of the United States is endeavoring to improve and elevate the condition of these dependent tribes to whom it sustains the relation of guardian." One commentator, Rice, suggested that the Courts of Indian Offenses "derive their authority from the tribe, rather than from Washington," but this attempted justification has never become a popular explanation because of the documented abuses of Indians in these courts by the agents.

These courts have become known as CFR courts since they operated under the written guidelines as set down in the Code of Federal Regulations. But when surveying the literature concerning their operation it is difficult to determine whether they were really courts in the traditional jurisprudential sense of either the Indian or the Anglo-American culture or whether they were not simply instruments of cultural oppression since some of the offenses that were tried in these courts had more to do with suppressing religious dances and certain kinds of ceremonials than with keeping law and order. The sacred Sioux ceremony of "keeping the soul," eloquently described in *The Sacred Pipe* by Black Elk to Joseph Epes Brown, which was basically a condolence rite, was banned by these courts on the Dakota reservations to the consternation of the people.

Although the CFR courts were staffed by Indian judges, they served at the pleasure of the agent, not the community. The Indian agent appointed his judges as a patronage exercise, which rewarded the Indians who seemed to be assimilating while depriving the traditional people of the opportunity to participate in this vital function of the community. Even though the judges invested a good deal of energy and prestige in serving on these courts, too frequently the ultimate decision rested with the Indian agent, who often acted as though the people had no right to understand the reasoning behind his arbitrary decisions. Interestingly, there was never any real statutory authority for the establishment of the CFR courts and their legitimacy was rationalized under general powers that were lodged in the office of the commissioner of Indian affairs. At its zenith, the CFR court system was operating on about two-thirds of all reservations (Kerr, p. 321). With the authorization of the IRA corporate form of tribal government, all but a few tribes assumed judicial functions as a manifestation of self-government and rid themselves of this hated institution. Since these courts did not have the sanction of the whole tribal community, even the most beneficial parts of their operations have been eyed with suspicion by Indians and historians alike.

Modern Tribal Courts

As with tribal governments, the Indian Reorganization Act of 1934 heralded the beginning of the modern tribal court system. Under the IRA, not only could tribes draft a constitution and by-laws for self-government, but they could also establish their own judicial system. This opportunity afforded the Indians a chance to abandon the already disintegrating CFR court system and replace it with a legal system more responsive to tribal needs and under tribal control. More important, it provided an opportunity to resurrect the traditions and customs that had been so important to Indian culture before being dissipated by the bureaucratic controls from Washington.

The years of assimilation that Washington had thrust upon Indian Country, however, had taken their toll. Most tribes were not in a position to re-create the old traditional courts of justice that had functioned prior to the CFR era. Instead, tribal governments established legal systems closely fashioned after a BIA model. A few tribes simply retained their old CFR court system slightly modified to eliminate the objectionable features that had hampered it and made it seem a foreign institution. The old methods of handling disputes could not really be brought back into the lives of the people because most of them depended upon religious ceremonies that were no longer practiced. And Indians who were now converted and church-going Christians were generally suspicious of the effort by the New Dealers to guarantee religious freedom to traditional people. Thus, custom law, unless it involved a deeply personal responsibility, could not again become the base for community cohesion and law and order.

The newly created tribal court system, then, was designed to operate under and enforce the new tribal codes, which were designed to meet contingencies of today rather than recast traditions of the past. Their jurisdiction over civil disputes among tribal members was extensive and the courts could exercise some criminal jurisdiction over reservation offenses that had not been pre-empted by the federal government under such legislation as the Major Crimes Act. Generally, one could characterize the variety of offenses that became the province of the tribal courts as those falling into the misdemeanor class rather than the felony category.

Robert Coulter has provided an excellent description of the

tribal court system created by the Oglala Sioux (Coulter, pp. 66–69). This court is not untypical of the general characteristics and procedures of many tribal courts today.

The court is composed of three associate judges and one Chief Judge, each elected by a two-thirds vote of the tribal council. Provision is also made for the appointment of a "special judge" who must be a licensed attorney. Aside from the "special judge" there is no requirement of legal training. However, judges must be able to read and understand English, and all but the "special judge" must be members of the Tribe and able to read and understand Lakota, the tribal language. This feature of the Oglala Sioux Court is representative; most Indian judges are non-lawyers; however, training programs are being developed to aid them, and some tribes have hired non-Indian professional attorneys to serve as full-time judges. . . .

Although the Oglala Sioux Tribal Code provides for admission to a Tribal Bar, there is ordinarily no professional counsel present in the tribal court. Practice and procedure in the Oglala Sioux Court, as in most Indian courts, is casual. The general absence of professional attorneys often leads the judge into an active role in hearings and trials. Occasionally, judges even rely on their personal knowledge of the facts of the case before them. In reaction to the relative looseness of the tribal court procedures, some officials of the court are prone to overemphasize unimportant technicalities. . . .

Appeals from trial court decisions are rare, though most tribes provide some means for review of both civil and criminal cases. Judgements of the tribal courts may usually be appealed either to a panel of tribal judges, to the tribal council sitting judicially, or to a single judge of the tribal court. Prior to the Indian Bill of Rights, tribal court decisions could not generally be reviewed outside the tribal system. The principal reason for the paucity of appeals is that most cases handled are simple misdemeanors, with sentences of six months or less. Other reasons may be that parties are unaware of their rights, that appeals are discouraged by the tribal judge himself, and that appeal may be futile, since the same judge may be sitting on the appellate panel.

In this study, Coulter points out that a tribal court like the Oglala hears about 2,500 cases annually and that most of these are alcohol-related misdemeanors and alcohol-related domestic relations controversies often revolving around divorce and child custody problems that have been aggravated by social conditions on the reservation. He also notes that many of the criminal cases heard by the tribal court could just as well be heard in a civil court setting but that injured parties are more inclined to swear out criminal complaints than to file civil suits. This tendency can certainly be traced back to the propensity of the old Courts of Indian Offenses to visualize everything as a violation of basic agency rules and to the lack of sophistication of reservation people in using civil remedies.

The vast majority of cases heard in tribal courts begin with an initial plea of not guilty with the plea changed at the trial to guilty and an expectation of leniency from the judge. Bail is usually very low and generally is a personal recognizance bond since the offenses under consideration are generally minor violations of the tribal code. Few cases actually ever go through the complicated appeals system that the tribes have established, and many criminal defendants see the courtroom as only an anteroom leading to a term in the tribal jail. Divorce cases do not generally take much time since the break in the marriage has already been verified by other means and the tribal court provides a useful and inexpensive forum to accomplish the disengagement the people have already experienced emotionally. Custody cases generally involve a bit more care and have some unusual complications when the parents are from different tribes. Even in this area of law, however, it is unusual to have a difficult or lengthy and complicated case in tribal court.

Modern-day tribal courts have thus taken on some of the trappings of the Anglo-American judicial system. Judges sometimes wear robes, witnesses are called to testify, attempts are made to keep testimony relevant, the litigants are permitted to have judicial advocates, and tribal court decisions are subject to appeal. But with all these similarities, there are still significant differences that bring a unique flavor to the tribal court system.

As Coulter reveals in his portrayal of the Oglala Sioux tribal court system, tribal judges are not usually attorneys. What legal training they receive comes through seminars and training sessions sponsored by the National American Indian Court Judges Association and other organizations. In some tribal court proceedings, lawyers are not permitted to participate; rather, the parties are represented by Indian advocates who are frequently assisted by Indian Legal Services attorneys. The judge often controls the flow of a trial by asking questions of witnesses and even assisting the parties with the presentation of their positions. The atmosphere of the trial courtroom is markedly informal and relaxed as compared to that of the Anglo-American system. Tribal courts are not generally courts of record and seldom is a written opinion handed down. Since the existence of Indian nations precedes the adoption of the U.S. Constitution, provisions of the Bill of Rights do not rigidly apply to tribal court proceedings. And if a tribal judge commits some type of prejudicial error during the trial, his or her verdict can be appealed to a higher Indian authority. In some instances, however, the tribal judge who allegedly committed the error also will sit on the panel of appellate judges hearing the appeal.

Given the marked differences between tribal court proceedings and Anglo-American courts, a question might arise concerning the integrity of tribal court decisions. Are they fully recognized throughout the overall American legal system? Since the development of the tribal court system has been sanctioned, indeed encouraged by Congress, there is little room for argument concerning the legitimacy of tribal court orders. However, since Indian nations do not fall within the definition of a state but are viewed as "domestic dependent nations," the tribal court decrees are not entitled to the "Full Faith and Credit" recognition that the orders of state courts are accorded under the Constitution. (Full Faith and Credit requires that each state extend the same force and recognition to the court orders of sister states as if those orders had been issued in the home state.)

The Full Faith and Credit issue was recently decided in the case of *Red Fox v. Red Fox*, 23 Ore. App. 393, 542 P.2d. 918 (1975). While noting that the Full Faith and Credit Clause of the Constitution did not apply to Indian nations, the Oregon appellate court did reason that tribal court decrees were entitled to the same deference shown the decrees of foreign nations as a matter of *comity*. Comity is a legal doctrine under which deference is extended to foreign court orders as a matter of courtesy, not of legal right or obligation. The critical question in granting comity, the court opinion continued, is whether the parties had a fair and impartial trial within the tribal court system. If the court had jurisdiction, the parties had an opportunity to present their sides of the question, the proceedings reflected civilized jurisprudence, and a record was kept, then there is a prima facie case for a fair trial.

It would appear that many tribal court proceedings would have little difficulty satisfying the requirements of *Red Fox* such that their court orders would be extended comity by both state and federal courts. There is even some evidence of late that a trend may be emerging in the direction of extending Full Faith and Credit to tribal court decrees. Congress passed a statute stipulating that "acts, records, and judicial proceedings (of any State, Territory or Possession) shall have the same full faith and credit in every court within the U.S. and its Territories and possessions as they have by usage in the courts of such State, Territory, or Possession from which they are taken" (28 U.S.C.A. §1738). Several cases have indicated that Indian tribes constitute a "territory" under the terms of this act such that tribal court orders would fall within the purview of the Full Faith and Credit doctrine (see *Jim v. CIT Financial Services Corporation*, 87 N. Mex. 362, 533 P.2d 751 (1975), and *In Re Buehl*, 87 Wash. 649, 555 P.2d 1334 (1976)). And in 1978, the Supreme Court in dicta in *Santa Clara Pueblo v. Martinez*, 436 U.S. 49 (1978), indicated that tribal court judgments have been regarded under some circumstances as entitled to receiving Full Faith and Credit. While the intricacies of this legal argument apparently need more time for resolution, it is clear that tribal court judgments that presently depend upon recognition through comity are sufficiently legitimate to be an acceptable and integral part of the overall American system of law.

The greatest challenge faced by the modern tribal court system is in the harmonizing of past Indian customs and traditions with the dictates of contemporary jurisprudence. Tribes are reluctant to abandon their past traditions by placing too much reliance on the whites' legal procedures and practices. While borrowing some Anglo-American notions about the system of justice, tribal courts are struggling to preserve much of the wisdom of their past experiences. Many tribal judges continue to operate as the head of a family might in solving problems. The desired resolution of an intratribal dispute is one that benefits the whole Indian community (family) and not one designed to chastise an individual offender. Non-Indian critics may not understand such a concept of justice, but within Indian traditions it is an accepted and expected norm. Given the importance of the tribal judge's notion of justice in the modern-day Indian court system, a further exploration of his or her role is in order.

TRIBAL JUDGES

It is impossible to identify an established uniform procedure whereby all tribal judges are chosen because the methods of selection vary significantly from tribe to tribe. One of the most common methods of judicial recruitment is simply appointment by the tribal council of people in whom they and the community have confidence. But other judges are selected by the religious leaders of the community or directly by the tribal members in a general election. Many Indian judges function in a judicial capacity because of their position as tribal leaders. In some pueblos, for instance, the governor, who is the titular head of the community, also serves as the tribal judge.

Most Indian judges are appointed or elected for a specific period of time. The terms obviously vary—one, two, or four years—depending upon the tribal constitution and by-laws that establish the tribal court. Some judges, such as the Navajo, are appointed for a life term not unlike federal judges. Once having completed a short probationary period, the judge can be removed only for cause, the grounds of which are spelled out in the Navajo Judicial Code. Since there are very few Indian attorneys, potential judicial candidates do not have to possess a legal education prior to their selection. Candidates qualify because they are men and women of stature and integrity in whose judgment the Indian community has confidence. Familiarity with tribal custom is more important than a knowledge of the law. Judges, however, usually are fluent in both English and the native language of the tribe.

The Indian judicial selection process should not be viewed just within this utopian framework. Stature and integrity are very important considerations in the recruitment of tribal judges but so is politics. The selection of tribal judges is every bit as political as is the selection of judges within the Anglo-American judicial system. The politics may not necessarily involve loyalty and service to a political party but politics is nevertheless present. Like all organized communities, Indian tribes are split into political factions and in every action that tribes take the astute observer can trace out the political compromises that made a consensus possible. The conflict may be between two powerful familes who contend with each other for political control of the tribe every election and have done so for generations. Politics may also revolve around the changing of the generations, with the younger, educated Indians wishing to replace their elders and to upgrade existing tribal institutions, including the courts, and the elders resisting this kind of change and advocating the continuance of tribal elders as judges with the belief that these people will prevent a rapid adoption of white customs and values.

Unlike the judicial appointments in the Anglo-American system, the lack of legal training and experience is not a handicap in receiving an appointment as a tribal judge. One starts from the proposition that there are few Indians attorneys and that these few have not been active in the profession for very long. Those Indian attorneys who are active are generally badly needed by tribes and organizations to pursue litigation on various important subjects, leaving few attorneys who could or would act simply as judges in a tribal court. More important, legal education within the Anglo-American system does not provide either an understanding of or an appreciation for Indian customs and traditions that are still vital to the decision-making that takes place in tribal courts and reservation communities. Lawyers live in their own little world, speak their own technical language, which bears little resemblance to either English or any of the tribal languages, and do not adjust well to strange situations and foreign systems of law. Instead of bending gracefully to fit into the alien system, lawyers have a tendency to reshape the foreign system in which they find themselves so that it quickly fits their idea of how the world should operate. If attorneys were to take over the system of tribal justice, it would not be too long before Indian customs and traditions, the studied informality of the tribal courts, and the particular attention that tribal judges pay to family situations and responsibilities would be replaced by a variety of model codes written by and for the convenience of the attorneys. That result, which we find with increasing frequency in non-Indian society, Indians feel is too costly to consider.

While the requirement of a formal legal education and experience is not a prerequisite to the appointment of tribal judges, they cannot function in a courtroom possessing only the qualities of community leadership, integrity, and political influence. Tribal judges must operate within a legal setting, albeit one fashioned primarily to meet needs insofar as the Anglo-American system can be adapted to do so, which affects and is affected by a variety of internal and external influences and considerations. The many requirements of federal programs that interfere with normal community activities, the jurisdictional conflicts with state governments and agencies, the growing interdependent relationship between Indian and non-Indian business enterprises and development schemes—all these factors contribute to the complex legal arena in which tribal judges must perform their assigned tasks. Unless the people chosen as tribal judges have a fairly good grasp of the complexity of all these areas of Indian life, they are unable to match and meld the circumstances under which the tribal members live and the violations with which they are charged in order to reach decisions that will be understood and accepted by the Indian community.

It is virtually impossible for a tribal judge to meet the challenge of contemporary tribal life without some kind of legal training. There is no doubt that the incorporation of certain Anglo-American procedures has streamlined tribal court operations and made them seem more sophisticated in the eyes of non-Indians and the federal officials who have responsibility to provide funds for tribal court activities. But these mechanisms must be adopted in such a manner that they do not destroy the traditional components and familiarities of Indian law that still linger in a vulnerable condition. Adoption of these procedural formalities must not be allowed to intrude upon and dominate the informality of tribal courts, which reassures tribal members that the judge continues to work with the old traditions of solving problems rather than seeking retribution. The fancy footwork of television attorneys is definitely rejected by both tribal judges and Indian people since it seems to indicate a "win at any cost" value, which they see and reject in the whites' world.

A number of governmental and private agencies have made efforts of late to provide tribal judges with the legal training needed to handle their functions. The federal Law Enforcement Assistance Administration (LEAA) provided funds for training programs, but these have been greatly reduced recently. The Native American Rights Fund co-sponsors, along with the Legal Services Corporation, the Indian Law Support Center, which holds legal training conferences for Indian judges, attorneys, and paralegal personnel. Perhaps the most influential of these "training" organizations is the National American Indian Court Judges Association. Recognizing the need for a special blending of Indian tradition with that of legal procedure and substance, the Indian Court Judges Association has conducted a number of educational seminars for its members. Federal judges and United States attorneys, as well as experienced local and tribal attorneys, have participated in these seminars so that the tribal judges have had the benefit of discussing their problems with first-rate, experienced people in the field.

In addition to providing a legal educational experience for tribal court personnel, the National American Indian Court Judges Association has critically examined some of the problems confronting tribal judges. In a recent report entitled *Justice and the American Indian*, the association identified at least six major problems that demand attention (National American Indian Court Judges Association, vol. 2, pp. 30–37).

Political pressure from tribal and religious leaders. Tribal leaders who have been instrumental in securing a judge's appointment often indicate to a judge how cases should be decided. Since tribal judges serve short terms in office and occasionally are subject to recall by the appointing officials, they are placed in a vulnerable position. A lack of judicial independence from highly politicized tribal officials increases a judge's insecurity and clearly erodes the administration of justice.

Lack of judicial training.   As noted earlier, few tribal judges are attorneys. Most are simply learned in the customs and traditions of the tribe. Periodic seminars designed to socialize judges and to provide them with a fund of legal expertise are imperative to enable the judges to deal with the intricacies of the Anglo-American law hybrid of legal issues.

Lack of staff, administrative organization, and mechanical support.   Tribal judges frequently must hold court in unsuitable or inadequate quarters. There is little privacy, no room for juries, a minimum of basic mechanical equipment, and almost always the complete absence of modern technologies that are used in the more sophisticated courtrooms in the non-Indian world. There are few, if any, staff members and those who are available are usually untrained. Judicial operations in many instances are intertwined with law enforcement functions. Budgets are combined with police, corrections, and probation divisions. Indeed, in some tribal court systems, police act as the prosecuting attorneys for the tribe. Judges too frequently find themselves performing the tasks of clerk, bailiff, prosecutor, and defense attorney.

Inability to enforce court orders.   It is one thing to decide a case and issue a court order. At times it is quite something else to see that the order is enforced. In some tribes, the religious or political leaders simply overrule a tribal judge's decision. There are occasions when criminal offenders surrender themselves to other tribal officials, who in turn release them or resolve the issue without judicial assistance. Confidence by tribal leaders in the Indian system of justice has not reached the point on all reservations that tribal court orders are extended sufficient deference and respect so as to be enforced automatically without political intrusion.

Tribal court relationships with law enforcement.   Tribal courts and law enforcement branches on reservations are often too closely related to each other. On smaller reservations there may be no police or prosecutor and these functions must of necessity fall on the tribal judge. In other areas, the tribal judge is the only person with any knowledge of the law. Hence, he or she becomes the legal advisor to the police. This proximity, although in many instances a harmless cooperative effort to ensure that *some* system of justice indigenous to the people is preserved, creates the impression that the tribal judge and the tribal police are working hand in hand and have no real differences to speak of. The advice that the judge provides might well result in a legal issue that may later be brought before him or her to rule upon as a judge. This operational convergence of the prosecutory and judicial functions never would be tolerated in the Anglo-American system of law. But it is a practical necessity on some reservations if there is to be any systematic legal control over the law enforcement function by Indians themselves.

Tribal court relationships with the Bureau of Indian Affairs. Tribal court relationships with the Bureau of Indian Affairs pose special difficulties. Some tribal judges are in fact employees of the BIA or have their salaries paid by the BIA. With regard to the CFR courts, the BIA actually appoints these judges or at least must approve the tribal council's choices. It is not uncommon for a BIA special officer (investigator) to bring pressure on a judge to decide a case in a particular way. Further complicating the situation, a judge's authority with regard to the agency superintendent is precarious. If a tribal judge rules on an issue involving trust property or money that is under the supervision of the agency superintendent, the superintendent may have the discretion to accept or reject the judge's decision. This superior power and its arbitrary exercise by the superintendent hardly contribute to judicial independence. Some of these difficulties, such as the tribal judge–BIA employee dependency, have been minimized by having the tribe enter into a subcontract with the BIA so that the tribe can run its own court system. In general, however, when tribal judges are also BIA employees, they are judges on a part-time basis and their primary administrative duties are not related to their activities as judges of the tribal court.

While the problems confronting tribal judges persist today, it must be remembered that the Indian court system is still in its embryonic stage. Time and the exercise of more local tribal power should bring an ever-increasing sophistication to the operations of the tribal court system. The continued production of more Indian attorneys and the increasing sophistication of this generation of tribal judges will also eventually produce a more stable system of justice on the reservations as people become familiar with how courts are supposed to operate and adjust to their presence in the community.

TRIBAL COURTS AND THE 1968 INDIAN
CIVIL RIGHTS ACT

In 1953, former California Governor Earl Warren was appointed chief justice of the United States Supreme Court. Under the leadership of Warren, the country experienced what many scholars have characterized as a "constitutional revolution." During the fifteen years in which Warren directed the Court's activities, many of the important provisions of the Bill of Rights—the right to legal counsel, the privilege against self-incrimination, the right to trial by jury, to mention but a few—were made applicable to the states. Millions of citizens who previously had not been covered by these constitutional guarantees at the state level were now extended this ultimate protection. American Indians, however, were not among those citizens who received these constitutional benefits with respect to their relationships to tribal courts.

It would seem self-evident that tribal courts, organized under federal laws, often supported with federal funds, and generally supervised by federal officials, would be rigorously subject to the Constitution, but they occupy a peculiar position relative to the enforcement of constitutional rights that bears considerable explanation because it derives from the status of Indian tribes as defined by John Marshall in the *Cherokee Nation Cases* and it testifies to the continued "foreign" political relationship, originally identified by Justice Thompson in the *Cherokee Nation v. Georgia* case, of tribal governments. The treaty relationship that binds Indians to the federal government recognizes the arm's-length relationship that tribes had to have enjoyed at the time of treaty negotiations in order for the process to have been considered a real treaty. That is to say, Congress was not conducting a sham procedure when it considered and ratified the Indian treaties; it really was dealing with an entirely foreign political entity and this entity possessed then and partially possesses today some elements in itself that have not been and cannot be subsumed under any federal law or policy.

During those decades in which the tribes exercised traditional judicial functions without interference from the federal government, they evolved certain procedures, created particular institutions, and established some definite precedents that characterized their own court systems. Particularly among the Five Civilized Tribes this pattern of development moved away from tribal traditions and attempted to adapt (with certain modifications) institutions, forms of organization, and procedures quite similar to those of the non-Indian legal system. Since there remained even in these tribes a great deal of cultural cohesion until very late in the nineteenth century, no appeals of any consequence were ever made from a tribal court to a federal court involving the very complicated question of whether, since the individual tribal members were considered to be wards of the federal government, protections of the United States Constitution applied to them in their relationship to their own tribal governments. This question clearly involves a difficult question regarding the nature of the relationship of tribal governments to the federal government that cannot be answered casually.

The issue arose in 1895 in the case of *Talton v. Mayes*, 163 U.S. 376 (1895). The Supreme Court was faced with the question of whether or not the Fifth Amendment Grand Jury provision applied to the criminal laws of the Cherokee Nation. Talton had been convicted of murder by an Indian grand jury of less than twelve people and he had argued that this indictment and conviction violated his constitutional rights. The Court concluded not only that Talton's rights were not violated by the tribal court but also that the powers of local self-government as exercised by the Cherokees existed *prior* to the adoption of the United States Constitution and had never been subsequently modified or surrendered. The tribal laws were neither created by nor flowed from the Constitution. Hence, Indians living on a reservation, with respect to the relationship they enjoyed with their own tribal governments, were not accorded constitutional protections but were assumed to rely upon tribal customs and traditions. This decision meant that such constitutional guarantees as free speech, the free exercise of religion, the right to an attorney in a criminal case, and similar benefits were not available to American Indians unless specifically provided for in a tribal code or constitution.

During the seventh decade of this century, questions were raised in a number of sectors as to why American Indians, who were citizens of the United States as well as being citizens of their own tribes, should be guaranteed basic civil rights in a national setting but denied these basic human rights when dealing with their own local community institutions. One of the chief spokesmen voicing this concern was Senator Sam J. Ervin, a powerful southern Democrat who sat on the Senate Judiciary Committee and conducted hearings in Washington and in the field at various locations to determine the conditions of Indians vis-à-vis governments at all levels and the protection of their human rights. Part of the controversy involving Indian civil rights originated in the case of *Colliflower v. Garland*, 342 F.2d 369 (9th Cir. 1965), in which Madeline Colliflower, a Gros Ventre and a member of the Fort Belknap tribes of Montana, was successful in filing a writ of habeas corpus against the tribal court. The federal court, after listening to the case and recognizing the precedent it was confronting, ruled in Colliflower's favor but limited the scope of its ruling to the Fort Belknap tribal court alone on the justification that it was a court established through the provisions of the Indian Reorganization Act and therefore, in a sense, a court sanctioned by and playing the role of a federal agency—a status to which the long arm of constitutional protections could reach.

The ruling stunned tribal leaders since it meant that tribal courts would no longer be immune from the inquiries of federal courts. Even more profound in its implications, the *Colliflower* case spurred Senator Ervin and the Senate Judiciary Committee into action and inspired them to move forward with the Indian Civil Rights Act. The Indian community, however, was far from unanimous in its support of this legislation. A major source of Indian apprehension over the legislative proposals was the fear that the imposition of an Indian Bill of Rights on tribal court proceedings would go a long way toward transforming them into dark-skinned replicas of the non-Indian courts and would require massive expenditures of funds to ensure constitutional protections to defendants, which would bankrupt many small tribes. The Pueblos in particular were worried about the intrusions of the civil rights idea, that of pitting an individual against his or her society, in the traditional judicial system they favored, which was highly religious and required a fine sense of Indian customs. The Pueblos initially refused to attend hearings on the proposed legislation believing that it would not apply to them without their consent, and later, after the bill was enacted, the Pueblos stormed into Washington accusing the Senate Judiciary Committee of attempting to destroy their theocratic foundations. With erratic and inconsistent support and opposition such as this being the only Indian comments received by Ervin on the legislation, he finally concluded that the legislation should be enacted. He cleverly attached the Indian Civil Rights Bill to a housing bill during the spring of 1968 when the assassination of Martin Luther King gave that piece of legislation a certainty for passage. The Indian Civil Rights Bill thus became federal law as an amendment to another piece of civil rights legislation (25 U.S.C.A. §§1301 et seq.).

Sections 1302 and 1303 of the 1968 act contain its most important provisions and are reproduced below. The act is further broken down in Table 2 so that the reader can compare the Indian Bill of Rights guarantees with those specified in the United States Constitution.

TABLE 2. 1968 Indian Civil Rights Act and Its Equivalent U.S. Constitutional Provisions

1968 Act Provision	*U.S. Constitutional Provision*
Free speech	1st Amendment
Free exercise of religion	1st Amendment
Free press	1st Amendment
Peaceful assembly and petition	1st Amendment
Unreasonable searches and seizures	4th Amendment
Double jeopardy	5th Amendment
Self-incrimination	5th Amendment
Just compensation	5th Amendment
Speedy and public trial	6th Amendment
Right to confrontation and cross-examination	6th Amendment
Right to counsel (at defendant's own expense)	6th Amendment
Trial by jury (criminal only)	6th Amendment
No excessive bail	8th Amendment
Cruel and unusual punishment	8th Amendment
Equal protection of the laws	14th Amendment
Due process of law	5th Amendment
No ex post facto law	Art. 1, § 9
No bill of attainder	Art. 1, § 9

1968 Indian Civil Rights Act
Public Law 90-284, 82 Stat. 77
25 U.S.C.A. §§ 1302–1303

1302. Constitutional rights

No Indian tribe in exercising powers of self-government shall—(1) make or enforce any law prohibiting the free exercise of religion, or abridging the freedom of speech, or of the press, or the right of the people peaceably to assemble and to petition for a redress of grievances;

(2) violate the right of the people to be secure in their persons, houses, papers, and effects against unreasonable search and seizure nor issue warrants, but upon probable cause, supported by oath or affirmation, and particularly describing the place to be searched and the person or thing to be seized;

(3) subject any person for the same offense to be twice put in jeopardy;

(4) compel any person in any criminal case to be a witness against himself;

(5) take any private property for a public use without just compensation;

(6) deny to any person in a criminal proceeding the right to a speedy and public trial, to be informed of the nature and cause of the accusation, to be confronted with the witnesses against him, to have compulsory process for obtaining witnesses in his favor, and at his own expense to have the assistance of counsel for his defense;

(7) require excessive bail, impose excessive fines, inflict cruel and unusual punishments, and in no event impose for conviction of any one offense any penalty or punishment greater than imprisonment for a term of six months or a fine of $500, or both;

(8) deny to any person within its jurisdiction the equal protection of its laws or deprive any person of liberty or property without due process of law;

(9) pass any bill of attainder or ex post facto laws; or

(10) deny to any person accused of an offense punishable by imprisonment the right, upon request, to a trial by jury of not less than six persons.

1303 Habeas corpus

The privilege of the writ of habeas corpus shall be available to any person, in a court of the United States, to test the legality of his detention by order of an Indian tribe.

There are obviously some constitutional provisions that have not been incorporated into the 1968 act. Indictment by a grand jury, the Establishment of Religion Clause, and the restriction against quartering troops in homes are a few protections missing in the Indian Civil Rights Bill that are found in the Constitution. It should also be noted that some of the provisions that have been adopted are qualified versions of the American constitutional guarantees. The right to retain an attorney, for instance, is only guaranteed if the accused has the funds to hire an attorney, making the guarantee of this right wholly dependent upon the ability of the accused to pay for legal counsel. Attorneys are not automatically provided to indigent offenders as they are under the federal constitution. Even with these qualifications, a substantial body of U.S. constitutional law is now applicable to tribal court proceedings. This introduction of Anglo-American doctrine cannot help but restrict the power of tribal court judges and suggests a further erosion of traditional Indian practices.

FEDERAL REVIEW OF TRIBAL COURT DECISIONS

One of the most controversial issues that the 1968 Indian Civil Rights Act attempted to resolve was the nature and scope of review that federal courts could exercise over decisions of tribal courts. Historically, tribal courts have dealt exclusively with matters of local government in the civil area and misdemeanor offenses in the criminal area. Appeals have been minimal because of the drawn-out nature of appeals. Many Indian litigants felt that it was easier to accept the verdict of the tribal court and get the matter behind them than to appeal and prolong what was really a minor incident in their lives. In the case of Madeline Colliflower there was sufficient personal interest by the defendant to reform the procedures of the tribal court to make such an appeal an attractive alternative.

Historically, also, the federal courts seemed to accept the idea that the Congress had not extinguished certain powers of self-government that had accrued to the tribes prior to their contact with the United States, and *Talton* gave the Supreme Court an opportunity to make this belief a concrete expression of historical fact. In *Native American Church v. Navajo Tribal Council,* 272 F.2d 131 (10th Cir. 1959), the issue raised concerned the right of the Navajo Tribal Council to prohibit the exercise of the peyote religion within the reservation boundaries. Again, the federal courts supported the idea that tribes were in a special legal-political category, this time the court going so far as to characterize tribes as "higher than states." Not that appeals had never been taken from tribal courts. Indeed, *Talton* itself, beginning in the Cherokee National Supreme Court, went through the federal system to arrive at the Supreme Court. But almost all previous appeals had dealt with subjects peripheral to individual rights and involved property and treaty rights.

The *Colliflower* court had suggested that "it is pure fiction to say that the Indian courts functioning in the Fort Belknap Indian community are not in part, at least, arms of the federal government" (342 F.2d 369 (1965)). But this relationship was implied by the court because the Fort Belknap Reservation had been organized under the Indian Reorganization Act and the corporate nature of the tribal government, as recognized by the approval of the secretary of the interior, meant that it had a specially sanctioned status; thus, it was not difficult for the court to find corresponding responsibilities in the federal government to ensure an equitable functioning of the respective parts of that tribal government. *Colliflower* was thus an intrusion into tribal affairs although of an admittedly restricted nature since the appellate court would not venture to suggest that the doctrine be applied indiscriminately to other tribes. The importance of the case was that it occurred at a time when the Congress was finishing its examination of possible reforms in the administration of justice by the tribal courts and the public impact of *Colliflower* was to give dramatic support to what became section 1303— provisions for applying the writ of habeas corpus to tribal courts by specific congressional directive. This section was immediately tested (see *Settler v. Yakima Tribal Council*, 419 F.2d 486 (9th Cir. 1969)) and found constitutional.

A writ of habeas corpus is only a limited remedy but it is a direct attack on the integrity of the procedures of the court decision it challenges. It can be invoked only to contest the illegal detention of a person, but for tribal courts with their limited scope of punishments it stands as a major weapon for reform. It was not long, however, before an attempt was made to expand the scope of federal review to include more than just the habeas corpus avenue. Indeed, efforts were directed toward obtaining federal court review not only of a tribal court order but to contest the validity of tribal council policies as well.

In the first case to arise under the 1968 Indian Civil Rights Act, a federal district court reviewed a tribal council decision that had not been brought to it under a habeas corpus petition. In *Dodge v. Nakai*, 298 F. Supp. 26 (D. Ariz. 1969), the Navajo Tribal Council excluded Theodore Mitchell, a non-Indian and the program director of the DNA Legal Services, from the reservation. Mitchell, who had been embroiled in a dispute with the tribal council concerning how much independence his attorneys should have from the council, sought an order from the federal district court to enjoin the tribal council from this action. The federal judge struck down the tribal council's action as violative of due process of law, as an abridgment of free speech, and as constituting a bill of attainder, all of which were prohibited by the 1968 Indian Civil Rights Act.

In enjoining the tribal council order, the federal court went beyond the expressed provision of section 1303 (habeas corpus) and thus opened the door to challenging tribal government decisions by a variety of civil remedies, such as injunctions, declaratory judgments, and the like. The fears that many Indians held that the 1968 act would significantly intrude into the independence of tribal courts were certainly substantiated by the *Nakai* decision. Indeed, the federal court had gone even beyond the express provisions of the 1968 act, which had mentioned federal review over tribal actions only with reference to writs of habeas corpus petitions. It seems strange that the first person to use the Indian Civil Rights Act was a non-Indian.

This federal incursion into an area that Indians had thought to be immune from federal review finally came to the attention of the United States Supreme Court in the case of *Santa Clara Pueblo v. Martinez*, 98 S.Ct. 1670 (1978), a decade after the Indian Civil Rights Act was passed and after a number of law review articles had been published suggesting the scope of actions possible under this act. Unfortunately, none of the legal scholars anticipated that the act would become embroiled in a very difficult case that involved two explosive contemporary issues: the status of women within the tribe and the right of a tribe to determine its own membership.

Julia Martinez brought a cause of action in a federal district court to prevent the Santa Clara Pueblo from enforcing an ordinance denying membership in the tribe to the children of women who had married outside the tribe. The children of male members who married outside the pueblo were permitted to maintain their tribal membership, so there was no question that the ordinance had dimensions of discrimination by gender. The issue before the court had practical as well as legal consequences. The original issue concerned whether or not Martinez could get a HUD house that was part of a tribal housing program and whether or not her children could also get an interest in that house although they were not then enrolled in the tribe. The Indian Health Service had also asked the pueblo to certify the Indian blood of one of the Martinez children so that it could provide health services. The tribal government refused to do so fearing that this certification would be interpreted as the equivalent of recognition as a tribal member. The testimony concerning the pueblo tradition also conflicted. There was some evidence that, prior to the passage of the patrilineal enrollment ordinance, in the late 1930s, the tribe had had a matrilineal system for determining its membership. This shift in eligibility raised the question of whether ancient or more recent tribal "traditions" would be determinative of Indian custom. The case, therefore, in almost every respect, was important for outlining a contemporary theory of the tribal right to determine tribal membership apart from other factors.

Although the pueblo was thought to have a sovereign immunity against any suit of this kind, the federal district court found that it had jurisdiction over the case. It held that the Indian Civil Rights Act of 1968 had by implication waived tribal sovereignty and immunity and thus permitted the issue to be heard. The court then proceeded to conclude that the Santa Clara Pueblo could determine its own membership and that this determination could be predicated upon the traditional values of patriarchy, which were still important to the tribe's cultural existence. Julia Martinez lost her case but persisted and appealed the cause to the United States Supreme Court alleging that the tribal classification, which was based on differences of gender, violated the equal protection provision of the Indian Civil Rights Act of 1968.

In delivering the majority opinion in the *Martinez* case, Justice Thurgood Marshall did not even address himself to the equal protection issue involving the charge of discrimination on the basis of gender. Rather, Marshall limited the Court's consideration to the question of federal review of tribal policy. While noting that Indian nations possessed a separate sovereignty that pre-existed the U.S. Constitution (thus falling beyond the constraints of the Constitution), Marshall reasoned that the traditional powers of Indian self-government could be modified or eliminated by congressional enactment. Congress then, through its plenary power, could lawfully pass the 1968 Indian Civil Rights Act imposing certain restraints upon tribal governments. But Marshall then reasoned that it was significant that the *only* appeal remedy that Congress provided in the ICRA was the writ of habeas corpus. Indian tribes had long enjoyed sovereign immunity from suit. But it is well settled that a waiver of this sovereign immunity cannot be implied but had to be unequivocally expressed. Clearly, Congress, in providing the writ of habeas corpus as the only remedy in the 1968 act, did not expressly waive this right. In the absence of a clear legislative intent, the Court would not imply civil remedies as a basis to challenge tribal policies.

To support this conclusion, Marshall provided the following rationalization of the Court's position:

> Our reluctance [to imply civil remedies] is strongly reinforced by the specific legislative history underlying 25 U.S.C.A. 1303. This history, extending over more than three years, indicates that Congress' provision for habeas corpus relief, and nothing more, reflected a considered accommodation of the competing goals of "preventing injustices perpetrated by tribal governments, on the one hand, and, on the other, avoiding undue or precipitous interference in the affairs of the Indian people."
>
> After considering numerous alternatives for review of tribal convictions, Congress apparently decided that review by way of habeas corpus would adequately protect the individual interests at stake while avoiding unnecessary intrusions on tribal governments. Given Congress' desire not to intrude needlessly on tribal self-government, it is not surprising that Congress

chose at this stage to provide for federal review only in habeas corpus proceedings.

By not exposing tribal officials to the full array of federal remedies available to redress actions of federal and state officials, Congress may also have considered that resolution of statutory issues under 1302, and particularly those issues likely to arise in a civil context, will frequently depend on questions of tribal tradition and custom which tribal forums may be in a better position to evaluate than federal courts. Efforts by the federal judiciary to apply the statutory prohibitions of 1302 in a civil context may substantially interfere with a tribe's ability to maintain itself as a culturally and politically distinct entity. (*Santa Clara Pueblo v. Martinez*, 98 S.Ct. 1670, 1681 (1978))

In *Santa Clara Pueblo v. Martinez*, the Supreme Court has brought a good deal of clarity to the issue involving federal court review of tribal policies. The 1968 act does not provide litigants with a host of civil remedies to challenge tribal policy in the federal courts. One and only one avenue exists—the writ of habeas corpus—and the occasions for its use are severely limited to unlawful detention, which is at best peripheral to major policy decisions and their programmatic expressions. This restriction does not mean that Congress in the future could not broaden the review power by providing additional remedies, but until Congress acts, and acts with clear specificity, avenues to the federal and state court are limited. Nor does this narrowness in remedies preclude Indian litigants from challenging the orders of tribal councils. They have access to the tribal courts and have the right to at least one appeal within the Indian court system.

The *Martinez* decision is important in another respect. The initial discussion of federal review related to the review of tribal court decisions. But the *Martinez* case reaches beyond the narrow realm of tribal court orders and pertains to tribal policy-making per se. It is immaterial whether that policy emanates from a tribal court or from a tribal council.

Does this restriction significantly limit the future grievances of tribal members? The answer must be "no" if one has any confidence in the integrity of the tribal court system. Policy issues may be contested in the tribal court but more often, with the rising tide of traditionalism, they are more likely to be made the subject of tribal constitutions. Indian litigants receiving adverse judgments at the tribal court level have the right to an appeal within the tribal court system. While the appellate system of review admittedly needs sophistication, to alter it by permitting review by non-Indian institutions would gravely threaten the continuing quest from maximizing tribal self-government.

THE TRIBAL COURT SYSTEM: AN ASSESSMENT

The tribal court system is coming of age. The number of tribal courts has increased tremendously in the past decade as funds have become available to provide them with training and a financial base and they are functioning with confidence and some measurable degree of popular support. In 1978, the National American Indian Court Judges Association assessed the strengths and weaknesses still inherent in the system (National American Indian Court Judges Association, 1978, pp. 88–102). A brief look at these assets and liabilities will assist in ascertaining just where administrative efforts to improve the system should be placed in the future.

Strengths of the System

Deference by federal courts.   Federal courts are beginning to recognize the authority of tribal courts over matters arising in Indian Country. This recognition has in turn provided tribal judges with more self-assuredness and has resulted in efforts by tribal judges to improve the Indian system of justice even more.

Quick access to a fair forum.   Indian reservations embrace a vast geographical area. Access to courts was greatly restricted prior to the establishment of the tribal court system. The elimination of these geographic barriers has opened the doors to many isolated Indians who heretofore have been effectively excluded from the legal arena.

Growing support from federal agencies, tribal leaders, and organizations.   This support is not restricted to a general support of the tribal court system per se but includes financial support from such organizations as the Law Enforcement Assistance Administration, the Bureau of Indian Affairs, and private foundations and church groups.

Ability to bridge the gap between law and Indian culture.   The ability of the tribal court to interpret law to the Indian people and to interpret Indian culture to other legal institutions may be the most important of all assets flowing from the tribal court system. In the absence of an Indian court system, the remaining vestiges of tribal culture and values might soon disappear, being swallowed up by the ever-encroaching norms and procedures of the dominant (white) majority within the country.

Dedicated judiciary. The career of the Indian judge has not been an easy one. In the non-Indian society, judges are extended respect, tenure in office, adequate compensation for their services, and substantial community prestige. Indian judges are underpaid, can anticipate few retirement or fringe benefits, frequently possess little or no security in their positions, and are often treated disrespectfully by tribal leaders. In spite of these career disabilities, Indian judges persist and are devoted to their jobs. As the National American Indian Court Judges Association report notes, what these judges lack in formal education they make up in a dedicated and serious approach to their work.

Weaknesses of the System

Susceptibility to political influence. Indian judges do not possess the independence enjoyed by judges in the Anglo-American judicial system. Many tribal judges are appointed by tribal leaders and hence serve at the pleasure of these political leaders. While non-Indian judges serve under the same conditions, this proximity of the judiciary to the other arms of the political structure is much more apparent in a small community and therefore has considerably more impact on everyone concerned. Complaints of political interference are commonplace and recalls and impeachments are not infrequent. More needs to be done to provide tribal judges with the independence that will immunize them from political pressures.

Summary justice. In the field of criminal law, tribal justice leaves much to be desired. Arrests result in a high rate of guilty pleas and convictions. Indians have a tendency to avoid confrontations and so plead guilty in most instances whether they are really guilty or not. There are few defense attorneys available to defendants and the attitude that "you can't beat the system" is prevalent on reservations. Tribal judges possess and exercise an enormous amount of power in the criminal area with few practical institutional checks. It is one thing for Congress to pass an Indian Civil Rights Act and quite another to have the act be effective in the absence of funds, personnel, and a judicial "libertarian" atmosphere that would make its presence felt in the Indian court system.

Inadequate tribal laws. Since tribal governments in their present form are still a comparatively new experience, it is not surprising that tribal constitutions and codes are deficient. Not only are the laws badly written and ill defined at times, but there are also great gaps in these laws. Many laws are not even codified. Few tribes have special provisions relating to juveniles and other special personages, such as the mentally ill. But these things will come in time: patience and persistent attention to these matters are needed.

Dearth of civil cases. The great variety of civil cases handled by the Anglo-American courts is not found in the tribal context. Indeed, few civil cases are brought before the courts of the reservations. This absence is not because of a lack of civil problems on the reservations. It is more attributable to the fact that Indians are not a litigous people. Most of the civil issues coming before tribal courts relate to domestic relations, such as divorce and child custody, and truancy.

Need for qualified personnel. We have already discussed at some length the lack of legal training possessed by tribal judges. Most tribes require no qualifications at all for the post. This absence of standards combined with problems of political influence, low salaries, and career instability have resulted in a high turnover of personnel. Moreover, the same problems are true with reference to court administrators, where these positions exist. Much work needs to be done to upgrade the salaries, respect, and technologies that are necessary for a viable and successful system of justice.

Lack of dispositional alternatives. When a judge sentences an Indian defendant, his or her options are few indeed. Other than jail-like detention facilities, there is little in the way of alternative forms of punishment and correction. The absence of juvenile facilities, alcohol centers, and other institutional mechanisms to deal with special problems places substantial restraints upon a judge's ability to wisely dispose of a case.

Lack of planning. Like most political communities, Indians have responded to reservation problems only after they have become apparent. The customary "band-aid" solution to political and legal problems inevitably takes precedence over planned action. This natural expediency has been true in the development of most tribal court systems from their inception. While the awareness of a necessity for long-range planning is always discussed, it seldom receives any real attention.

6. The Role of Attorneys, Advocates, and Legal Interest Groups in the Indian System of Law

Americans are a litigous people. They use the courts to solve their problems more often than any other people in the world. Perhaps that is why there are proportionately more attorneys in the United States than in any other nation. Critics of the legal profession might suggest that we are prone to seek legal redress more in this country simply because we have more attorneys—nearly half a million—to feed. A New Mexico territorial judge, more than a century ago, aptly summarized the effect that attorneys have on a community: "Take the case of a peaceful community, where they have not had a lawyer or a lawsuit for half a century, and let a young lawyer put up his law books on nice shelves, hang out his sign, O. Gammon, Esq, Attorney and counselor at law, and in less than six months, one half the village will have hatched up a lawsuit against the the other half; no man will pass the counselor's law office without trying to arrange in his mind a lawsuit for the counselor" (*United States v. Lucero*, 1 N.M. 422 (1869)). This description, more satirical than real, does characterize the opinion many people have of the legal profession. Regardless of one's perspective, it is an irreducible fact that the law and lawyers play an important role in American life.

Lawyers have played an important role in Indian affairs from the very beginning. They have been the solitary voice in many instances in which the tribes would have suffered grievous wrongs had not there been an avenue of protest in the judicial arena admirably manned by an attorney working on their behalf. On the other hand, some of the gross injustices perpetrated on Indians have been at the hands of unscrupulous attorneys. Even a neutral appraisal would be difficult to make concerning the role of attorneys in Indian life. The issues with which they have had to contend have been extraordinarily complex and for many generations there were no good sets of rules and doctrines upon which they could rely. American Indian law is unlike any other body of knowledge in that it does not have a central core of doctrines that are capable of allocating many subgroupings of theories in comfortable and comprehensible fields and every case contains within it pitfalls and conceptual traps, which often prove fatal to the proper resolution of the dispute.

Until the last decade, the people working in Indian law have been predominantly non-Indians. The Five Civilized Tribes very early trained some of their young people as attorneys and one can trace a number of competent attorneys in the Cherokee Nation for several generations. The western tribes, and more particularly the southwestern tribes, have not produced any significant number of attorneys until the very recent movement of young Indians into the legal profession. One Omaha attorney, Thomas Sloan, achieved an outstanding record as a lawyer during the first few decades of this century, but generally speaking the legal profession has been one career that did not attract Indians. Today there are an estimated 450 Indian attorneys working in a variety of jobs and approximately 35 new Indian attorneys join the growing number of Indians working in the legal profession every year.

The status and role that attorneys assume in the Indian system of law are unique. In many tribal court proceedings, for instance, attorneys are not permitted to participate directly. Still, they perform an important advisory function and often serve as judges or appellate judges in the tribal court system. Outside the reservation judicial system, attorneys play a direct and indispensable role in promoting Indian rights in both state and federal courts. To gain a comprehensive perspective of this complicated role that attorneys assume when dealing with Indian legal problems, let us look first at the activities in which they are engaged in the institutions of American society that bear directly on the protection and preservation of Indian rights, and then turn to the role of lawyers functioning in the reservation milieu.

INDIAN ATTORNEYS AND AMERICAN SOCIETY

Although the relationship between American Indians and the federal government has been established by treaty, lawyers have played an important role in the process of discovering the parameters of that relationship. Their participation has been a very active one aggressively pursuing the bits and shards of legal doctrine to ensure that the maximum benefits accrue to Indians from the multitude of legal documents that chart the development of the relationship between particular tribes and the United States. The articles of treaties are not particularly enlightening in a legal sense because they were written in a form of covenantal relationship that relied upon the good will of the parties for their fulfillment. Promises made during treaty negotiations, although in most instances sincere, are not framed in the language of contract and consequently present untold difficulties when presented in a judicial forum as the basis for establishing Indian rights.

The same general commentary could be made respecting the agreements, the statutes, and the rules and regulations that have been promulgated over the centuries in an effort to distinguish and clarify the rights of Indians. In the case of federal statutes the attorneys must hypothesize from congressional hearings, correspondence, and miscellaneous documents the probable will or intent of Congress in considering and then finally passing a particular law. The interpretation constructed by the attorney must adequately explain the nature of the change that Congress intended to generate and must suggest that the intent was to benefit Indians according to the requirements laid down in the theory of the trust or ward-guardian model. From this complicated argument, then, the attorney must infer and convince the court that certain safeguards or protections inevitably follow—and must be upheld by the court.

Attorneys thus "make" federal Indian law in a very fundamental way that cannot be compared to their function with respect to any other body of law. In two centuries of American political existence attorneys have developed numerous interpretations of law that have become acceptable to the federal courts and the Congress and have been used as guidelines to assist everyone in finding and following the proper legal doctrines. The trust relationship, the protection of the tribe against state incursions into tribal sovereignty and self-government, the articulation of the time and manner of treaty fishing rights, the definition of individual rights under the Indian Civil Rights Act, and the scope of the federal discretionary powers with respect to Indian lands and natural resources—all of these complex and technical subjects have been developed by attorneys working in the field of Indian law.

The arena in which this activity takes place is the larger American society and its judicial and legislative institutions. Attorneys working on behalf of Indian tribes must use the same judicial forums as those working for other Americans use. They must formulate their causes of action, their theories of the case, and their evidence in the same manner and under the same restrictions as attorneys practicing in other fields of American law. There are basically three major areas in which we find attorneys practicing federal

Indian law: (a) attorneys engaged in private practice, (b) attorneys employed in federal agencies who deal with Indian matters, and (c), more recently, attorneys working in public interest law firms of a nonprofit nature who work on more abstract but equally important special issues that are chosen with the intent of furthering the development of legal theory involving American Indians.

Since there are so few Indians now practicing as attorneys in comparison with attorneys already established as specialists in federal Indian law, it should come as no surprise to learn that several large law firms have been active in the field of Indian law for some time. These law firms basically grew up as a result of the efforts made by tribes in the first half of this century to seek redress for violations of their treaties. Indian tribes were barred from entering the U.S. court of claims on causes of actions involving treaty claims about the time of the Civil War and the only access they had to this forum was by special jurisdictional acts passed by Congress authorizing them to file suit for specific grievances. Attorneys specializing in federal Indian law, particularly in the sophisticated techniques of lobbying a jurisdictional bill through Congress in order to secure entrance to the court of claims, eventually formed law firms specifically for that practice and developed a regular formula whereby they could pursue claims on behalf of Indian tribes. The more successful firms then continued to build up this practice and eventually became regular counsels for tribes having other difficulties, such as leasing lands, development of mineral resources, and sale of timber.

The passage of the Indian Claims Commission Act gave great impetus to firms wishing to work in the field of Indian law. The act that established the commission (60 Stat. 1049) intended it to become an independent, investigating, and flexible forum that could consider the equitable, humanistic nature of the claims and find a reasonable solution to them. But law firms accustomed to working in the court of claims, where rigid rules of evidence and well-established procedures for appraisal of actual losses were commonplace, could not adjust to the liberality and informality that Congress had intended the Indian Claims Commission to have. The result was that the procedures and schedules for hearing cases of the court of claims, which had dismissed a significant number of Indian claims on mere linguistic manipulation and technical flaws, were transferred almost intact to the new forum and established law firms became the only people authorized to pursue claims against the government.

Indians, fearful that incompetent or inexperienced law firms would not be able to successfully pursue their claims, generally hired the already established law firms. Additionally, there is sub-

stantial evidence that some law firms actually created claims or so-
licited tribal business—albeit successfully because there was never
any effort by the Interior Department, which had to approve tribal claims attorneys' contracts, or the American Bar Association,
which should have been suspicious of the sudden frantic activity in
this field, to investigate what was actually happening with Indian
claims. The attorneys working on Indian claims received approximately 10 percent of the award and in some cases this amount
proved to be substantial. An award to a tribe of $15 million would
return to a law firm around $1.5 million free and clear since the
tribe had already paid for the expenses of the case by borrowing
funds from the Interior Department to pursue it and to compensate
their attorneys for the ongoing costs of expert witnesses, travel, research, and time spent in discussing the case. The law firms, real-
izing that a sudden gain of $1.5 million would place them in an
awkward position regarding taxes, secured a special section of the
Internal Revenue Code that allowed them to spread their award over
a ten-year period, which substantially reduced the tax burden they
had to bear for their success.

It is not difficult to understand, then, that Indian law is dominated by a few large and very successful law firms with considerable
influence in the nation's capital and courts. With successful claims
awards already in the bank, many firms simply continued to represent tribes in their business affairs. The availability of federal funds
during the expansion of social welfare programs under the Great Society meant additional work for the large law firms representing Indians. With their Washington contacts and influence in the informal
politics that characterizes our nation's capital, some law firms were
extraordinarily successful in getting federal grants for their tribal clients. One incident illustrates the power these firms represent. Ap-
plications for grants in the Poverty Program (OEO) were supposed to
be drawn up, discussed, designed, and submitted by the "grass-
roots" people on the reservations since the program was meant to
respond to the perceived needs of the poor. One tribe's application
for a grant was handed in to the Office of Economic Opportunity the
very day that the forms for such a proposal were made available to
the general public. Both the tribe and the lawyers involved had to do
some tall explaining of how they had gotten the forms, held the
proper discussions, and written and submitted the grant application
within several hours of the time the forms were released. As one
might suspect, the inquiry into this fortunate set of circumstances
was very quickly aborted by some informal discussions among the
Washington power brokers.

The large private law firms that represent Indian tribes are mostly staffed with non-Indian attorneys. In the past there was an unwritten law that Indian attorneys would not be hired by these firms and several tribal leaders, seeking positions with the tribe's legal counsel for their sons graduating from law school, have been politely but firmly informed that there is no room in the firms for additional attorneys. A definite pattern emerges when one traces the entrance of Indian attorneys into these law firms. A significant number of attorneys once worked for the Department of Justice, sometimes against the tribal claims, other times on behalf of the Indians whom the department was representing. After a period of what could be called an "internship" during which the attorney made valuable contacts and perhaps favorable stipulations during the course of a case, the attorney would resign from the government and either establish his or her own practice or be admitted to one of the law firms practicing in the field of Indian law.

The power of non-Indian attorneys in prestigious law firms cannot be underestimated. Reservation Indians feel fortunate to have large firms with luxurious offices in the nation's capital and over the decades since they have had any real and lasting involvement with Washington firms have come to trust them implicitly. The attorneys now seem to possess an aura of authority that is absolute and many tribes take their word on legal matters without any further inquiry. Attorneys in return understand the fear Indians have of the federal government, and their ignorance of how it works, and some cleverly have their office clerks reproduce pages of the *Congressional Record* dealing with Indian matters and mail them to the tribes. Tribal leaders, receiving these materials, think their attorneys are carefully watching the government and protecting their rights. In the world of private practice in Indian affairs, a few large firms have a virtual monopoly over what happens and who is represented.

With the rapid increase in Indian attorneys in the last two decades, in part due to repeated Indian pleas during hearings on higher education that law be made a priority field of study, this dismal situation is gradually changing. Tribes are now beginning to hire Indian attorneys as their local counsel to do much of the routine legal representation on leases, zoning, taxation, and grant proposals instead of relying on the large firms, which charge considerably more than local attorneys for this kind of work. Without exception, however, the important cases continue to go to the large law firms with Washington influence. Recently three Navajo attorneys opened their own all-Indian law firm in Window Rock, Arizona, the capital of the Navajo Reservation. The tribe, much to the chagrin of the three young attorneys, is still represented by a non-Indian firm, but the three Navajo lawyers believe that the tribe will eventually decide to have an all-Indian firm represent its interests. The Navajo tribe is a multimillion dollar client and thus its business is highly sought after.

A number of Indians who are licensed to practice law have decided not to seek tribes as their major or primary clients. They have instead elected to build an ordinary practice in civil and criminal law in the states in which they reside. Generally, these Indian attorneys in private practice inspire the confidence and respect of the Indians in their community because they are seen as having a special understanding of Indian problems. Some of these lawyers are already achieving a good reputation for working in the Indian cause.

The second major area in which attorneys specializing in federal Indian law work is the federal government. Although every federal agency that has dealt with tribes must have some legal counsel to keep it informed about the complexities of the Indian legal and political status, in general two departments hire the majority of attorneys working directly in the field of Indian law. The Departments of Justice and Interior both provide a substantial number of positions for attorneys interested in Indian work. In their way, each of these departments has significant influence on the manner in which federal Indian law has been developed.

Most Indians have no contact with the United States Attorney's Office in the Department of Justice. It is only those that run afoul of the law in committing major criminal offenses who face the misfortune of federal criminal prosecution by U.S. attorneys. Each of the federal judicial districts scattered around the country has at least one U.S. attorney assigned to that district. The U.S. Attorney's Office is charged with prosecuting offenders who have allegedly violated federal criminal law. Since under the Major Crimes Act, all Indians committing a major felony in Indian Country fall under federal law (as opposed to tribal jurisdiction or state jurisdiction), the U.S. Attorney's Office is responsible for their prosecution.

A number of administrative problems hinder law enforcement in Indian Country (this is discussed in detail in Chapter 7). U.S. attorneys seldom have contact with tribal police or other Indian law enforcement personnel. Their interaction is with the FBI agents who operate as a connective linkage between tribal police and the U.S. Attorney's Office. There are virtually no Indian law experts in these legal offices and few attorneys are conversant with the diverse Indian cultures with which they occasionally have to deal. Indian language barriers also hinder these government lawyers in the performance of their duties.

U.S. attorneys fall under the administrative supervision of the

Department of Justice. Overall policy is thus set in Washington and not at the federal district level, although this centralization of policy and decision-making functions does not generally affect day-to-day prosecution decisions. It must be remembered that the U.S. attorneys are primarily trial attorneys. Once the criminal trial has been completed, appeals are handled, not by the U.S. Attorney's Office, but rather by the Solicitor General's Office in the Department of Justice. The Solicitor General's Office is the chief appellate counsel in the Department of Justice for both civil and criminal cases. The attorneys in this office are the ones who argue cases before the United States Supreme Court as well as before the various U.S. courts of appeal. Any Indian contemplating appeal in a criminal case therefore will be faced with a great deal of legal expertise on the other side.

In addition to the Solicitor General's Office, the Department of Justice has other divisions within its halls that deal with Indian matters. There is an Indian Resource Section within Justice's Land and Natural Resources Division; an Indian Claims Section, which represents the United States in cases the tribes bring against it; and the Civil Rights Division, which deals with issues of discrimination. Additionally, there is the nongovernment, independent Legal Services Corporation, which provides civil legal services to Indian reservations. The legal bureaucracy touching upon Indian affairs is indeed extensive.

Indians do not have much contact with U.S. attorneys today in comparison to the attention they once received. Until 1954 it was against federal law to sell liquor to an Indian who was in wardship status (which came to mean an Indian with trust land). Prosecuting persons, Indian and non-Indian, who were engaged in bootlegging activities on the reservations was a large part of the U.S. Attorney's Office's tasks in those federal districts that had reservations within them. A glance at the types of cases that were successfully brought against bootleggers indicates that the law was sporadically enforced. A significant number of cases involved condemnation proceedings against automobiles used to carry liquor onto reservations rather than against the persons involved in this clandestine trade. Since it is a simple matter to trace the registration of an auto, one concludes after reading a number of these cases that the unspoken policy was simply to make the trade costly to the bootleggers by confiscating their goods and not to seek rigorous enforcement of the law.

Another major assignment to these offices was that of prosecuting Indians who misappropriated federal funds during the Depression years. This era provides a sad commentary on the state of Indians when one is confronted with the rigid enforcement of federal law against them. During the Depression a program to rehabilitate Indians was initiated that involved giving Indian small ranchers several head of cattle with "I.D." conspicuously branded on them. The Indian rancher was supposed to raise the calf crop every year until he had stabilized a good herd and had enough surplus cattle to return to the Interior Department the number of cattle he had originally been granted. When some Indians killed these cattle to feed their families, as many had to do in order to stay alive, they were prosecuted for rustling or misuse of federal property.

Indians in the last decade have had many confrontations with the U.S. Attorney's Office in the trials coming as a result of activist protests, particularly the occupation of Wounded Knee. U.S. attorneys prosecuted Russell Means and Dennis Banks for their role in the activities at Wounded Knee. But they were too eager to secure a conviction against these Indian leaders and committed a number of misdeeds in violation of the federal laws governing their conduct. Finally, the judge in the Means-Banks trial dismissed the counts against the two activists, announcing that the U.S. attorneys and the FBI had so polluted the fountain of justice as to make further prosecution of these people unjust. Surveying all the trials that were held prosecuting Indian activists and the behavior of the U.S. attorneys during these trials, it is apparent that they are not serving the interests of justice or the best traditions of the Department of Justice when they conduct prosecutions against Indian activists.

During the life of the Indian Claims Commission, lawyers for the Department of Justice had to defend the United States against some six hundred claims by Indian tribes. Their task was extraordinarily difficult because it was apparent that they would lose most of these cases since the claims of the Indians were in most instances well-documented cases of fraudulent dealings by the United States. Some lawyers worked more than twenty years on a single set of cases and finally became experts in Indian history and culture and knew more about some tribes than they knew about themselves. On the whole, these attorneys established a proud and just record in their representation of the United States and did not become emotionally "anti-Indian" although the pressures to adopt personally the postures they were expected to carry into the courtroom must have been tremendous. Some attorneys continued to work on Indian claims although most of the present claims now under litigation are from causes of action arising in recent times and thus have more similarity to other work the attorneys might be doing than did the original large number of claims based upon treaties of the century before.

In addition to the Department of Justice, Indian legal issues can be affected by the Solicitor's Office in the Department of the Interior. In general, the Solicitor's Office performs all the legal work in Interior. The Indian Affairs Division has a staff of about twenty Indian law specialists. These attorneys issue legal opinions and memorandums, prepare litigation for the government on behalf of the Indian tribes, and serve as an advocate of Indian interests within Interior.

The Solicitor's Office exercises a good deal of power through the issuance of "Opinions of the Solicitor." These formal pronouncements are not unlike the opinions issued by the Attorney General's Office. If an administrator in Interior wished to obtain the answer to a legal question without going to court, a request can be made to the solicitor to issue an advisory opinion on the matter. These opinions are very persuasive and serve as the definitive statement of the law until a court speaks specifically to the issue involved. The opinions are usually interpretations of the law that can serve as guidelines for present and future policy. One problem with them is that, like other legal subjects, there are always a multitude of viewpoints on any particular issue. Consequently, in the course of several administrations solicitor's opinions can be issued on the same or similar topics that conflict with each other although expressing the policy directives and intents of the succeeding administrations. Such a sequence of opinions simply creates an atmosphere of confusion regarding the nature of federal Indian law.

Interior has recently published a two-volume set of "Opinions of the Solicitor" ranging from 1917 to 1974. This comprehensive compendium of legal advice covers nearly 2,200 pages. The impact of these legal statements can materially affect the course of conduct contemplated by an Indian tribe. The power of the Solicitor's Office is not to be taken lightly. Students of federal Indian policy could not do better, in seeking to trace the various concerns that have motivated and informed Indian matters in this century, than to read the solicitor's opinions chronologically to see the twists and turns and tidbits of legalese that detail the inconsistencies and lack of direction of these opinions.

ATTORNEYS AND ADVOCATES IN AN INDIAN SETTING

When Indians living off the reservation run into legal conflicts with people in white communities regarding business transactions, accidents, and the like, they simply contact a licensed attorney and embark upon what is usually a long and expensive road to a solution. If the controversy cannot be settled out of court, the issue is taken before a judge and/or a jury and the courtroom battle is conducted by opposing counsel. It is the attorneys who act as the catalyst in the courtroom and keep the action flowing. Such is not the case when a legal issue is taken before a tribal court.

Tribal court proceedings are unique. The legal setting is different, the nature of the issues and the attendant law are different, the actors are different, the language is different. There truly is a marked contrast between a tribal court proceeding and that of an Anglo-American hearing. The reason for this variance is that tribal law demands a special blending of traditional customs, which have evolved over centuries and are tenaciously held by reservation people as the proper way to resolve certain kinds of disputes, with modern notions of jurisprudence, which the whites have imposed upon the tribes.

Perhaps the most important distinction between tribal court proceedings and those of Anglo-American courts is that, in the vast majority of tribal hearings, attorneys do *not* generally participate directly. Instead, the traditional role of the attorney is assumed by an Indian advocate, or lay counselor as they are sometimes called. The attorney may be present and provide assistance to the Indian advocate, but it is usually the advocate who directs the presentation of evidence and conducts the cross-examination. The Indian advocate is usually a tribal member who has command of the tribal language, is familiar with tribal customs and traditions, and has been licensed by the tribe to function in his or her advocacy position. Advocates do not possess law degrees but sometimes have been provided with some legal training in order to qualify for their license. Quite often the advocate will be allowed to practice because he or she has a good reputation in the community, knows the people and their problems well, and has at one time served in some capacity in the tribe's judicial activities. Some training from Indian Legal Services attorneys may have been received by advocates who work on the reservation. Or the advocates may have attended conferences and seminars offered by such organizations as the Indian Law Support Center, a component part of the Native American Rights Fund. The advocate is assisted at tribal hearings by a licensed attorney. Thus the advocate not only provides his or her independent Indian knowledge for the proceedings but also has access to independent legal advice.

There are a number of reasons why tribal hearings rely upon the use of advocates rather than direct participation by attorneys. In addition to the fact that most white lawyers would be prohibitively expensive in comparison with the seriousness of the issue under consideration, the white lawyers know little of the traditions of Indian tribes and the values that would be the major motivating influence of individual actions. Motives wholly consistent within Indian culture, when suggested to a non-Indian trained in the rigors of common law and Western culture, would appear insignificant, incoherent, and perhaps inconsistent absent the tribal cultural context, in which they make a great deal of sense. There is also the problem faced by tribal judges, the vast majority of whom do not possess law degrees. If licensed attorneys were permitted to participate directly in the court proceedings, the attorneys, as is their tendency, could well take control of the court proceedings by sophisticated use of procedural maneuvering. Since tribal courts are concerned with resolving human problems and preserving community well-being instead of winning, such tactics would defeat the whole purpose of conducting the tribal court.

Tribal judges, lacking legal expertise and being accustomed to modestly retreating in the face of white authority figures, might be tempted to rely too heavily on the white attorneys, seeking their advice and counsel. The general temperament of tribal judges is that of the benign patriarch who sincerely wishes to resolve disputes with a minimum disruption of human lives—the kind of image once portrayed by Judge Hardy in the Mickey Rooney movies of several decades ago. In this role tribal judges are likely to stop the proceedings when they notice a tribal elder in the courtroom and ask his or her opinion on a matter of Indian tradition, which involves a lengthy conversation before the trial can proceed. This behavior is considered normal among Indian people, for the whole purpose of the trial is to do justice and every bit of information pertinent to the solution of the case is welcomed. Such an interlude, in the face of an objecting attorney concerned primarily with excluding any consideration that might place his or her client in a weaker or more compromising situation, would surely defeat the whole purpose of preserving self-government as it is understood by the Indian people, which is the reason why tribal courts exist.

Thus, attorneys are placed in the role of advisor and counselor so that there will be no judicial abdication, so that the proper reliance on tribal customs and traditions can be maintained, and so that the tribal court can reach a solution satisfactory to everyone involved. Alternatively, it is possible that a tribal judge, harassed by continuing sophisticated motions of procedural relevance only, might be forced into a constant defensive posture, which would encourage him or her to render an arbitrary decision in an effort to maintain order in the courtroom.

The threat posed to tribal integrity by the direct participation of licensed attorneys is sufficiently great to justify restrictions upon their activities. The solution that most tribes have agreed upon is to permit the lawyer to participate indirectly by assisting the Indian advocate. In this way the advocate can provide the traditional input into the proceeding and the attorney can assist in handling the legal nuances and other aspects of the trial for which legal training can be most helpful. It should be noted that, while most tribes have adopted this type of system, the extent of the role assumed by attorneys does vary significantly. On the Rosebud Sioux Reservation in South Dakota, for instance, Legal Services attorneys have brought a strong flavor of the Anglo-American system to the tribal court proceedings. But on the Navajo Reservation, a concerted attempt has been made to keep alive the traditional vestiges of the tribal legal culture (Price, 1969, p. 174).

In addition to the important role assumed by Indian advocates, the power of tribal judges is conspicuous in tribal court proceedings. Depending upon the judicial personality, a tribal judge often will run the hearing as he or she sees fit. Tribal proceedings are very informal yet possess sufficient dignity to be considered as serious occasions. Indian judges may ask questions, sometimes dominate the handling of witnesses, call for evidence that the advocate has not thought of submitting, and pretty much operate the courts as they deem it necessary to see that justice prevails. This notion of Indian "justice" may vary considerably with its Anglo-American counterpart. Mediation and the solving of familylike (tribal) conflict may well take precedence over a strict adherence to the law. Given this goal, the rules of evidence used by tribal judges are much more liberal than those acceptable in a non-Indian court. All this is a reflection of the Indians' attempt to preserve a fund of their legal heritage.

INDIAN LEGAL SERVICES ATTORNEYS

While Indian advocates are the primary actors in tribal court proceedings, this does not mean that attorneys do not play an important role in the Indian legal arena. Most of the attorneys practicing on reservations are funded by the Legal Services Corporation. This agency evolved from the first legal aid programs, which were funded by the Office of Economic Opportunity (OEO). The Economic Opportunity Act of 1964 (78 Stat. 508) was designed to coordinate programs to make low-income Americans more self-sufficient. While a legal assistance program was not initially mentioned in the act, in

1965 a Legal Services Program was established as a separate division of OEO. This division provided funds for attorneys to function in areas of poverty. Neighborhood Legal Services offices were created in barrio, ghetto, and reservation neighborhoods so that legal assistance could be extended to the poor as well as the affluent.

Indian reservations, of course, were prominent recipients of Legal Services programs. While the tribal court proceedings continued to rely heavily upon Indian advocates, there was a large and important role that Indian Legal Services attorneys could play in the developing court systems on the reservations. Indeed, the role extends beyond the courtroom into the community at large. These young attorneys have been active in community action work on the reservations, in community education programs, and in bringing aspects of legal reform to the Indian system of justice as a whole.

One of the best illustrations of the Indian Legal Services program is found on the Navajo Reservation. The Navajo program, known as DNA, was established in 1967. (DNA stands for Dinebeiin a Nahiilna be Agaditahe, which translated means "Attorneys That Contribute to the Economic Revitalization of the People.") The DNA program, which is more Indian oriented than most programs, uses a combination of judicial actors with primary emphasis on Indian advocates. All motions and arguments presented before the tribal court must be made by the advocate or by an attorney under the direct personal supervision of an advocate. Attorneys may assist advocates throughout the proceedings, but they must be licensed by the Board of Legal Examiners: in addition to qualifying by being admitted to the practice of law in the state where the reservation is located, an attorney must also satisfy certain tribal requirements, including continuous domicile on the Navajo Reservation for four months prior to applying for a tribal license.

The DNA program is administered by a 22-person Board of Directors. Seventeen of these directors are Navajos and 5 are non-Indians. Ten of the directors are elected directly by the tribal members through five agency committees (Swan, p. 607). Often these tribal boards of directors will include law school professors and county judges among their members in order to preserve access to non-Indian judicial expertise. There are 17 attorneys and 28 advocates functioning under the DNA program. In addition to the main agency in the capital of Window Rock, Arizona, the program has offices located in each of the five geographic areas to provide services to the widely distributed Navajo communities. Other Legal Services programs, attempting to solve the problem of servicing the back-country districts of large reservations, have their staff "ride the circuit." Journeys on the Papago Reservation in Arizona, for example, are made in conjunction with the Indian Health Service for the convenience of the isolated tribal members.

Indian Legal Services attorneys have made a significant contribution to tribal court systems of justice. There is the risk that the presence of these lawyers may impose more of the whites' institutional procedures upon Indian proceedings than is desirable, but this risk is counterbalanced by other factors. The educational function that the attorneys have provided to Indian advocates has been a material contribution. The attorneys also have benefited tribes by making them aware of additional policy avenues that can be pursued in the promotion or preservation of Indian rights. While the Indian world is foreign to the whites, so is the white community and its political institutions a puzzlement to Indians. Legal Services attorneys can direct tribal authorities to the proper channels and can assist in the development of political strategies to secure policy goals.

In most instances Legal Services attorneys have worked well and successfully with tribal court authorities although there have been conflicts at times, more with the tribal councils than with the lay advocates. As discussed earlier, in one rather notorious case Theodore Mitchell, director of DNA, was ordered off the reservation by the tribal council. While the problem initially centered around a dispute concerning the operation of the tribal school system, it was climaxed when Mitchell, along with several Indians, laughed rather boisterously at a question raised by a council member at a meeting in which a group was attempting to have Mitchell evicted from the reservation. The issue ultimately was taken to a federal district court, which held that Mitchell's exclusion was illegal and invalidated the action of the tribal council (*Dodge v. Nakai*, 298 F. Supp. 26 (D. Ariz. 1969)). This case of "indiscrete laughter" has been the exception to the general rule that Indian Legal Services attorneys have worked harmoniously and productively with tribal government personnel.

Indian Legal Services attorneys function on reservations primarily for the purpose of representing individual Indians. At times, however, the tribe will want to employ an attorney to represent the tribe as a whole in prosecuting a claim against the federal government or the states or in pursuit of other tribal matters. The tribal council, however, is not completely free in the selection of such legal representation. A federal law provides that "no agreement shall be made by any person with any tribe of Indians . . . unless such contract or agreement be . . . approved . . . [by] the Secretary of the Interior and the Commissioner of Indian Affairs" (25 U.S.C.A. §§

81–82). This "approval power" divests Indian tribes of a good deal of their autonomy in the selection of a lawyer, a prerogative that is thought to be inviolate under Anglo-American law. It also opens the door to politics.

There are those who believe that the "approval power" of the secretary of the interior and the commissioner of Indian affairs is an unconstitutional burden that has been thrust upon Indian tribes. At least one federal district court, however, not only has upheld the validity of this federal statute but also has gone on to note that the secretary also has the power to cancel a contract between a tribe and its chosen attorney (*Udall v. Littell*, 366 F.2d 668 (D.C. Cir. 1968)). The court's decision was predicated upon the broad authority the secretary has in fulfilling his or her trust responsibility for Indian tribes, particularly in light of the long history of concern over tribal relations with attorneys.

The "approval power" of the secretary of the interior and the commissioner of Indian affairs continues to concern Indian tribes. It is a blatant violation of the notion that everyone, including Indian tribes, should possess freedom of choice in selecting legal representation. The federal statute smacks of the continuing paternalism of the historical past and is certainly discordant with the contemporary theme of Indian self-determination. Congress has placed a small modification on the "approval power" of Interior. In 1968 a law was enacted stipulating that an application for legal assistance must be granted if it is not denied within a period of ninety days (25 U.S.C.A. § 1341). Although this change seemed to indicate a willingness of Congress to place some restriction on the powers of the secretary, in fact it can be a useful tool in manipulating attorneys. During the hearings on this legislation one Bureau of Indian Affairs official sitting in the audience remarked in a low confidential voice, "Hell, now we can wait for 89 days, disapprove of the contract for a minor flaw, and send it back to be revised and keep doing that until the attorney gives up."

One of the major problems in requiring secretarial approval over the employment of the major tribal legal counsel is that attorneys must inevitably cooperate with Interior officials. No bureaucrat is going to approve the contract of an attorney who will vigorously attack the bureaucratic institutions on behalf of his tribal clients. Nor will Interior approve the contract of a very competent and aggressive attorney who will seek lands rather than money in some of the claims based on treaties. Consequently, informal "agreements" or "understandings" have arisen between attorneys and Interior officials. Attorney contracts get approved and renewed and certain kinds of law suits never get filed. It is difficult to prove any collusion in this critical area but there is no question that some informal arrangement has been worked out so that tribal attorneys and the Interior Department do not come into many serious conflicts even though there is ample evidence that serious breaches of federal law are continuously committed by Interior personnel.

INDIAN LEGAL INTEREST GROUPS

Legal interest groups, such as the National Association for the Advancement of Colored People, the NAACP Legal Defense and Educational Fund, and the American Civil Liberties Union, have played a prominent role in the development of American constitutional law. These nonprofit organizations have concentrated primarily on the courts as the major political institutions by which to promote their policy preferences. In seeking to clarify, defend, or question certain doctrines of law and political policies, these groups have forced substantial changes in the way in which we think about certain issues. While most people think of Congress as the appropriate branch of government charged with making policy, the courts also play a significant role. One might say that Congress articulates the general principles under which the nation lives while the courts tell us how these principles apply when they are seen in concrete human situations.

The style and strategy used to persuade judges may be somewhat different from that used to convince legislators of the appropriateness of a given path of action, but influence is brought to bear nevertheless. Submitting *amicus curiae* briefs on a particular issue demonstrating interest and support for a particular principle of law or a particular interpretation of a principle, developing test cases that can phrase the legal principle under consideration in such a manner as to invoke or elicit a particular response, providing expert witnesses and research data—all these services and activities are techniques that can be used to provide input into judicial policymaking. Such organizations as the NAACP and the ACLU have been extremely successful in using the courts as an avenue by which to promote their interests.

Indian interest groups have long been active in the pursuit of certain political goals on behalf of the tribes. During colonial days the Society of Friends assigned certain well-respected members of their congregations to attend treaty negotiations to ensure that the tribes were not defrauded. Perhaps the first significant use of the federal courts by Indian friends was the willingness of Samuel Worcester and his group of missionaries to violate the laws of Georgia in order that the Cherokee treaties could be heard in the Supreme Court. In 1883, as an ongoing part of the Quaker concern, the Indian Rights Association was formed. Although the IRA spent a great deal of its energies lobbying and working on legislation, it did furnish the resources for two of the most important cases of the first decade of this century: *Lone Wolf v. Hitchcock* and *Quick Bear v. Leupp.* More Indian interest groups were formed during the 1920s and 1930s but, like their predecessor the IRA, they focused primarily on legislation. The National Congress of American Indians, formed in Denver in 1944 and destined to become the oldest of contemporary interest organizations composed predominantly of Indians, provided funds in the late 1940s and early 1950s for voting rights cases in Arizona and Utah.

Until the late 1960s with the funding of Legal Services programs on the reservations there was only sporadic interest in establishing a national organization devoted to pursuing a specific litigation strategy for Indian rights. The NCAI met briefly with Jack Greenberg of the NAACP Legal Defense and Educational Fund to discuss establishing an independent nonprofit organization that could develop a litigation program similar to that which had materially assisted the black community in its desegregation fight, but the tribes preferred to continue their own independent actions as each cause arose. Some of the early Indian activists had to rely on their own resources or use National Lawyers Guild members when they needed legal counsel. But the idea of such a program was already planted in the minds of numerous Indian attorneys.

The Native American Rights Fund, commonly referred to as NARF, was founded in 1970. It is the oldest and largest national Indian interest law firm in the United States. NARF began as a project of the California Indian Legal Services program. Pursuant to a Ford Foundation grant in the summer of 1970, it quickly emerged as a prominent advocate of Indian legal interests. The purpose of NARF is not simply to represent individual Indians in an attempt to rectify personal grievances. Rather, its function is to advocate the Indian position on *major* policy issues of a legal nature. The cases that it selects are those that will affect the greatest number of people and at the same time have a significant impact on Indian policy. Each year NARF handles about two hundred cases and other legal matters. In 1979, it provided representation to over eighty-nine tribes and other Indian clients in thirty states although much of this work was consultation rather than extensive litigation.

NARF is operated like most other nonprofit public interest law firms. It has a legal staff of approximately fifteen attorneys, two-thirds of whom are Indian. While it is headquartered in Boulder, Colorado, it has opened an office in Washington, D.C., in order to be closer to the heartland of federal agencies that affect Indian people. The organization is directed by a thirteen-member Steering Committee, which meets twice a year and establishes the guidelines for determining the types of cases that NARF will accept. A four-member Executive Committee brings continuity to the organization by meeting more frequently as needs require. The Executive Committee can reconsider general policy decisions, develop recommendations to be brought before the Steering Committee, and administer the burdens of finance and fund-raising.

The work of NARF is dependent solely upon grants, contracts, and donations from foundations and private individuals. A donor file of about sixteen thousand people has been compiled. In 1979, of the $1,945,416 raised for the NARF annual budget, 28 percent came from private foundations, 59 percent from federal government sources, 9 percent from private contributions, and 4 percent from other sources (Native American Rights Fund, p. 81). Approximately 75 percent of these funds go for litigation and client services.

Direct litigation is not the only service that NARF provides. In conjunction with the Legal Services Corporation, NARF has established the Indian Law Support Center. Under this rubric NARF acts as co-counsel with local Indian Legal Services attorneys on major Indian cases and issues. In this way, the Native American Rights Fund can provide reservation attorneys with data and expertise that otherwise would not be available. In 1978, NARF acted as co-counsel in fourteen of these Legal Services cases. In many instances where NARF is not functioning as a co-counsel, it responds to general requests for legal information from Legal Services attorneys. In 1978, the center spent more than 784 hours answering such requests (Native American Rights Fund, p. 7). The Indian Law Support Center has been active in holding Indian law training conferences designed to improve the legal capabilities of reservation attorneys, Indian advocates, and paralegal personnel. While basic legal education is important, the thrust of these conferences together with the overall objectives of NARF have resulted in the establishment of certain organizational goals and priorities. These include the following:

1. *Tribal existence*—ensuring tribal independence and preserving Indian practices.
2. *Tribal resources*—protecting lands, water, minerals, and other resources from abuse.

3. *Human rights*—securing rights to education that complements Indian culture; adequate health care; equitable treatment of Indian prisoners.
4. *Accountability*—assuring that federal, state, local, and tribal laws are properly enforced.
5. *Indian law development*—assuring an orderly development of Indian law and work to improve Indian legal resources.

In support of these objectives, NARF has developed a National Indian Law Library. The library was established in 1972 pursuant to a grant from the Carnegie Corporation and is located at NARF headquarters in Boulder. The library has been of great benefit to tribes and Legal Services attorneys, who frequently request information. All of the library's holdings are published in an NILL catalogue, which contained in 1978 some 2,750 library items. These holdings include books, law review articles, and other relevant publications that shed light on Indian legal issues. Today NARF possesses much of the prestige enjoyed by the large private law firms that have handled tribal legal problems for many decades, yet NARF has the advantage of Indian, as opposed to Anglo, attorneys who work on Indian problems. Tribal contracts with the large private firms will obviously not become extinct because of the presence of NARF, but the combination of the two types of organizations makes for a formidable adversary in the conflict that persists in the legal arena.

While the Native American Rights Fund has been extended a great deal of respect, it has not escaped criticism. Like most legal public interest groups, NARF does not represent paying clients. Indeed, the issues that the organization's Steering Committee chooses to pursue are not determined by clients, as is the case with a private law firm, but are decided upon by an elitist group of thirteen Indians. Michael Gross, a former consultant to NARF and DNA attorney for the Navajo tribe, has chastized NARF for its independent detachment from an Indian clientele (Gross, p. 78). Gross argues that NARF sets its own goals and that these may or may not be harmonious with its general Indian clientele. The Indians who serve on NARF's Steering Committee are different, both economically and socially, from most Indians, and while this is true of the attorneys associated with the large private firms handling Indian business, at least the firms must respond to the demands of their clients. This direct link between clients and counsel insofar as control of a case is concerned is not true of NARF.

Undoubtedly, there is some truth in Gross' criticism of NARF, but it is a criticism that can be levied at all legal interest groups. The fact remains that the overall impact that such legal interest groups as the NAACP and the ACLU, as well as NARF, have had upon major policy issues has been immense. Of more importance as a criticism of NARF is the contention being increasingly voiced that heavy reliance on federal funding makes NARF less willing to enter cases that have some controversial element in them. Particularly with respect to the work done on eastern Indian land claims and recognition problems, NARF has received a substantial amount of federal dollars but has not provided the same aggressiveness in pursuing its work, particularly with respect to recognition, that it once did.

Part of the ongoing controversy within tribes is the contest between the traditional Indians and the Indians who have sufficiently assimilated to be willing to work within the political institutions that the Bureau of Indian Affairs has forced the tribes to adopt. With the rise of Indian activism in the early 1970s, particularly the American Indian Movement (AIM), traditionalism became very popular and many people began to question the basis for their IRA constitutions and governments. As Indians probed into the background of some of their land claims they also discovered some very unsavory activities by the Washington law firms and the recognized tribal governments and claims committees. Consequently, the need arose for a small independent and aggressive group of lawyers to begin to challenge the very foundations of the Indian-federal establishment. Probing into this traditional quid pro quo relationship is not guaranteed to open the doors of career opportunity for attorneys because it means calling into question the basis upon which informal activities are conducted within the small arena of Indian affairs.

The Indian Law Resource Center was established in 1977 to do such work and has become one of the most fearless and probably controversial groups in Indian affairs. It has assisted the Mohawks and traditional people of the Six Nations in their occupation of a state park in upper New York State and has helped them prepare their case for presentation at a United Nations inquiry into the conditions of Indians in the Western Hemisphere and before the Fourth International Russell Tribunal. Naturally, these forums are unusual and are bound to generate a great deal of hostility from conservative Americans who would prefer to think that American Indian problems should be confined to benign discussions within the domestic sphere. Thus, the Indian Law Resource Center has received more direct emotional attacks on its activities than the other legal interest groups in the United States. But its presence serves a very useful purpose of offering an alternative to Indians, particularly traditional Indians who reject the cozy and sometimes conspiratorial activities that seem to permeate the relationship of Indians and the United States government in the important area of legal counsel.

Evaluating the performance of attorneys in those areas where they most importantly affect Indian rights is difficult indeed. Although attorneys have been critically important in preserving Indian rights, it has often been an enriching experience for them, and when one weighs their enrichment against the gains made by Indians, one is still left with an uneasy feeling. We would certainly not condemn a whole profession for the thoughtless or unethical practices of a few persons. Certainly, there is no way to predict how the legal profession will respond to its challenges in any one generation. Nevertheless, there has been no corresponding accumulation of sound legal doctrines in the decades in which the tribal lawyers have represented the tribes. In the past decade with the emergerce of public interest nonprofit legal organizations, such as NARF, there has been even less emphasis on developing coherent theories of law that can serve another generation well.

Indian law, and the attorneys, advocates, and legal interest groups that compose its active functioning parts, is in a period of extreme crisis. By charting the wins and losses in the United States Supreme Court against the issues most critical to Indians, one can detect a pattern of failure in recent years. Indians have won cases when their public image was most favorable and they have lost when the tide of public opinion began to run against them or callousness made Indian rights a moot issue with opinion-makers. Almost all the groups now working in this field seem to choose their cases according to the possible impact they will have on their fundraising activities. Thus "sexy" cases involving sacred lands, treaties, and neglected communities rank high while difficult cases involving land titles and other aspects of treaties rank low.

The NAACP, when it began to litigate its segregation cases, and the ACLU, when it worked on the death penalty, on search and seizure, and other constitutional issues, both had specific goals in mind. It was relatively simple to determine, after a decade or more of work, how close they had come to achieving their avowed goals. With Indian legal interest groups, now after their first decade of active work, it is impossible to tell if there has been any thought at all given to the development of litigation strategies, establishment of goals, or movement toward stabilizing certain rights for American Indians. One might hope that some articulation of theory, some introduction of new concepts, or some elaboration of existing rights might emerge from the frantic activity that today characterizes the Indian interest law organizations. Perhaps another generation will perform this difficult philosophical work so that all the activity that we have seen in recent years will begin to take shape and make sense.

7. The Criminal System of Justice in Indian Country

Jay Morningstar, an enrolled member of the Antler tribe, spent most of a summer evening drinking beer in the Mill Creek Tavern located in Summit Hill, Colorado. Summit Hill is a small, non-Indian town located within the Antler Reservation but under state jurisdiction. Having toasted friend and foe alike too many times, Jay Morningstar began to brawl with several patrons who also frequented the Mill Creek Tavern. Before the raucus ended, Jay had pulled a knife and stabbed an innocent bystander. The bartender put out an urgent call to local law enforcement authorities and, within a period of twenty minutes, three different groups arrived at the tavern to arrest Jay Morningstar. Since Jay was a reservation Indian the tribal police arrived to take him into custody believing that Jay had violated tribal law. But a state trooper was also on hand to make an arrest since Summit Hill was a town falling under state jurisdiction. Joining the group was a federal agent, who was convinced that Jay Morningstar had violated a provision of the federal Major Crimes Act and hence should be taken into custody by federal authorities. The ultimate question involved is which of these groups had jurisdiction in this case—the tribal authorities, the state, or the federal government?

While the saga of Jay Morningstar may not be the typical criminal case arising in Indian Country, it illustrates some of the jurisdictional problems that make the Indian criminal justice system exceedingly complex. Trying to ascertain which governmental authority possesses the power to apprehend and try criminal offenders in or near Indian Country can be likened to bringing order to a jurisdictional maze. Three important areas of concern need to be explored if one is to gain a meaningful understanding of the criminal justice system in Indian Country. The first requires an examination of the major statutes that Congress has passed that have defined the parameters of the criminal justice system. The second focus of attention involves a general examination and classification of the jurisdictional authority possessed by each of the competing governmental entities (the tribal governments, the states, and the federal authorities). Finally, it is necessary to examine some of the basic problems inherent in the law enforcement and criminal prosecution functions that the tribal governments face in their attempts to cope with the issue of crime.

FEDERAL STATUTES AND CRIMINAL LAW

Traditionally, as we have seen, Indian tribes dealt with criminal offenders in a variety of ways. Criminal problems were resolved with an eye toward restitution, not retribution, although there were certainly instances when the family exercised its right to punish the wrongdoer without any penalty or social stigma from the rest of the tribe. But the primary consideration was to provide compensation for the victim's relatives and to return the tribe, insofar as it was possible, to the original state of social equilibrium. Were we to attempt to draw parallels between the variety and seriousness of crimes in Indian society and those we recognize today as violations of the acceptable norms, we might be hard pressed to find sufficient parallels to warrant our research. People felt free to use other people's property within reason and only a continuous and careless use of property invoked any kind of social sanctions. Lying, on the other hand, was regarded as extremely heinous and many tribes saw it as a fundamental breach of the social contract. Banishment, not execution, was regarded as the most serious punishment since an individual without a community or relatives literally did not exist as a human being for many groups.

When the white settlers appeared in America the Indians expected them to live according to similar codes. Their efforts to compensate whites who had lost relatives in the frontier skirmishes were insultingly rebuffed and demands for execution of wrongdoers seemed unduly harsh to the Indians. The Iroquois once lost two warriors to a group of French trappers and, sending a delegation to Montreal, they demanded compensation. The French officer commanding the fort sought out the guilty parties and, arresting them, invited the Iroquois to send a delegation to watch their execution. When the Iroquois observers discovered that the French intended to execute all five, they fervently pleaded with the commanding officer to spare three lives, remarking that they had only lost two men. Try as he might, the French commander was unable to explain the European concept of guilt to the Indians. In the European mode of thought, all five were guilty since they had shared the deed equally. The Indians, on the other hand, viewing things from a tribal perspective, saw only that they had lost two men and that the French intended to punish five for the misdeed.

The Europeans lived in continual fear of the Indians. Culturally distinct, unable to understand the complexities of the Indian clans, villages, and tribal relationships, the settlers began to assume that the Indians were incorrigible and incapable of understanding the laws of "civilized" peoples. Skirmishes on the frontier usually did not wait until a clear identification was made between two parties and the constant complaint of the tribes was about the unlawful and callous killing of people in the forests separating the two peoples. Settlers coming upon an Indian, incapable of identifying his tribe and its present posture toward the settlement, preferred to shoot first and ask questions later. Preserving even a semblance of peaceful relations on the edge of expanding and aggressive settlements became next to impossible and only the traders who were well experienced in dealing with the Indians stood between many settlements and extinction.

The first treaties carefully delineated the lines of landownership and the general rule adopted was one of banning Indians and settlers beyond certain agreed-upon landmarks. If Indians were found inside the boundaries of colonies without good-conduct passes provided by the military authorities, it was assumed they would be fired upon. By the same token, white settlers who crossed certain watersheds were literally taking their lives in their hands. The famous Treaty of Lancaster in 1744 made provisions for a careful articulation of boundaries beyond which individuals of the colonies and the tribes could not pass. So important was this conference that the colonies of Maryland, Virginia, and Pennsylvania were represented as were the Iroquois, Shawnee, Miami, and other large confederations of tribes.

The problem of frontier frictions was not resolved when the United States achieved its independence. Traditional rules were followed and, although the federal government was more inclined to support the right of settlers to move into lands that had not yet been formally ceded by the Indians than had been the colonial governors, still there were frequent conferences to establish rules and regulations that would govern the violations of law by the citizens of either side. Some of these treaty articles are very interesting in that they demonstrate that actions we would regard today as violations of the criminal code were regarded in the early days of the Republic as national violations and recourse was first to the constituted authorities of the tribe and the federal government with little thought about the application of federal or state laws on the tribal member committing the act. The treaty with the Wyandot and other tribes in 1785 has two articles that illustrate the manner in which crimes were handled:

> *Article V.* If any citizen of the United States, or other persons not being an Indian, shall attempt to settle on any of the lands allotted to the Windot and Delaware nations in this treaty, except on the lands reserved to the United States in the preceding article, such person shall forfeit the protection of the United States, and the Indians may punish him as they please.

> *Article IX.* If any Indian or Indians shall commit a robbery or murder on any citizen of the United States, the tribe to which such offenders may belong, shall be bound to deliver them up at the nearest post, to be punished according to the ordinances of the United States. (7 Stat. 16, 17)

The treaties of 1785 had what amounted to basically reciprocal rights to punish for criminal violations. The tribes pledged to surrender their wrongdoers and in some instances they did. More often, unable to find the wrongdoers and not willing to provoke an Indian war, federal officials had to be content to deduct from the annuities due the tribe a reasonable sum to be paid as compensation to the families or survivors of the victims.

Clearly this frontier situation was unsatisfactory from the non-Indian point of view. Schooled in the stern and inexorable concepts of justice derived from Old Testament Mosaic laws, the settlers demanded their revenge and it was not long in the treaty-making process before the federal government demanded and got an admission by the tribes of the primacy of federal laws in this area. The Pickering treaty of 1794 with the Iroquois, for example, had a provision whereby the matter of violations would eventually be referred to congressional guidance and one can assume that, if the United States was able to get the Iroquois to agree to these provisions, the other tribes would have already given in on this point since the Six Nations comprised the most formidable group of Indians confronting the United States at this time. Article VII of the 1794 treaty provided:

> Lest the firm peace and friendship now established should
> be interrupted by the misconduct of individuals, the United
> States and Six Nations agree, that for injuries done by individ-

uals on either side, no private revenge or retaliation shall take place; but, instead thereof, complaint shall be made by the party injured, to the other: By the Six Nations or any of them, to the President of the United States, or the Superintendent by him appointed; and by the Superintendents or other persons appointed by the President, to the principal chiefs of the Six Nations, or of the nation to which the offender belongs: *and such prudent measures shall then be pursued as shall be necessary to preserve our peace and friendship unbroken; until the legislature (or great council) of the United States shall make other equitable provision for the purpose.* (7 Stat. 44, 46; emphasis added)

Once this particular point had been ceded, the logic of increasing federal involvement was inevitable and the groundwork had been laid for federal intrusion into domestic tribal relations in the field of criminal law.

The Indian Intercourse Acts of 1790 and continuing amendments and renewals until 1802 attempted to spell out the types of actions that would be regarded as violations of federal law in the relationship with Indians. Not until the Act of March 3, 1817 (3 Stat. 383), did the federal government attempt to pass a statute that established a system of criminal justice applicable to Indians as well as non-Indians within Indian Country. The act provided that Indians or anyone else committing offenses within Indian Country would be subject to the same punishment that would be applicable had the offense been committed within the United States itself. Federal courts were given jurisdiction to try anyone indicted under this statute. But section 2 of the act contained an important exception regarding tribal jurisdiction over offenses of a domestic tribal nature: ". . . nothing in this act shall be so construed as to affect any treaty now in force between the United States and any Indian nation, or to extend to any offence committed by one Indian against another, within any Indian boundary." The exception was important because it constituted a recognition of the internal sovereignty of the tribe and eventually led to that line of reasoning which clearly defined the preconstitutional aboriginal rights of self-government as articulated in *Talton v. Mayes* and *Native American Church v. Navajo Tribal Council.*

The westward movement of the frontier produced considerable alterations of the federal perception of criminal laws applicable to Indian tribes. The successful removal of the eastern Indians to Oklahoma and Kansas and the establishment by most of the migrating tribes of forms of government similar in many ways to the federal government eliminated the need for further incursions into the domestic relations of tribes. Now, confronting the nomadic and militant people of the plains and southwestern deserts, the federal government had to revert once again to its position of allowing great flexibility in the application of federal laws to Indians. The 1802 act was largely obsolete. It was virtually impossible to impose any semblance of systematic law enforcement on tribes who roamed over thousands of miles of open prairie or who lived in the remote canyons of the southwestern deserts. In 1834, when the existing federal laws dealing with Indian matters were reconstituted and revised in the Trade and Intercourse Act of June 20 (4 Stat. 729), the House Indian Committee reporting on the legislation commented:

> It will be seen that we cannot, consistently with the provisions of some of our treaties, and of the territorial act, extend our criminal laws to offences committed by or against Indians, of which the tribes have exclusive jurisdiction; and *it is rather of courtesy than of right* that we undertake to punish crimes committed in that territory by and against our citizens. And this provision is retained principally on the ground that it may be unsafe to trust to Indian law in the early stages of their Government. It is not perceived that we can with any justice or propriety extend our laws to offences committed by Indians against Indians. (H. Rpt. No. 474, 23rd Cong. 1st Sess. May 20, 1834, pp. 13–14; emphasis added)

This hesitancy, in the face of previous federal assertions of superior sovereignty and ultimate supremacy, seems to indicate a reluctance to grapple with the complex issues involving conflicting jurisdictions, both apparently secured by federal law and constitutional duties.

The General Crimes Act

The 1834 Trade and Intercourse Act provided a basic framework of relationships for dealing with Indians, but it shied away from a direct confrontation about the ultimate source of the domestic law that would govern Indians within their own territory. The act was amended twenty years later by the Act of March 27, 1854 (10 Stat. 269), and the cumulative provisions of the two acts, as expressed in the 1854 statute, became known as the "General Crimes Act," which was designed to govern, if only temporarily, the conditions on the frontier insofar as they were amenable to resolution by federal and territorial courts. The 1854 act removed from the jurisdiction of federal courts the offenses committed by Indians against non-Indians in Indian Country who had "been punished by the local law of the tribe." But it outlined two specific offenses: arson and assault by individuals of one race against individuals of the other with intent to kill or maim. Presumably, Congress believed that these provisions would forestall violence on the frontier. If one banned burning and killing between Indians and whites, what else would they be able to do to each other of a criminal nature?

The General Crimes Act was not capable of really resolving disputes because rapidly changing conditions in the west made it virtually impossible to deal on a piecemeal basis with jurisdictional problems. Some Indians in the tribes on the Missouri and Arkansas rivers, having established governments upon their removal to the west, were already moving into civilized ways that required new protections they had not previously needed. The Act of June 14, 1862 (12 Stat. 427), for example, attempted to resolve the increasing difficulties experienced by Indians who had taken agricultural allotments. It authorized the superintendents to protect them and made trespass upon their lands by unallotted Indians a criminal offense, going so far as to depose for a short period of time any chief or headman who trespassed.

Congress recognized that this piecemeal approach to legislation dealing with criminal jurisdiction could not produce the conditions it desired in the western lands where some tribes still reigned supreme and others were but shadows of their former selves. The same condition existed on other federal lands and so a special act was passed (March 3, 1873, 17 Stat. 579) that provided for the preparation and presentation to Congress of the revision of the laws of the United States that were applicable to post roads, military installations, and Indian affairs. A year later, in the Act of June 20, 1874 (18 Stat. 113), the revised laws were published. They contained, for the first time in a codified form, sections pertinent to Indian jurisdiction. Sections 2145 and 2146 were particularly relevant:

Section 2145—Except as otherwise expressly provided by law, the general laws of the United States as to the punishment of offenses committed in any place within the sole and exclusive jurisdiction of the United States, except the District of Columbia, shall extend to the Indian country.

Section 2146—This section shall not extend to offenses committed by one Indian against the person or property of another

Indian, nor to any Indian committing any offense in the Indian country who has been punished by the local law of the tribe, or to any case where, by treaty stipulations, the exclusive jurisdiction over such offenses is or may be secured to the Indian tribes respectively.

Although some contemporary commentators have described the revised statutes as intrusions on tribal sovereignty, it is not difficult to see that considerable leeway existed in the enforcement of these provisions. The establishment of some form of government consistent with at least some of the principles of the local region would be sufficient to pre-empt federal jurisdiction, and allocation of a particular subject matter to the tribes by treaty would also take the offense out of the hands of federal officials. At least that is what people believed until a cause célèbre made federal jurisdiction imperative within the reserved lands of the Indians.

The Major Crimes Act

In 1883 a Sioux Indian named Crow Dog killed a very popular Brûlé Sioux chief by the name of Spotted Tail and unleashed a storm of controversy and concern regarding the application of traditional tribal laws to actions that, in the non-Indian society, would be regarded as serious breaches of the peace. Spotted Tail had been a pliant and peaceful chief who acted as a buffer between the United States and the more aggressive Sioux leaders, such as Red Cloud, Sitting Bull, and Crazy Horse. He always counseled for peace and provided the progovernment faction within the tribe. Spotted Tail was amply rewarded for his efforts on behalf of the government, receiving a nice two-story house at the agency named after him on the Rosebud Creek in present midwestern South Dakota. But this demonstration of favoritism greatly angered the traditional Sioux and, when Spotted Tail extended his chiefly privileges to include the wives of some of the traditional leaders, there was no question that he was a marked man even with the aura of federal protection around him.

Following the killing, Crow Dog's relatives met with the family of Spotted Tail as was the Sioux custom and the two families, eager to resolve their problems and avoid a continuing feud within the Brûlés, accepted the compensation that the Crow Dog relatives proposed. But word got out that Spotted Tail's killer had not been executed, had not, in fact, even appeared before the court of law for his misdeed. A raging storm of protest over the killing of this well-known chief made it imperative that the federal government do something and so Crow Dog was arrested, taken to Deadwood, Dakota Territory, to the federal territorial court, and tried and convicted by the federal jury for the murder of Spotted Tail. Crow Dog convinced the federal marshal that he should be released to go home and settle his affairs and he was released to go back to the Rosebud Agency.

It was snowing the day Crow Dog was supposed to report back to the federal marshal at Deadwood and everyone wagered that the Sioux medicine man would not appear. But he walked into the federal marshal's office and gave himself up at the appointed time; newspaper accounts chronicled this remarkable feat—no white man, placed in a similar situation, would conceivably have done the same thing. Suddenly Crow Dog was a hero in the newspapers and attorneys volunteered to take a writ of habeas corpus on his behalf to the Supreme Court. Congress eventually paid the expenses of this suit. The country, still puzzled over the nature of Sioux justice and the extraordinary behavior of the condemned Crow Dog, awaited the Court's decision.

In *Ex Parte Crow Dog*, 109 U.S. 556 (1883), the Supreme Court concluded that the defendant's plea was not without merit. While much of the opinion revolves around judicial interpretations of the relevant statutes involved, a large portion of the opinion deals with the idea that Indian offenders who commit crimes in Indian Country should be tried by the tribal governments involved and not by federal authorities. To justify a departure from the general notion of tribal jurisdiction in such cases, there had to be a clear expression of such an intention by Congress. None of the statutes or treaties involved revealed such an intention and so the Court concluded that the Brûlé Sioux tribe, not the federal government, possessed jurisdiction over the murder of Spotted Tail. The writ of habeas corpus was issued and Crow Dog was set free.

Congress continued to feel the pressure of public opinion in this instance. Friends of the Indians were at that time earnestly seeking the allotment of all Indian reservations with the confidence that making the Indians agricultural and sedentary would assist in converting them to Christianity and would make them good citizens. To allow a "primitive" form of justice to flourish in the case of the most serious crimes was unthinkable. To allow the Indians to continue to regulate their own domestic relations was considered a mild form of insanity. The slogan that characterized federal Indian policy was "break up the tribal mass" and this particular custom, to give compensation for a murder instead of invoking the death penalty, was considered a symbol of continued savage resistance to the overtures of sincere "civilized" efforts to assist the Indians. All that people knew, or understood, was that the federal government was releasing rather than executing an admitted murderer.

In 1885, as part of the general appropriation act of that year, Congress attached a short paragraph dealing with seven major crimes. Although there were no hearings or expressions of Indian opinion, or even congressional opinion for that matter, and although the rider did not seem important at the time, this section has come to be called the Major Crimes Act (23 Stat. 362, 385) and has formed the basis for profound and extensive federal intrusions into tribal self-government. The practical thrust of the Major Crimes Act was to divest Indian tribes of their jurisdiction over major criminal offenses committed within Indian Country. Under the act the federal government would assume jurisdiction over these offenses. Initially, the act only included seven major crimes, but it has since been amended and judicially interpreted so that today fourteen felonies fall within its scope. The major portion of the amendment now reads as follows:

> *Any Indian* who commits against the person or property of *another Indian or other person* any of the following offenses, namely, murder, manslaughter, kidnapping, rape, carnal knowledge of any female, not his wife, who has not attained the age of sixteen years, assault with intent to commit rape, incest, assault with intent to commit murder, assault with a dangerous weapon, assault resulting in serious bodily injury, arson, burglary, robbery, and larceny *within the Indian country*, shall be subject to the same laws and penalties as all other persons committing any of the above offenses, within the exclusive jurisdiction of the United States. (Emphasis added)

Strangely, this act was never enforced with respect to the Five Civilized tribes in Oklahoma nor did it apply for many years to the Western Shoshones of the Nevada deserts. It also did not specifically amend the provisions of the 1868 treaty with the Sioux, which had been the basis of Crow Dog's assertion of exclusive tribal jurisdiction over the offense.

Several features of the act merit attention. In the first place, the statute only applies when the criminal offender is an Indian. The victim of the crime, however, may be an Indian or any "other person." The phrase "other person" has been defined by the court to include non-Indians (*Henry v. United States*, 432 F.2d 114 (9th Cir. 1970)). The criminal act, of course, must be committed within Indian Country, as designated in the statute.

The constitutionality of the Major Crimes Act was contested in

United States v. Kagama, 118 U.S. 375 (1886). Although the factual situation in this case is not sufficiently strong, nor are the logic and constitutional citations used by the Court sufficiently impressive to constitute a significant testing of this allocation of jurisdictional authority to the federal government, it has come to be regarded as the major case on criminal jurisdiction. Two Indians were indicted under the act for murdering another Indian on the Hoopa Valley Reservation in California. The Supreme Court concluded that Congress had ample power to pass the act. The Court reasoned that Indian tribes were wards of the United States and that their communities were dependent upon the federal government for protection. Under this extension of the guardianship theory, it was not difficult for the justices to find that the government not only had the right but also owed the duty to the Indian nations to provide such protection. The passage of the Major Crimes Act, therefore, could be justified on the basis of fulfilling this "guardianship" obligation.

It is interesting to note the omissions of the case as well as its positive assertions. First, the Hoopas had no treaty that would have taken this crime out of the general revised statute provisions of 2146, absent the passage of the Major Crimes Act. Second, the Hoopas had no existing tribal government that could have enforced the tribal penalty had they wished to exert tribal jurisdiction over this particular crime. Given the absence of any viable tribal institutional alternative and unwilling to surrender Indians to the state of California, which had a notoriously bad reputation regarding Indian rights, the Supreme Court acknowledged the jurisdictional vacuum and then argued that it must reside in the federal government because there was no place else where the power to punish this crime could be lodged.

The impact of the Major Crimes Act upon the exercise of tribal power over criminal affairs is immense. Under the *Crow Dog* doctrine, tribal courts exercised exclusive jurisdiction over serious crimes committed by Indians on the reservations. But the Major Crimes Act put an end to this jurisdiction. Theoretically, one could argue that tribal courts still may exercise concurrent jurisdiction along with the federal government, that the Major Crimes Act only added federal jurisdiction to an already-existing tribal jurisdiction. At the very least tribal authorities could argue that they should be able to prosecute serious crimes when the federal government fails to prosecute offenders, but this argument is not very persuasive from a practical standpoint. Under the 1968 Civil Rights Act, tribal courts may impose sentences on defendants only up to $500 in fines and/or six months in jail. Serious criminal activity usually demands penal-

ties of a more severe nature than these provisions. Thus, for all practical purposes, the tribal governments have been stripped of their
power to deal with major criminal activity on the reservations.

An additional feature of the Major Crimes Act had diluted the
ability of tribal courts to maintain their prosecutorial functions over
criminal activity. This feature relates to the "lesser included offense" doctrine, which is an outgrowth of the common law. The
lesser included offense doctrine permits juries to convict a defendant of a less serious offense if that offense falls within the general
classification of the crime. For instance, if a person is charged with
murder, he or she may be found guilty of murder in the first degree
or of several lesser included offenses, such as second degree murder
or manslaughter.

Tribal authorities are troubled over a decision the Supreme
Court handed down that permits Indians who are prosecuted under
the Major Crimes Act to be convicted of lesser included offenses.
This idea was promulgated in *Keeble v. United States*, 412 U.S. 205
(1973), a case in which an Indian defendant was charged with and
convicted of assault with intent to commit serious bodily harm, a
crime specified in the Major Crimes Act. At his trial, Keeble insisted
that the judge instruct the jury to consider finding him guilty of a
simple assault charge (a lesser included offense) instead of the initial
charge of assault with intent to commit serious bodily harm. The
government argued that the crime of simple assault was not even
designated in the Major Crimes Act. Moreover, since the Major
Crimes Act was a careful, limited intrusion of federal power into the
otherwise exclusive jurisdiction of tribal courts, it would be improper for the court to broaden that encroachment by expanding the
category of crime by including lesser included offenses. The judge
accepted the government's interpretation of the act and Keeble
appealed.

The Supreme Court rejected the federal government's argument. It reasoned that Indians were to be extended the same treatment as other defendants and that Congress had never intended to
disqualify Indians from the benefits available to white defendants,
one of which was the availability of the lesser included offense doctrine. While Keeble, a Crow Creek Sioux, had his conviction overturned by the Supreme Court, the long-range consequence of this
decision to Indian judicial authority was more detrimental than beneficial. Permitting federal courts to use the lesser included offense
doctrine in Major Crimes Act prosecutions will result in cases being
disposed of by federal courts at very low conviction levels—levels
that in the absence of the doctrine would have been handled by the
tribal courts. This situation is simply another step in the continued

erosion of tribal authority in the field of criminal law. The National American Indian Court Judges Association has characterized this decision as a usurpation of tribal court authority.

The Assimilative Crimes Act

The Assimilative Crimes Act is a congressional enactment that indirectly applies minor state laws to all federal enclaves where state laws cannot be enforced. For instance, if the federal government builds an air base in Tucson, Arizona, that base is not subject to local or state jurisdiction since it is situated on federal land. Thus, none of the state criminal laws can reach people living within the federal enclave. This situation can cause a great deal of local hostility to the presence of federal activities. To burden one group of people with a network of criminal laws while exempting their neighbors simply because they live in a federal enclave is to ask for unnecessary trouble. To remedy this problem, Congress enacted the Assimilative Crimes Act in 1898 (Act of July 7, 1898, 30 Stat. 717, and later amendments), which reads, "whoever . . . is guilty of an act or omission which, although not made punishable by any enactment of Congress, would be punishable if committed or omitted within the jurisdiction of the State, Territory, Possession, or District in which such place is situated, . . . shall be guilty of a like offense and subject to a like punishment" (18 U.S.C.A. § 13).

But the problem is much greater than simply a public relations matter although maintaining the proper relationships between state and federal governments is important. Federal criminal law is generally linked to federal or "national" purposes. Interstate transportation of stolen automobiles, for example, is a federal criminal offense because only the federal government can adequately deal with a multiplicity of jurisdictions in what is essentially a movable criminal activity. Therefore, federal criminal law does not contain the full range of criminal activities necessary to keep order in a local community. Rather than adopt a full criminal code, which would certainly involve many areas of conflict when enforced in the midst of local jurisdictions and state codes and county ordinances, the Assimilative Crimes Act adopts the solution of making the state criminal code determinative for federal enclaves for a variety of minor offenses.

What the Assimilative Crimes Act does is to permit the federal government to apply (assimilate) minor state criminal laws to federal enclaves, such as Indian reservations, where no definitive statement on such activity had previously existed. This extension and assimilation of a state criminal statute is another intrusion by the federal government into tribal affairs. It can assume jurisdiction over criminal offenses under the Assimilative Crimes Act that have never been specifically prohibited by either federal or tribal law. Admittedly, the offenses usually involve minor violations of state law, but the power still permits state and local communities to extend their policy preferences involving law and law enforcement indirectly upon the reservation judicial system.

The Assimilative Crimes Act appears to be quite a drastic intrusion into Indian matters. Actually, the encroachment is fairly restrictive. In the first place, since the Assimilative Crimes Act is made applicable to the reservations through the General Crimes Act, it is limited only to interracial crimes. Hence, it does not apply to offenses that are committed by and between two Indians on the reservations. There must be an Indian–non-Indian relationship involved before the act comes into effect. Second, the Supreme Court in *Williams v. United States*, 327 U.S. 711 (1946), indicated that the Assimilative Crimes Act applies only when no federally defined crime exists. This restriction means that state criminal acts cannot be substituted for federal criminal statutes. Only in the absence of a federally defined statute can the state ordinance be applied to the reservations. When the act is applied, the court simply adopts the state definition of the crime and applies it to the reservation.

An example of the application of the Assimilative Crimes Act is revealed in the case of *United States v. Marcyes*, 557 F.2d 1361 (9th Cir. 1977). Marcyes operated a fireworks stand on the Puyallup Indian Reservation. The state of Washington had a law that precluded the sale and use of fireworks. While neither the federal government nor the Puyallup tribe had laws pertaining to the sale of fireworks, Marcyes was prosecuted and convicted under the Assimilative Crimes Act for violating the Washington law. The main issue that occupied the attention of the federal court actually revolved around the nature of the Washington law and not whether it applied to the Indian reservation via the Assimilative Crimes Act. Marcyes had argued that the Washington statute was regulatory in nature, as opposed to prohibitory, and thus fell beyond the scope of the Assimilative Crimes Act. The federal court rejected this contention concluding that the law was prohibitory and properly fell within the purview of the Assimilative Crimes Act. Leaving aside this issue, the Marcyes case is an excellent illustration of how a state criminal law can be made applicable to Indian Country.

The Indian Civil Rights Act of 1968

The Indian Civil Rights Act of 1968 has already been discussed at length in an earlier chapter exploring the power of tribal courts, but it is important to re-examine it briefly with respect to criminal law issues. As will be recalled, the 1968 act placed a number of procedural restrictions upon tribal courts in the handling of criminal cases. Most of the guarantees found in the Bill of Rights were codified and made applicable to tribal court proceedings. The right to retained counsel, the privilege against self-incrimination, the right to confrontation and cross-examination of witnesses—all are procedural requisites that Indian defendants are assured under the 1968 act.

There is little doubt that the ICRA imposes a variety of non-Indian norms and values on tribal court proceedings. A real fear of tribal judges is that incorporation of these values and norms will erode even further the attempt by Indians to preserve many of the traditions and customs of Indian culture that remain today. The "win or lose" approach of Anglo-American law together with the concept of retribution and deterrence as the primary sentencing goals are still somewhat foreign to traditional Indian thought and communities. And the imposition of many of the provisions of the 1968 Indian Civil Rights Act is predicated upon precisely this type of Anglo-American jurisprudence.

Perhaps the most important limitation emanating from the 1968 act relates to the available sanctions that tribal judges may impose in criminal cases. Paragraph seven of section 1302 of the act limits tribal judges to criminal penalties, which do not exceed a fine of $500 or six months' imprisonment, or both. This limitation effectively eliminates tribal courts from regulating serious criminal activity in Indian Country. For all practical purposes, the act indirectly bestows exclusive jurisdiction on the federal courts in the handling of major crimes. This result is especially disconcerting, as we shall see later in this chapter, because the role of the federal government in dealing with serious criminal conduct on the reservations has been far from satisfactory.

Public Law 280

The final piece of federal legislation that needs to be examined in this discussion of crime in Indian Country is Public Law 280 of the Eighty-third Congress. In the sixth decade of this century, the Eisenhower administration adopted the policy of terminating federal supervision over Indians and their property with the ultimate goals of assimilating them into American society and eliminating the reservation enclaves of Indian culture. One of the legislative devices to accomplish this goal was the passage of P.L. 280. The statute transferred both civil and criminal jurisdiction over reservation Indians to certain states and gave permission to other states to amend their constitutions (which had a disclaimer clause required as a condition of their admission to the Union) so that they could assume jurisdiction if they desired. Initially, five states were specifically named: California, Minnesota (except the Red Lake Chippewa Reservation), Nebraska, Oregon (except the Warm Springs Reservation), and Wisconsin (except the Menominee Reservation). Because the states could not touch either Indian hunting and fishing rights or tribal and individual property held in trust by the federal government, the assumption was basically a unilateral demand that states pay additional funds to assume the federal responsibilities without the benefit of any additional income to balance the account.

Since 1953 a variety of state statutes have been passed giving at least partial civil or criminal jurisdiction to a number of other states. Prior to 1968, tribal consent was not needed before such a transfer of responsibilities could be effective. Some states, such as Arizona, attempted to extend their jurisdiction without making any formal legislative statement of their intent to do so. The plenitude of tax and jurisdictional cases that marked the 1960s and 1970s in Arizona is due specifically to this failure to act in accordance with the provisions of P.L. 280. In many states tribes and state governments negotiated agreements whereby state governments would assume certain functions in the absence of tribal capabilities to act. Old age programs, confinement of the mentally ill, provisions for orphans, and other basically social welfare activities were generally subjects of cooperative ventures or cessions of jurisdiction.

The impact of P.L. 280 on tribal governments located in the participating states was devastating. Tribal court authority and law enforcement on the reservations involved were eliminated and replaced by state authority. Whereas the federal encroachments into Indian control over reservation crimes had been significant, under P.L. 280 state displacement of tribal authority was even more complete. Many states, particularly at the county level, refused to provide any real police protection or court services until they were allowed to tax the reservation lands. Since Congress refused to allow state taxation, this impasse meant that law enforcement was a catch-as-catch-can operation and wholly arbitrary on the part of state officials. No one actually knew whether or not a complaint would be heeded and law became a sporadic episode in a context where rigid enforcement had once held sway.

Hunting and fishing problems seemed important in states that had accepted the P.L. 280 provisions, and state fish and game agencies insisted on reading the federal law ceding civil and criminal jurisdiction as if it had given them absolute control over these resources. These problems became more complicated with the increase in the number of non-Indians turning to outdoor recreational pursuits, and the runs of fish decreased rapidly under the impact of increased commercial and recreational fishing. Tribes eventually had to adopt their own codes for fish and game management and go to the federal courts to prevent state intrusions in this critical area.

No one really had much understanding of how P.L. 280 was supposed to work. It had been rushed through Congress without much thought and its sponsors, when queried about its impact, answered with the traditional conservative doctrine that states were much more efficient than the federal government in dealing with people's problems. Whether such a response was philosophically true or not, it did little in the way of offering guidelines for practical law enforcement. Tribes were particularly traumatized because P.L. 280 appeared to be simply the first shot in a prolonged and arbitrary war against them. Having little real understanding of the nature of the legislative process, even after the jurisdictional provisions were amended in 1968 to provide for tribal consent prior to the assumption of state jurisdiction, tribes kept demanding that P.L. 280 be repealed. Noting that it was still on the books (albeit as a historical curiosity after the ICRA), tribal leaders demanded that it be completely repealed. What they really sought, perhaps, was expungement of the federal statute books, but their confusion over the status of P.L. 280 contributed no little to the continued puzzlement on the part of everyone concerned about what the law really meant in the contemporary world. Thus part of the confusion and concern over P.L. 280 comes from the emotional heritage that the federal relationship with its frequent twists and turns has bequeathed to us.

While an examination of federal legislation can be less than an exciting endeavor, it is extremely important if one is to gain a real understanding of tribal control over criminal activity in Indian Country. These five statutory enactments—the General Crimes Act, the Major Crimes Act, the Assimilative Crimes Act, the Indian Civil Rights Act of 1968, the Public Law 280—have all encroached severally and separately upon tribal powers to deal with crime on the reservations. At one time tribes had exclusive jurisdiction over such issues. Today, their authority is but a skeleton of past powers and prestige. With this condition in mind, let us now proceed to look into some of the general jurisdictional problems faced when attempting to determine which level of government is entitled to try criminal offenders.

CRIMINAL JURISDICTION: BRINGING ORDER
TO A COMPLEX MAZE

The jurisdictional maze that has clouded the Indian system of justice has confused layperson, lawyer, judge, and bureaucrat alike. The basic question to be resolved is which level of government assumes jurisdiction over criminal offenses in Indian Country—the federal government, the state governments and their subdivisions, or the tribal governments. The answer to this question revolves around the interrelationship of three factors: (a) the location where the crime is committed, (b) the particular statute that has been violated, and (c) the type of persons involved in the crime (Indian/non-Indian). Only by carefully examining each of these factors can one bring some type of order to this jurisdictional maze. Table 3 presents a jurisdictional chart interrelating all three of the factors discussed above.

The first factor to be examined in attempting to identify which level of government has jurisdiction over reservation crimes relates to the location where the crime is committed. The critical question to be asked is whether or not the offense geographically falls within the confines of Indian Country. If the answer is no, the tribal courts generally have no jurisdiction at all, with one exception. The exception to this rule involves the preservation of tribal rights to fish at "usual and accustomed places." Unless the fishing site is an allotment in trust, and most are not generally allotments, the fishing site would not be Indian Country in a precise technical sense but the violations of the tribal fishing codes would be matters for tribal consideration. At any rate, most of the offenses committed outside Indian Country fall within state jurisdiction since the states are the primary units charged with law enforcement. Still, there are federal criminal laws and if an accused has violated a federal law the federal courts would assume jurisdiction over the matter.

If the offense involved does occur in Indian Country, one must look to the relevant statutes (discussed in the preceding section) to determine where the jurisdiction lies. The first statutory inquiry is to see if Public Law 280 applies. Remember, P.L. 280 vests criminal jurisdiction of reservation crimes in the states in which the reservations are geographically located. Though this law applies to but a few states, where it does apply, only the states have jurisdiction. Tribal and federal authority are extinguished or superseded, with the exception that some state statutes permit tribal courts to exercise concurrent jurisdiction.

If a crime occurs in Indian Country and P.L. 280 is not applicable, jurisdiction is then determined by matching the relevant statute

TABLE 3. Criminal Jurisdiction and the Indian System of Justice

Location Where Crime Is Committed	Federal Jurisdiction	State Jurisdiction	Tribal Jurisdiction
I. In non-Indian Country			
A. Federal law involved	Yes	No	No
B. State law involved	No	Yes	No
C. Tribal law involved	No	No	Maybe
II. In Indian Country (where P.L. 280 or specific statute applies)	No	Yes	No
III. In Indian Country (no P.L. 280)			
A. Crimes by Indian v. Indian			
1. Major Crimes Act	Yes	No	No[b]
2. Other crimes	No	No	Yes
B. Crimes by Indian v. non-Indian			
1. Major Crimes Act	Yes	No	No[b]
2. General Crimes Act	Yes	No	Yes[c]
3. Assimilative Crimes Act	Yes	No	Yes
C. Crimes by non-Indian v. Indian			
1. General Crimes Act	Yes	No	No
2. Assimilative Crimes Act	Yes	No	No
D. Crimes by non-Indian v. non-Indian	No	Yes	No
E. Victimless and consensual crimes			
1. Crimes by Indians	No	No	Yes
2. Crimes by non-Indians		Yes[a]	
a. General Crimes Act	Yes	Yes[b]	No
b. Assimilative Crimes Act	Yes	Yes[b]	No

Source: Based on material in Getches, Rosenfelt, and Wilkinson, pp. 385–389.
[a]Some statutes permit concurrent jurisdiction.
[b]The law is unsettled in these areas.
[c]If prior punishment by tribal court or as provided for by statute.

involved with the type of persons involved in the offense. Four defendant-victim classifications are possible:

1. Crimes by an Indian against an Indian.
2. Crimes by an Indian against a non-Indian.
3. Crimes by a non-Indian against an Indian.
4. Crimes by a non-Indian against a non-Indian.

Table 3 provides a breakdown of these categories and relates each to the important criminal statutes involved—the Major Crimes Act, the General Crimes Act, and the Assimilative Crimes Act. Even a casual glance at Table 3 reveals the dominant role taken on by the federal government in assuming jurisdiction in Indian Country. Tribal court jurisdiction is astonishingly limited. Its primary case-load falls within the category of "other crimes" where one Indian has committed a crime against another Indian (see Table 4), and these "other crimes" are restricted to the minor criminal infractions that occur. Technically, tribal courts can assume jurisdiction over some offenses under the General Crimes Act (if prior punishment is involved or if specifically designated by statute), as well as crimes falling under the Assimilative Crimes Act and victimless and consensual crimes. But these instances do not account for much of the tribal caseloads.

The lack of tribal court jurisdiction over many of the offenses that occur in Indian Country has been exceedingly disconcerting to Indian nations. This is particularly true with reference to crimes committed by non-Indian defendants against Indian victims. In the past many tribes have attempted to assume jurisdiction over these interracial cases, but in 1978 the Supreme Court finally precluded them from exercising this power. In the case of *Oliphant v. Suquamish Indian Tribe*, 435 U.S. 191 (1978), several non-Indians were arrested for criminal disturbances that occurred on the Port Madison Reservation during the Chief Seattle Days celebration. Over the objections of the non-Indian defendants, the tribal court assumed jurisdiction and each of the defendants was found guilty. Upon appeal to the U.S. Supreme Court, the convictions were reversed with the High Court finding that the tribal courts were without jurisdiction.

In delivering the majority opinion, Justice William H. Rehnquist engaged in a historical discussion of the development of the tribal court system in the area of criminal law. This review, coupled with his interpretation of past statutes and congressional hearings, resulted in a conclusion that Indian tribal law was enforceable only against Indian defendants. Non-Indians therefore fell outside the jurisdiction of tribal courts. They could be tried only by the state or federal courts, depending upon the statute involved. Only Congress

TABLE 4. Tribal Court Jurisdiction: Types of Criminal Offenses

Primary Caseload	Minor Caseload
1. Crimes by Indian v. Indian (nonmajor crimes only)	1. Crimes by Indian v. non-Indian a. General Crimes Act (if first punishment or statute provides) b. Assimilative Crimes Act (possible concurrent jurisdiction) 2. Crimes by Indians that are a. Victimless b. Consensual

could confer tribal courts with jurisdiction over offenses committed by non-Indians on reservations and Congress had not conferred such power on the Suquamish tribe.

Of the 127 tribal courts in operation in 1978, 33 had purported to extend their jurisdiction over non-Indian offenders. The *Oliphant* case does not necessarily invalidate all these jurisdictional provisions since each case must be decided in light of the statutory context in order to determine if Congress has or has not empowered the tribe to exercise this kind of jurisdiction. In the absence of an affirmative delegation of power by Congress, however, tribal courts cannot assume jurisdiction over crimes committed within Indian Country. In his opinion, Justice Rehnquist did note that many tribal courts were becoming more sophisticated and that the 1968 Indian Civil Rights Act had eliminated many of the non-Indian fears about the tribal administration of justice. Still, the Court indicated that the issue was a policy issue for Congress to decide and not one for resolution by the judiciary.

Like tribal court jurisdiction, state court jurisdiction is also highly restricted. Excluding the victimless and consensual crimes category (where the law is unsettled), state courts have jurisdiction over reservation offenses only when a crime is committed by a non-Indian against another non-Indian. This provision has proved to be somewhat controversial in that many tribal authorities have felt that Indians, not the states, should regulate law enforcement within the confines of Indian Country.

The modern definition of state jurisdiction over non-Indian v. non-Indian crimes emanated initially from an 1881 decision of the Supreme Court in *United States v. McBratney*, 104 U.S. 621 (1881).

The case involved a white man who murdered another white man on the Ute Reservation in southern Colorado. In the *McBratney* opinion the Court concluded that the federal government did not have jurisdiction over cases involving the criminal activity of one white man against another white man even though the crime took place on an Indian reservation. Many lower courts simply interpreted this decision to mean that state courts were to assume jurisdiction over this kind of case. While this conclusion is not precisely the rule of law in *McBratney*, it has become the accepted statement of the law as it relates to non-Indian offenses against non-Indian victims in Indian Country.

The vast jurisdictional authority that the federal courts possess in the area of criminal law should not be surprising. It fits harmoniously into the overall governmental structure that pervades the life of American Indians. Although there are reasonable arguments supporting this extraordinary exercise of federal power, especially when compared to the alternative of state jurisdiction, it has resulted in the confinement of tribal court authority to but a narrow area of criminal activity in Indian Country. With this jurisdictional background in mind, it is now time to examine the criminal system in operation to see what problems exist in the field of law enforcement and criminal prosecution.

LAW ENFORCEMENT AND CRIMINAL PROSECUTION

In 1974 the National American Indian Court Judges Association published several studies exploring the difficulties inherent in the law enforcement and criminal prosecution aspects of Indian justice ("Federal Prosecution of Crimes Committed on Indian Reservations," in *Justice and the American Indian*, vol. 5). This study is probably the most comprehensive and insightful analysis available to date and hence much of the material in this section will call upon the association's report and findings.

As Indian communities vary from reservation to reservation, so do the methods and devices used to cope with law enforcement problems. Some Indian communities employ their own tribal police and generally these are the larger tribes who have a substantial tribal budget and large geographical areas to patrol. Others use a traditional method of voluntary law enforcement. Still other tribes get their law enforcement from the Bureau of Indian Affairs, which supplies the reservation with officers. Finally, some tribes have assumed police functions with the assistance of grants from federal agencies and have supplanted federal police officers although with federal funds and continuing federal supervision. BIA police are actually employees of the Department of the Interior and are thus responsible to the agency superintendent and not to the tribal authorities. Using BIA police obviously results in a number of difficulties.

Like the recruitment of tribal police, the procedures used by Indian communities in apprehending and prosecuting criminals also vary. Admitting the vulnerability of generalizing, the procedure in a typical case is probably similar to the following:

> The initial complaint or call for assistance is made to the reservation police who respond to the scene. Where the offense involves an Indian, either as a subject or victim, and the offense is a felony, reservation police call a criminal investigator from the Bureau of Indian Affairs who generally is stationed on the reservation. He initiates the investigation and during this stage notifies the nearest F.B.I. office. Many times, the F.B.I. does not respond for several days. When the F.B.I. arrives, the agent will generally re-interview the subject and any principal witnesses. The agent will then present the case to the U.S. Attorney, generally by telephone. There is a duplication of effort and responsibility between criminal investigators of the BIA and agents of the F.B.I. The results are that, while felonious offenses on Indian Reservations may be timely investigated by the BIA, the action stops at this point, awaiting the F.B.I. and his telephone report to the U.S. Attorney. Generally, a good deal of time has elapsed since the investigation by the BIA and community feelings rise as to why the serious crimes are not handled in a timely manner. In most situations the offenders are Indians and are arrested initially on tribal charges and sometimes sentenced to tribal jail to remove them from the community while the federal government takes considerable time to decide what, if anything, it will do by way of prosecution. ("Federal Prosecution of Crimes Committed on Indian Reservations," p. 12)

Apart from the significant lapse in time between the apprehension of the wrongdoers and the indictment in federal court for the felony, several major problems arise in this context. The FBI agent seldom speaks the tribal language and must rely heavily upon the skills and evidence initially obtained by the BIA special officer but more often gathered by the tribal police. The FBI agent is always almost wholly reliant on Indian personnel for his or her information and understanding of the situation. The determination of whether or not the case shall be prosecuted rests with the U.S. attorney, who is often hundreds of miles from the reservation and is generally burdened with the immediate problems of his or her office which he or she generally regards as more important than crimes committed on the reservation. Political considerations often enter into the process if a person prominent in the tribe or a relative is the suspect. Particularly in cases of fraud, embezzlement, misappropriation of funds, or any of the white-collar crimes usually associated with administration, the propensity is to overlook or to neglect vigorous prosecution of the crime. Law enforcement on the reservations, then, is somewhat similar to that in most American cities—the politically powerful most generally escape and the poor who have committed violent crimes become the people against whom the law is enforced.

Dealing with the commission of a major crime on an Indian reservation is undoubtedly a complicated matter. Unlike the typical city experience where the lines of responsibility are well drawn and closely coordinated, on an Indian reservation there are a number of disparate agencies with different lines of command and responsibility converging on the scene and protective of their own interests. The tribal police, the law enforcement division of the BIA, the Federal Bureau of Investigation, and the United States Attorney's Office all become involved in most reservation felony cases. Each of these government units has a role to play in the resolution of the criminal case.

Tribal police.   Although their actual powers are severely restricted, the tribal police are the most important step in resolving the criminal case. They almost always discover the crime, interview the initial and best witnesses, and know the personalities and circumstances involved. Their role is one of continuing assistance throughout the entire case and every other agency is dependent upon them for its information and understanding of the case. Their recommendations are respected, particularly by the decision-makers above them in the prosecutorial role since their evaluation of the seriousness of the crime and its likely impact on the community is usually very accurate.

Bureau of Indian Affairs.   From a practical standpoint, the BIA assumes a large role in law enforcement on Indian reservations. Not only does the agency frequently provide the reservation police force, or fund some of its functions, but it also plays a very important role in criminal investigation. The Law and Order Branch of the BIA is headquartered in Washington, D.C., where it is headed by a chief of

its division. The branch has seven area offices and eighty-seven offices on Indian reservations. Each of the area offices as well as the
agency offices have special officers (criminal investigators) attached
to them. Some of the upper-echelon personnel appear to be of a high
calibre but many of the agency officers have insufficient training in
law enforcement. Like most contemporary law enforcement organizations, the Law and Order Branch has a paramilitary orientation,
which means that it emphasizes the enforcement rather than the
peace-making function of the law officer and prefers additional
weapons training to community reconciliation workshops.

Structurally, the Law and Order Branch of the BIA is highly decentralized. While the branch chief is in Washington, he or she has
little control over the conduct of the special officers in the field. The
agency special officers are responsible to the agency superintendents
on the reservations and not the chief of the branch in Washington.
Hence, the chief cannot issue directives or enforce regulations without working through the agency superintendents. The branch cannot discipline the special officers nor does it even control its own
budget. It might be argued that, given the variety of Indian tribes,
decentralization of power in the hands of each reservation agency
superintendent is desirable. But a larger problem remains. The
agency superintendent is not a law enforcement officer nor does he
or she possess the necessary training to fulfill this function. Ultimately, this arrangement places the key law enforcement decisions
in the hands of a layperson, who is often more interested in preserving the façade of law and order than in the administration of justice.
This bureaucratic arrangement is hardly a step toward improved administration of justice on reservations.

Federal Bureau of Investigation.   The FBI poses something of a
burden on law enforcement on reservations. Few FBI agents are Indians and they seldom possess sufficient understanding of Indian life
to qualify them for such an important role in the area of Indian law
enforcement. FBI offices are located in cities some distance from Indian villages and areas where Indian-related crimes take place. The
problem is really one of isolation, cultural as well as geographical.
Since FBI agents only see Indians in the context of violent crime,
they quickly become hardened and unsympathetic to Indian problems. Much of the continuing difficulty during the Wounded Knee
occupation was caused by the arbitrary and inhumane actions of the
FBI on the reservations. Constitutional rights were continually violated, unlawful searches and seizures were made, and the FBI refused
to investigate some violent deaths or quickly closed investigations
before the facts were all known by the community. It was FBI mis-

conduct that made Judge Nichols declare the Means-Banks trial a mistrial, and several other trials were marred by extralegal FBI activity.

United States attorneys. Many of the criticisms that have been directed toward the FBI in Indian Country are also applicable to the U.S. Attorney's Office. There are no Indians working in the U.S. Attorney's Office although, briefly, a Sioux Indian was the U.S. attorney in South Dakota during the Carter administration. Like the FBI, the U.S. attorneys see individual Indians primarily in the context of criminal offenses and consequently have little knowledge of tribal customs, traditions, or current conditions. The offices are located distant from the reservations and there is little direct contact between the U.S. attorneys and tribal officials apart from criminal cases. The major interaction is generally between the FBI agent who brings the case to the attention of the U.S. attorney and the attorney charged with conducting the prosecution.

One of the basic complaints emanating from tribal officials regarding the U.S. attorneys relates to the lack of articulated standards used by them in determining when a case will be pursued and when it will be dropped. There are three situational crimes, for instance, for which cases always seem to be dropped: intoxication, family disputes, and juvenile offenses. Yet, as the National American Indian Court Judges Association points out, at least one of these elements is present in a majority of criminal felony cases arising on the reservations. Grounds for deciding not to pursue a case are not always given by the U.S. attorneys. Notification of declination is haphazard and frustrating to tribal officials. At times the U.S. attorney will notify the FBI; other times it will contact the BIA. Sometimes the notice is written; other times it is simply an oral communique. Declination of cases becomes important to tribal officials, for in some instances, if the federal government decides not to prosecute, the tribal government may initiate legal action. Allowing a case to remain open with no agency prosecuting, however, reduces respect for the law and badly hampers the effective use of tribal courts.

Effective law enforcement and prosecution can hardly be achieved in Indian Country given this multiple-agency approach. As the Indian judges have noted, the problems do not lie with individuals but are inherent in an inefficient and disorganized system. Established systems, however, are rarely abolished and even seldom reformed. When changes come, they come slowly and incrementally and sometimes are designed to solve problems that have long since ceased to exist. If there cannot be a reorientation of the system so as to place more responsibility into the hands of tribal authorities, there must at least be adjustments that will permit the participating agencies to work together more efficiently and harmoniously than is now the case.

SPECIAL PROBLEMS IN LAW ENFORCEMENT

In addition to the burdens that tribal authorities bear in maintaining law and order in Indian Country, several special matters demand attention. These problems include cross-deputization, fresh pursuit, implied consent, and extradition.

Cross-deputization. Wherever state and tribal lands meet, jurisdictional problems arise. And this is compounded by the fact that a number of townsites and small cities fall within the geographical confines of Indian Country. While these townsites and cities are governed by non-Indians, they often technically fall within the legal jurisdiction of Indian Country (18 U.S.C.A. § 1151). Consequently, an Indian who commits an offense within a townsite may still be prosecuted under federal or tribal law. State authorities, however, can also arrest non-Indians in the area for violation of state law. The state usually will not arrest Indians in these enclaves since Indians cannot be prosecuted under state law for crimes committed in Indian Country (*Seymour v. Superintendent*, 368 U.S. 351 (1962)). Confusion abounds in many instances since it is often unclear where Indian Country stops and state jurisdiction begins. When one realizes that many reservations have a "checkerboard" configuration, alternating trust land of Indians and fee simple land, the chaos is expectable but hardly comprehensible.

A solution has been proposed to minimize the law enforcement problems in areas where state and tribal lands are contiguous and intermingled. That solution is cross-deputization of law enforcement personnel. Under cross-deputization, tribal police are given deputy status by state authorities and state police are given deputy status by tribal officials. In this way, both the tribal police and the state law enforcement officers will have the power to arrest wrongdoers regardless of whether the offender is Indian or non-Indian and irrespective of the location of the violation. Theoretically, this arrangement is a splendid device for minimizing the difficulties of law enforcement growing out of this problem area.

Although this solution sounds reasonable, in practice cross-deputization leaves something to be desired. Cooperation between the two governmental authorities has not been good. Sometimes only one of the governmental units is willing to cross-deputize. On some reservations the tribal police are ill trained and this lack of expertise concerns state authorities. From the tribal perspective, many state law enforcement officers are insensitive and hostile to Indians and this attitude gives tribal authorities reason to pause. The benefits that can flow from cross-deputization are too great, however, not to explore the arrangement further. Until efforts are made to minimize these problems where they still exist, cross-deputization probably will remain a solution in theory only.

Fresh pursuit. A related problem to cross-deputization in border areas is that of on-the-scene criminal pursuit. Criminal offenders frequently commit a crime in one jurisdiction (the state, for instance) and then flee into another jurisdiction (an Indian reservation). Under the common law, officers may pursue a felon from one jurisdiction into another if they are in "fresh pursuit" and arrest the offender there. The culprit may then be returned to the jurisdiction where the crime was committed and prosecuted. Under some laws, the arrested person must be turned over to the nearest local official authorized to take the person into custody. Extradition proceedings may then be initiated by the state to have the felon returned.

The fresh pursuit doctrine poses problems to Indian–non-Indian border communities. In the first place, it is customary for each of the jurisdictions involved to have a working agreement by which to legitimize the fresh pursuit process. However, these working arrangements are not always present between state and tribal officials, and a number of tribes have complained that state officers engage in fresh pursuit even in the absence of such a working agreement. Another difficulty relates to the type of culprit being pursued. A state officer may pursue a non-Indian onto the reservation for violating a state law, but Indian judges believe that state officers should not be able to pursue Indians onto the reservation unless the state officer is cross-deputized and the Indian has violated a federal or tribal law. The state officer must stop the chase at the reservation line. Conversely, a tribal police officer must stop at the reservation border when pursuing an Indian who has committed a crime on the reservation. Why, then, Indians argue, should the state officer be allowed to continue into the reservation when in fresh pursuit of a violator of state law? If the tribal police officer is cross-deputized, an arrest may be made in the state area, but again only if the person has violated a federal or tribal law.

The National American Indian Court Judges Association appears to be opposed to the doctrine of fresh pursuit. It may be that it believes that this doctrine permits too much encroachment by the white community into Indian affairs and demonstrates an insensitivity to the existence of an Indian community in its locality. When this argument is placed in the context of maintaining both law enforcement and good community relations in border areas, it demands further sensitive thought. Criminal felons, whether Indian or non-Indian, should not be able to insulate themselves from arrest simply by fleeing across a jurisdictional border. Such an atmosphere not only facilitates crimes but also fosters a continued climate of hostility and distrust among the law enforcement authorities in both Indian and non-Indian communities.

Implied consent. One of the more frustrating problems faced by tribal governments is the notion that Indians lack jurisdiction over non-Indians who commit crimes on reservations. To overcome this problem, a number of tribes have adopted "implied consent" ordinances patterned after state motor vehicle statutes. Under these implied consent ordinances, any person who comes onto the reservation impliedly consents, by virtue of his or her entry onto the reservation, to the jurisdiction of the tribal police and courts (National American Indian Court Judges Association, vol. 5, p. 50). The first of such ordinances was passed by the Salt River Pima-Maricopa Indian Community in 1972.

It is not clear whether these implied consent ordinances are legal enactments. While both the secretary of the interior and the solicitor general have indicated that they believe such ordinances to be invalid, no action has been taken to do away with them. Tribal authorities, noting that the vast majority of states have implied consent statutes for motor vehicles, continue to believe that Indians should be permitted to use statutes like these to better control non-Indian criminal activity on the reservations. The Supreme Court, in the *Oliphant* case, refused to uphold an implied consent statute of the Suquamish tribe in Washington State, but the case for the Indians was not argued on an implied consent basis. The attorneys for the Indians emphasized inherent sovereignty and only peripherally touched on the fact that the white wrongdoers in that instance had full knowledge of the tribal court's jurisdiction and had seen a prominent sign at the borders of the reservation announcing the implied consent ordinance of the tribe. Because the case was badly handled, no clear indication on the status of implied consent emerged. Indians are puzzled because their ordinances are subject to federal approval and supervision and they remain as part of the tribal code in many instances.

Oliphant held that jurisdiction over non-Indians was "inconsistent with tribal status," meaning that only Congress can give such jurisdiction, not a consenting non-Indian defendant. The fact that tribes have not acted to repeal their implied consent ordinances or that these ordinances were federally approved prior to *Oliphant* most probably does not enable them to survive this ruling. Given the reasoning in *Oliphant*, it is difficult to see how a tribe can exercise jurisdiction over a non-Indian in the absence of a permissive treaty or statutory provision. However, when one views the decision of *Mazurie*, in which a liquor ordinance of a tribe was upheld, one can surmise that tribes may be anticipating a departure from the *Oliphant* decision in the near future (419 U.S. 544, 1975).

Extradition. Extradition is the surrender of a prisoner by one sovereign (the asylum state) to another sovereign (the demanding state) so that the criminal or fugitive may be dealt with according to the laws of the latter sovereign. The process is provided for in the United States Constitution, article VI, section 2, clause 2: "A person charged in any state with treason, felony, or other crime, who shall flee from justice, and be found in another state, shall on demand of the executive authority of the state from which he fled, be delivered up, to be removed to the state having jurisdiction of the crime." This provision applies to both states and territories. All but three states have adopted a Uniform Criminal Extradition Act, which designates the prescribed procedures to follow in such proceedings.

The idea of extradition has troubled a number of Indians because the Indian conception of justice frequently differs from that of the white community. Punishment is only a secondary consideration in many instances, with victim restitution being of primary importance. Hence, tribes are reluctant to send Indians back to the Anglo-American system, where the concept of justice is foreign to that of the Indian community. Complementing this idea is the notion that, if an offender has fled to avoid punishment, the Indian community is better off without him or her. Refusing to demand extradition, then, can replace the banishment that might have been the culprit's fate under traditional law. As Indians become more mobile and pan-Indian feelings increase, attitudes are also changing. People who view traditional customs as the proper standard of behavior tend to reject extradition as an unfair application of the white law. More assimilated Indians, to whom law and order in communities is critical to any continuing stability, generally recognize that the time has come for more rigorous enforcement of legal procedures to reduce the incidence of crime.

Extradition was never a popular idea among Indians. Some tribes, such as the Seminoles of Florida, originated with the flight of Indians, slaves, and indentured servants to the swamps of the Gulf of Mexico area, and early treaties featured prolonged and profound disagreements over extradition. In one of the earlier cases, *Ex Parte*

Morgan, 20 F. 298 (D.C.W.D. Ark. 1883), the chief of the Cherokee Nation requested that the governor of Arkansas extradite Frank Morgan on a charge of murder. When the issue was finally litigated, the court reasoned that the Cherokee Nation was neither a state nor a territory within the meaning of the Constitution and hence the extradition requirements did not apply to Indian nations. Why else, the court reasoned, were extradition provisions inserted into a number of Indian treaties? Since the chief of the Cherokee Nation was not the chief executive of a state or territory, he could not make a demand to have Frank Morgan extradited from Arkansas. The 1867–1868 treaties generally had provisions that, in lieu of the extradition of "bad Indians" from the tribe, it could choose to have annuities assessed to pay for whatever damages the criminal had caused.

More recently the courts have had another occasion to discuss extradition as it applies to Indian nations in a contemporary setting. In *Arizona ex rel. Merrill v. Turtle*, 413 F.2d 683 (9th Cir. 1969), Oklahoma attempted to extradite an Indian named Turtle from the Navajo Reservation in Arizona. The Navajos had entered into several extradition agreements, but only with the states of New Mexico, Arizona, and Utah, where their lands were located. Since no agreement had been made with Oklahoma, the Navajos refused the request. Oklahoma then attempted to get Arizona to extradite Turtle. Arizona arrested the Navajo Indian but the case went to court before Turtle could be returned to Oklahoma. The federal court concluded that Arizona could not comply with the extradition demand by Oklahoma. Arizona's laws could not be extended onto the reservation, absent a clear congressional authorization. To do so would encroach upon the self-government prerogatives of the Indian tribe and this was clearly prohibited under the *Williams v. Lee* doctrine (358 U.S. 217 (1959)).

The *Turtle* case would seem to indicate that as long as a tribe has enacted some type of extradition ordinance, thus evidencing an exercise of self-government, states may not intrude into this area unless authorized to do so by Congress. If, however, a tribe has not enacted an extradition law, the legal aspects of the issue are not clear. In the absence of a tribal extradition agreement, states may be able to argue that there is no invasion of Indian self-government since the tribe has not acted in this area of concern. Indeed, at least one lower court has ruled this way in *State ex rel. Old Elk v. District Court of Big Horn*, 552 P.2d 1394 (Mont. 1976); cert denied 429 U.S. 1030 (1976).

The status of extradition as it relates to Indian Country is unsettled. Recognizing the need to bring more clarity to this issue, the National American Indian Court Judges Association has called for congressional action to permit at least enabling legislation so that tribes may enter into extradition agreements if they so desire. Additionally, the association drafted a criminal extradition code that tribes could use as a model in case they chose to move in this direction.

Dealing with the problems of criminal law in Indian Country has been frustrating for tribal officials. To a large extent the federal government has pre-empted the field, leaving tribal courts to deal with but minor infractions. The whole thrust of federal legislation has been to whittle away at what used to be extensive tribal control over crimes committed in Indian Country. Equally perplexing is the difficulty in bringing efficient and effective law enforcement to the reservations. There is a lack of cooperation and attention given to Indian affairs, particularly by the Federal Bureau of Investigation and the U.S. Attorney's Office. Organizational and systematic changes are needed if tribes are to be assured adequate law enforcement. Most important, the future must bring a greater atmosphere of trust between state and tribal law enforcement agencies. Only by overcoming this hostile atmosphere will the two governmental entities be able to work in a climate of "interdependence" so as to minimize such problems as fresh pursuit, implied consent, and extradition.

Regarding our friend, Jay Morningstar, who is still awaiting the unraveling of the jurisdictional dilemma, we must refer to Table 3, the complicated outline of the various divisions of jurisdiction. Depending upon the specific facts of this case, the identity of the man he stabbed, the arrangements made between state and federal officials, and the viewpoints of the respective district and federal attorneys, Jay could be tried in either state or federal court. His chances, in view of the violent nature of the act, of being tried in court on a lesser charge, are, of course, minimal. We leave it to the reader to pick that set of facts which he or she believes necessary to resolve this jurisdictional conflict. In choosing the set of facts that will determine jurisdiction the reader can easily see that this area of law is fraught with arbitrary and unexpected choices determined partially by historical developments and partially by the inability of the various levels of government to reach a contemporary agreement.

8. The Civil System of Justice in Indian Country

Lawyers and laypeople alike are perpetually perplexed by the intricacies and complexities of jurisdictional problems. This confusion was readily apparent in the preceding chapter in which we explored the criminal system of justice. With so many competing entities exerting their political muscle to assume control of people, lands, and subjects, it is no wonder that even the expert in Indian law can but give an educated guess as to the result of any particular case under litigation. But the network of confusion in the civil area is equally frustrating. The immensity of the law as it relates to problems of water rights, real estate transactions, taxation, natural resources, motor vehicle accidents, and domestic relations can comfortably fit into an analysis of civil law and procedure. For those with a taste for the unusual, tracing the development of some of these more specific and exotic areas of interest might well consume a lifetime without much satisfaction except the knowledge that others were fearful of treading the same ground.

In order to provide a basic understanding of the civil system of justice in Indian Country, we shall first examine how tribes dealt with some of these problems in their original context and how accommodations were gradually made when the tribes came into contact with Europeans and then came under the control of the American version of the Anglo-Saxon legal tradition. Then we will explore the civil system in operation. Here attention will focus on how civil litigation is conducted within the tribal court system. Attempts will not be made, however, to sketch out the fine points of civil proceedings as they relate to Indians who are caught up in the federal, state, or local court systems. With a grasp of the operational aspects of tribal system in hand, we shall then examine two of the more important legal issues that affect the civil system of justice in Indian Country. The first of these issues deals with the problem of Indian Country immunity from the encroachment of state civil laws, while the second issue concerns the general problem of civil jurisdiction and Indian-state conflicts of law.

TRADITIONAL CIVIL LAW

Scholars attempting to pierce the veil of Indian customs to determine the nature of tribal criminal and civil law often find themselves searching for some concept, such as property, contract, or retribution—all ideas generated and taking their meaning from the western European intellectual heritage. When tribal customs are placed in this kind of analytical context, discovery of behavior that seems to foreshadow the development of something like property then leaves the observer to conclude that a particular tribe of Indians was well on its way to a "civilized" existence and that, given considerably more time to evolve, their society would some day have the same characteristics as the one in which the observer lives.

We must remember in viewing tribal customs that the traditional and familiar concepts of property, contract, and retribution are all fragments of the Western worldview that once had the unity and integrity of tribal perspectives. The reduction of human experience created by the emphasis on specific analysis produced these disparate ideas and made it appear as if they existed independently of other ideas and areas of human life. If we subsume property, contract, and retribution under the general idea of clan and family and come to understand that these functions of social and legal organization were viewed from a group rather than an individual perspective, we will be able to see how most tribes handled their civil law matters.

Tribes existed in a fairly homogeneous universe in the sense that every aspect of life involved the whole community and flowed naturally from one thing to another. The radical distinctions that exist in our society today did not exist for most tribes and the allocation of activities was more often linked with a religious ceremonial calendar and clan heritage than with individual decisions and the sudden intrusion of technological discovery. Nature was not a scientific concept and few tribes conceived of the physical world as something apart from themselves and their participation in it. Quarrels over something like natural resources, water rights, or real estate transactions, therefore, must be seen in the context of a universal sharing by our species with other life forms and a competition between two groups of people for specific areas that they could control over a short period of time. No tribe, however, felt that it had the absolute use and power to dispose of lands, animals, or waters.

If we were to translate the tribal concepts of custom into contemporary Anglo-American concepts of law, we would find water rights, real estate transactions, and natural resources coming under one general rubric. Most often this general idea would have its roots in a religious-historical tradition that involved an ancient prophecy that predicted a long period of wandering through the continent until the people arrived at a particular place that was given to them to live on. Migration stories of the tribes, then, served as their land title claims and in the traditions of the Hopi, the Sioux, the Crow, the Chippewa, and the Iroquois we find lengthy recounting of journeys to their promised lands. Arriving at the chosen spot, the peoples then center their universe on particular landmarks and establish the primary land use rights. The persistence of generations in one locale marks out the additional claims to ownership but also allows the inclusion of neighboring peoples who have an additional claim to some particular use of the same lands.

The multiple use of lands is best illustrated in the tribes and villages of the Pacific Northwest. In that land of bounty, tribes shared rivers and fishing sites with other tribes and villages. One river might contain several species of fish that inhabited the river and made their runs at different times of the year—king salmon in June and July, steelhead trout in the wintertime. Although one tribe might exercise primary political and economic dominance over the river, it allowed other tribes to use the river for the taking of certain species of fish or for catching and preserving the same species in different ways. On the plains one tribe might relish a certain root or food while other tribes had no taste for this delicacy but had the primary use right to harvest it. The root could be used in trade with tribes desiring it and inhabiting the same land and would be traded for important items that represented real wealth to everyone.

We can suggest, therefore, that the proper perspective on tribal civil law involved a sophisticated and ancient hierarchy of use rights to lands, plants and animals, and locations. The particularities of tribal preferences were sorted out over many centuries and each tribal group was able to develop its particular relationship to the land and to develop its own unique and exclusive usages. Particularity cannot be overemphasized because tribal traditions suggest that the food chain involved an ancient covenant between particular groups of people and specific animals. The northern plains tradition of the great race between the two-leggeds and the four-leggeds to determine which should feed the other is one explanation of how the physical universe was ordered and maintained. The two-leggeds won the race thanks to the wisdom and strategy of the magpie and the four-leggeds then agreed to feed the two-leggeds with the promise that when the two-leggeds died their bodies would become part of the earth and would then help grow the grass that the four-leggeds needed for grazing. The story is simple and direct and does help explain the ecological food chain in terms of responsibilities rather than rights.

Domestic law, such as marriage, divorce, child adoption, and social welfare, all were handled through clan and family, again with the emphasis on responsibility rather than rights. Some tribes, such as those on the northern plains, had elaborate customs that dictated the behavior to be expected between close relatives, and violating a kinship custom meant serious social consequences. The family was significantly extended—in some tribes when one reached the first-cousin relationship one had reached the outer limits of the family. The second cousin then became a brother or sister and linked up again with the central figures of the family unit. In such an intense ordering of personal relationships orphanage was unusual and linkage of blood families by kinship ties and responsibilities generally extended to include everyone in the tribe in one way or another. People could and did put aside their spouses but the frequency with which this occasion was likely to happen was minimal. Often, with multiple marriages to groups of sisters, there was no need or desire to break up the family unit.

The clan or family unit was generally dominated by women, which made the grandmother the primary figure in the local band, village, or community. As we have already seen, in the Iroquois Confederacy the women had the right to choose the chiefs and, when necessary, to remove them. A large number of tribes regarded the woman as the owner of the house and the man as the provider and protector. Since the women did the majority of house- or home-related work, including gathering of food, erecting shelters, preserving meats and berries, and making the clothing, it was proper that they should be regarded as owners of the tangible property that constituted the family's possessions. Men, on the other hand, engaged primarily in war, hunting, and political matters and owned the horses, the weapons, and the utensils necessary for proper religious observance of customs.

The change to reservation life involved a major reorientation of Indian family life. Reducing the large clan networks to nuclear families meant not simply eliminating extra wives but also severing the long-established ties between the grandparents and their children. Some chiefs were outraged when informed by the agents that they must divest themselves of their extra relatives. Quanah Parker, when told that he must give up his extra wives, took the agent out to look at his wives and children, tearfully informed the agent that he loved each and every one of them, and told the agent that, if he must give them up, he could not choose which one to surrender and that the agent must do it for him.

Allotments proved even more destructive to Indian family life. Quite often, in order to break the links with relatives, families would be given allotments in widely separate places on the reservations. Grandparents might be given lands forty or fifty miles away from their children; young people just establishing a family might have their allotments deliberately selected miles from where the majority of their relatives lived. Some agents gloated that they had devised a way to stop the perpetual "visiting" that characterized Indian life at the time. Today, after nearly four and sometimes five generations of allotment experience, Indians are astounded to learn that they have inherited interests in tracts of land on other reservations or miles from where they are presently located. The record-keeping on allotments alone must now cost $10 million a year to perpetuate, indicating that this initial desire to separate families had dire administrative as well as human consequences.

Most tribes have largely continued their clan and family traditions although keeping track of kinship responsibilities in the highly mobile society of today is a complex task and one that is proving increasingly difficult. Because domestic relationships have been so highly regulated by custom, and because the courts are still seen as implements of the whites' policy, few domestic relations cases of note actually arrive in tribal courts. Most Indians prefer to settle their disputes in the traditional manner by asking for the mediation services of a tribal or community elder. Since divorce involved considerable record-keeping with respect to legal status outside the reservation, tribal courts are seeing more formal divorce petitions since the paper that is issued is needed for such things as social security and welfare payments. A surprising number of Indians, however, continue to seek neither formal marriage nor formal divorce and thus avoid the problem altogether.

With this highly informal milieu in the civil area, each effort by the BIA or the tribal council or state and county governments to impose additional bureaucratic requirements and restrictions on personal freedoms is deeply resented. Many Indians see further record-keeping and appeals to tribal courts over civil matters as efforts by the government to program all human emotions in one large institutional structure and they believe this approach to human problems to be insane. The major problem in the civil law area, then, occurs when an Indian has to deal with the requirements and expectations of the outside world or when the tribe has adopted, for whatever reasons, procedures and institutions from the outside world as a means of developing the reservation and its communities. At that point tensions generally arise between those wishing to follow the old ways and the people who wish to operate the tribe in conformity with federal and state expectations. A fundamental question of community identity arises and we begin to see various symptoms of tribal and community social breakdown as people are unable to find the proper balance between old and new.

THE CIVIL SYSTEM IN OPERATION

The Supreme Court has described Indian tribes as "domestic dependent nations." As such they are endowed with all the requisites of internal sovereignty. The tribes are self-governing, capable of making their own constitutions, passing their own laws and ordinances, and setting up the judicial machinery to enforce recognized legal obligations among tribal members. When a legal obligation is breached, the injured party may go to the tribal court to seek redress.

For the tribal court to entertain a civil case, it must have jurisdiction over the subject matter of the action and/or personal jurisdiction over the contending parties. Determining jurisdiction is very difficult at times and often pits one court against another. A tribal court, for instance, may insist that it has jurisdiction over a particular action, while a state court may also lay claim to jurisdiction. It is not infrequent that one of the litigants will attempt to invoke the tribal court's authority while the other will strive to have the state assume control over the proceedings. These Indian-state conflicts of law will be dealt with later in this chapter. For the purposes of illustrating the tribal civil justice system in operation, we shall assume that the tribal court has jurisdiction over the subject matter (that is, the alleged civil wrong occurred within the confines of the reservation) and personal jurisdiction over the competing litigants (both parties to the proceeding are Indians living on the reservation). This set of circumstances invokes tribal jurisdiction in the purest sense of the word. Let's take a hypothetical case to illustrate some of the complexities. In the summer of 1980, Thomas Jayhawk purchased a tractor from Elton Johnshoe, the owner of the Yaqui Tractor and

Machine Company. Both Thomas Jayhawk and Elton Johnshoe are Yaqui Indians living on their home reservation. The commercial transaction took place at the Yaqui Tractor and Machine Company headquarters, which is located at Three Points, Arizona, the Yaqui Reservation capital. When Jayhawk first attempted to plow his north forty with the newly acquired tractor, he found it to be defective in a number of respects. When he brought this defective condition to the attention of Johnshoe and demanded his money back, Johnshoe insisted that the tractor was in good shape when he sold it and thus disclaimed any responsibility. Thomas Jayhawk felt he had been defrauded and decided to take some legal steps to get redress.

When one decides to pursue a legal grievance in the Anglo-American legal system, the first step is usually to consult an attorney, have him or her evaluate the chances of success in litigation, and have the attorney attempt to work things out amicably with a telephone call or visit. After a series of letters or visits in which there is no satisfaction, the aggrieved party usually authorizes the attorney to pursue litigation and a suit is filed in the state or county court. Locating an attorney is usually not the first step taken by an Indian party in attempting to get satisfaction. Informal inquiries are generally made regarding the honesty, attitude, and family relationships of the party with whom the problem exists. Relatives or community elders are asked, as a personal favor, if they will intervene in the situation and seek satisfaction on behalf of the person who seeks redress. In many instances, finding the proper person resolves the difficulty. The elder, visiting with the seller of the tractor in this instance, may well engage in a rambling discussion of their mutual childhood experiences, how things have radically changed since they were young, what good times they once experienced, and how now, in this circumstance, the elder knows that the person will treat his or her relative or friend properly.

These informal visits might seem to the non-Indian observer as useless and irrelevant to the problem at hand. But they are very useful in the Indian community context. Elders do not simply represent themselves or the aggrieved party but represent large families and lifetime relationships. Grievances between tribal individuals are not individual matters. Instead, they involve large numbers of people and, if not resolved, can cause bad blood between families for generations. Individuals accused of wrongdoing, therefore, think very carefully about their obstinance in making good on their contracts. They might start a feud that would last several generations and involve countless people not presently involved in any difficulties. Therefore, most disputes of a civil nature are resolved at this point in the

process because social pressures are very great and the two contending parties are seen as violators of the community peace and stability. Contrast this picture with the typical non-Indian community,
where disputes, although heated and quite emotional at times, do not
generally involve extensive family feelings or the possibility of a continuing feud between large groups of people over several generations.

Let us assume, however, that Johnshoe is unusually immune to
social and family pressures and that it appears as if Jayhawk will
have to file formal charges in the tribal court. Where the non-Indian
immediately authorizes an attorney to prepare and file the proper papers and places the prosecution of the suit largely in the hands of the
hired counsel, the Indian individual now seeks private counsel with
the tribal judge. During this informal discussion Jayhawk will inquire about the judge's evaluation of community attitudes. If his
case seems to appear frivolous to the judge, or the judge's gauge of
the community, most often Jayhawk will forget the matter and assume the loss himself. As an Indian he is well aware that in a small
community, even if one is absolutely in the right, pursuing an individual right to the point of disruption of the peace of the community
is regarded as extremely bad manners and may bring down the wrath
of the community on him—even though there is no question that he
is right in his contentions.

But let us assume that the tribal judge has heard of this problem
and that he or she has properly evaluated the attitude of the community. People do think that Jayhawk has been wronged, other people
have had this same experience with Johnshoe, and there are sufficient indications that the community would support some kind of
formal punitive measures against Johnshoe by the tribal court so
that his deviant behavior can be curbed. Jayhawk now has the assurance that his perceived personal injury is known and shared by
the community, that its sense of justice and redress is similar to his
feeling, and that should he be successful in his litigation, his victory
will not be regarded by the community as having taken unfair advantage of Johnshoe. Jayhawk will now proceed to push the case cautiously, relying on what he thinks will be a continuing feeling of in-
justice shared by the community, which will give him ultimate
justification.

Carefully evaluating community feelings is something akin to
appealing to a jury prior to the presentation of the case. But in Indian
society this careful approach is absolutely essential because one
needs support from the community in settling disputes that involve
community members. Were Jayhawk to move at once with sophisticated motions, extensive evidence, and complicated legal arguments

against Johnshoe, the community might well feel that he was using the law to take advantage of his opponent and that through trickery and manipulation of formal institutions Jayhawk had succeeded when his case did not warrant such a victory. When we contrast this need for community reassurance with attitudes toward law in the non-Indian community, we see a substantial difference in the attitude toward legal institutions. Non-Indians *expect* their lawyers to win at any cost, to use whatever procedural devices are available to win, and to press for the maximum advantage at every step of the process. Civil actions are generally regarded as private business in the white world; they are seen as community business in the Indian world.

If the Jayhawk-Johnshoe case does begin to look as if it must be resolved in court, the tribal judge will usually make an informal visit to Johnshoe and explain, as he did to Jayhawk, the consequences of community attitudes toward this quarrel. The presence of the tribal judge is usually a powerful deterrent to continued obstinacy. He or she represents not simply the law adopted by the tribe in its judicial code but also, and more important, the collected and distilled opinion of the community. The tribal judge's pleas for a peaceful resolution of the situation are generally not disregarded. Since the circumstances of the conflict are now community knowledge and since many of the relatives involved have already made up their minds about the final resolution of this problem, most generally there will appear at this stage of the conflict an indication that the judge should help seek a peaceful resolution of the dispute.

Unlike the non-Indian judicial system, which often seems to be a "winner take all" contest, seldom does one party win and the other lose in a tribal court. Instead a compromise is reached. The judge might suggest that Johnshoe provide free parts to remedy the defects in the tractor. He or she may also suggest that Jayhawk, along with his nephew who is a mechanic, and Johnshoe should work together to put the tractor into working condition. There may be some hurt feelings along the way. Some concessions entirely unrelated to the tractor may have to be made by both parties. And it may appear to the outside observer of the process that the solution to the dispute is actually an avoidance of the original cause of action. But generally the problem is solved and no one feels that he has been dispossessed of his possessions by the arbitrary and mechanical functioning of the legal process. What is most important in Indian tribal courts and particularly in Indian civil actions in tribal courts is that everyone perceives that there was some merit in both parties' arguments and that justice was done on behalf of the community.

The process described above still exists in many tribal courts although the contemporary efforts to upgrade tribal courts, to make them courts of record, and to ensure that full faith and credit will be given them by other judicial forums have meant that the informality of this process is under increasing attack by the requirements of formality that the non-Indian system demands. In some tribal courts today, Thomas Jayhawk might well seek legal redress by first contacting a Legal Services attorney working with the tribal judicial officers and discussing his complaint. If the attorney thinks that Jayhawk's claim is well founded, the attorney, together with an advocate, will file a formal complaint against Elton Johnshoe. Since most tribal courts do not permit attorneys to participate directly in tribal court proceedings, each party is assigned both an attorney and an advocate who will act as Jayhawk's representative. Upon being served with notice that he is being sued, Elton Johnshoe will employ an attorney and will find an advocate to make his presentation in tribal court.

As in the Anglo-American court system, the parties will initially try to settle the dispute without going to trial. Here the attorneys, advocates, and at times even the tribal judge will strive to negotiate the matter at an informal pretrial conference. If this fails, the conflict is taken to court. While the tribal proceeding is a bit more formal than the one previously described, even with the presence of attorneys assisting the parties it is still fairly unstructured. What has radically changed, however, is the fact that, once the proceedings begin, Anglo-American adherence to judicial procedure is fairly important and the litigation begins to resemble the "winner take all" contest of non-Indian society.

The competitive claims are presented to the tribal judge by the respective advocates, who are assisted by each of the attorneys. The advocates call witnesses, conduct direct and cross-examinations, present arguments, and comment on evidence. The tribal judge usually plays a much more active role in the proceedings than his or her counterpart in the Anglo-American system. If the judge wants to hear a particular witness that neither side has called, he or she summons the witness to court and conducts the interrogation. If one side has not presented the type of evidence that the judge feels should be submitted, he or she sends the advocate out to get the additionally required evidence. The rigid rules of evidence adhered to by Anglo-American courts are not necessarily followed by tribal court judges. Tribal court judges, of course, usually do not have law degrees and are concerned more with fundamental fairness in handling the case than with the intricacies of the rules of evidence.

As with the tribal judge in the more informal systems, the deci-sion-making style of almost all tribal courts is more mediation than adjudication. It should not be surprising, therefore, to learn that the tribal judge in this case concluded that the issue be resolved in the following manner. Elton Johnshoe should not be selling defective tractors to anyone. But, given the fact that Elton is having financial difficulties, he will only have to provide Thomas Jayhawk with the parts necessary to remedy the defects in the tractor. Jayhawk, with his nephew who is a mechanic, can use these parts and fix the trac-tor on his own. Incidentally, it probably would be a good idea if Elton Johnshoe gave them a hand as well just to show that he is imbued with the spirit of tribal brotherhood.

To the keen observer it might appear that this solution sounds a good deal like the one reached by the more informal tribal court sys-tem. Why then do tribal systems burden themselves with attorneys and advocates and procedures that sometimes frustrate all con-cerned? Why not just let the judge informally resolve legal disputes as the titular head of the Indian family? One answer to this question can be attributed to the fact that, in creating tribal court systems, the Washington bureaucracy has imposed many of the Anglo-American procedures on the Indian system. More important, perhaps, is the notion that regularized procedures designed to maximize full disclo-sure on each side of an issue cannot help but assist in bringing about a fair decision. As long as vestiges of the modern-day jurisprudence of the Anglo-American system can be blended with the tribal sys-tem without obstructing or hindering the "mediation" goal of the proceedings, the system will remain viable and true to its Indian purpose.

IMMUNITY FROM STATE ENCROACHMENT

One of the persistent themes that has tormented tribal governments throughout Indian history deals with aggressive attempts by state governments to extend their laws into Indian Country. With exten-sion of state legislation comes the assumption of state jurisdiction over legal disputes arising on the reservation and this intrusion has been no small concern to tribal authorities. In the early 1950s, the states were successful in convincing Congress to pass Public Law 280, which imposed state civil and criminal jurisdiction over some reservations in a number of identified states. On the whole, how-ever, tribal governments have been successful in maintaining a pro-tective shield from this threatened civil encroachment. Still, pressure from state governments has not subsided in this area of concern, especially in view of the fact that Indian Country holds so much in the nature of mineral wealth. The importance of this continuing Indian-state political struggle requires careful examination.

Earlier in this book we discussed several critically important Supreme Court decisions that provide the foundation for understanding the legal development of tribal immunity against intrusion of state civil laws. This quartet of important decisions includes *Worcester v. Georgia, The Kansas Indians, Williams v. Lee,* and *McClanahan v. Arizona State Tax Commission.* We shall not take the time to reiterate all the facts and doctrines articulated in these decisions but will simply refresh the reader's recollection with a brief summary of these cases. Each of the decisions promulgates an important principle that has expanded or contracted the ability of Indian tribes to remain free from state civil jurisdiction. Let us summarize them briefly.

Worcester v. Georgia, 31 U.S. (6 Pet.) 515 (1832): "Indian nations are distinct political communities possessing internal sovereignty. They are capable of self-government and are completely independent of and separate from the states. Hence, state laws cannot be extended into Indian Country nor may states exercise civil or criminal jurisdiction in Indian Country." The opinion of the Court in *Worcester* is abundantly clear. The judicial branch was erecting a protective barrier insulating Indian tribes from any type of state intrusion. States could not extend their laws into Indian Country nor could they assume civil jurisdiction of matters arising on the reservations. The constitutional allocation of Indian affairs to the federal government and its consequent denial to state governments of the power and right to deal with Indian tribes cannot be changed by any unilateral action on the part of state governments.

The Kansas Indians, 5 Wall. 737 (1866): "If the tribal organization is preserved intact, and recognized by the political department of the federal government as existing, then the Indians are a people distinct from others and to be governed exclusively by the federal government." The primary argument raised by state officials is that the change of conditions between the assumption of federal supervision and the present has so fundamentally altered the culture, status, and economic conditions of the Indians as to make further federal protection unnecessary. The Court articulated with some degree of precision the nature of the Indian-federal link as predominantly political and not cultural, social, or economic. Whatever other considerations might be made in deciding an Indian case, the basic fact remains that the relationship of Indians and the federal government is a wholly unique political tie that can only be severed or loosened by the specific and unambiguous action of the Congress.

Williams v. Lee, 358 U.S. 217 (1958): "In the absence of Congressional legislation, states may not extend their laws or exercise jurisdiction on a reservation if this would infringe upon the right of Indians to govern themselves." *Williams v. Lee* falls within the scope of the traditional federal protective umbrella shielding tribes from state actions but is viewed by some observers as a significant departure from the impregnable fortress that *Worcester* and *The Kansas Indians* provide. Under the *Williams* ruling it could be argued that states could extend their jurisdiction over certain subject matters on the reservations but only if their laws did not infringe on the exercise of tribal self-government. The critical question revolves around whether or not a conflict existed between the exercise of state jurisdiction and the self-governing powers of the Indians. If there is no significant intrusion, the states are free to extend their jurisdiction. Presumably, any effort by any state to extend its laws over certain subject matters on a reservation would call for immediate tribal action on the same subject matter attempting to pre-empt the field and eliminate what was perceived to be a vacuum in the exercise of tribal sovereignty.

In 1973 the Supreme Court moved some distance away from a doctrinaire interpretation of the *Worcester* concept. Indian sovereignty, while still an important concept, was relegated to a less important position, and a new doctrine, federal preemption of subject matter, was described as of primary importance in the case of *McClanahan v. Arizona State Tax Commission*.

McClanahan v. Arizona State Tax Commission, 441 U.S. 164 (1973): "The concept of sovereignty is to be used only as a 'backdrop' against which applicable statutes and treaties are to be read. If the statutes and treaties give rise to the fact that the federal government has 'preempted' the field, states may not exercise jurisdiction or otherwise intrude into Indian Country." There is little doubt that *McClanahan* and its principle of federal pre-emption have displaced *Worcester* as the primary consideration that federal courts will now make in determining when states may extend their laws onto the reservations. But as important as *McClanahan* is, the opinion fails to bring much understanding to just how tribal sovereignty as a "backdrop" for analysis should be used. Clearly the Court was not abandoning tribal sovereignty completely and there is significant evidence that much of its shyness in articulating a tribal sovereignty doctrine expansively came as a result of Indian militancy, which used tribal sovereignty as a rallying cry. But did the justices mean to place the doctrine on a back shelf, hoping that it would be lost in the dust of time?

In 1980 the Court provided an answer to this question. The state of Arizona had applied a motor carrier license tax and a use fuel tax on the operations of a non-Indian logging company that had contracted with the White Mountain Apaches to sell, load, and transport timber on the White Mountain Apache Reservation. The Indian tribe and the timber company joined forces in an attempt to have the taxes declared invalid. When the issue reached the Supreme Court in *White Mountain Apache Tribe v. Bracker,* 100 S.Ct. 2578 (1980), the Court held the taxes to be inapplicable as applied to the reservation activity on the ground that the federal government, having undertaken a comprehensive regulation of the harvesting and sale of tribal lumber, had pre-empted the field. This pre-emption precluded the state of Arizona from imposing its taxes on the reservation.

The *White Mountain Apache Tribe* case is extremely important in view of Justice Thurgood Marshall's discussion of the tests to be used in such disputes and the role of tribal sovereignty in making these determinations. Marshall reasoned that the "semi-independent position" of Indian tribes has given rise to two independent but related barriers to the assertion of state authority over tribal reservations. The first of these is that the federal government may have pre-empted the field (*McClanahan*). The second barrier is that state encroachment may unlawfully infringe on the right of tribal self-government (*Williams v. Lee*). Either of these barriers standing alone may be sufficient to invalidate the state intrusions. If there was any doubt as to how the Court was going to approach these problems prior to the *White Mountain Apache Tribe* case, it is clearly resolved by this decision.

In addition to delineating the role of *McClanahan* and *Williams* doctrines, Justice Marshall proceeded to elaborate further on the concept of tribal sovereignty: "Traditional notions of Indian self-government are so deeply engrained in our jurisprudence," Marshall noted, "that they have provided an important backdrop . . . against which vague or ambiguous federal enactments must always be measured." It is not helpful in cases involving American Indians to use the general laws of federal pre-emption that have emerged in other non-Indian areas of the law. The tradition of Indian sovereignty "must inform the determination whether the exercise of state authority has been pre-empted by operation of federal law." What Marshall is saying here is that tribal sovereignty as a "backdrop" for interpreting statutes assumes a meaningful role in judicial decision-making. Indian sovereignty is not to be relegated to a pleasant doctrine slowly vanishing into ambiguity. The "backdrop" requirement demands that treaties and federal statutes be interpreted "generously in order to comport with these traditional notions of sovereignty and with the federal policy of encouraging tribal independence." Under such an interpretation, federal pre-emption is much more easily demonstrated in the area of Indian affairs than in other fields of the law.

As the law stands today, then, a court, attempting to determine the validity of an attempt by a state to extend its jurisdiction into Indian Country must first examine the relevant treaties and statutes against a *meaningful* "backdrop" of tribal sovereignty to determine if federal pre-emption has occurred. If it has, then the states are foreclosed from intruding. If the court finds that federal pre-emption has not taken place, then the court turns to the *Williams* test to see if the state laws or activity conflict with tribal self-government. If they do, then the state intrusion again is invalidated. Only if there is no conflict can a state extend its jurisdiction and civil laws over the reservation.

Up to this time the Supreme Court has permitted state incursions into Indian Country in only two instances. Both cases, interestingly, deal with state attempts to extend tax laws to cover the sale of cigarettes in Indian territory. In 1976, the Supreme Court in *Moe v. Confederated Salish and Kootenai Tribes of the Flathead Indian Reservation*, 425 U.S. 463 (1976), held that the state of Montana could validly require Indian sellers on the reservation to collect a cigarette tax from *non-Indian* consumers. This collection was thought to be but a minimal burden on the Indian seller and, as a minimal burden, it would hardly interfere with tribal self-government. The tax, however, was only valid as collected from *non-Indian* consumers. The state could not extend its taxing power to Indian consumers, for this would conflict with federal statutes that had pre-empted the field and thus had been barred by *McClanahan*.

In 1980, the Supreme Court was faced with an almost identical situation. The state of Washington had imposed a tax on cigarettes sold by Colville Indians to both non-Indians and Indians who were not members of the Colville tribe. Since the cigarette sales took place on the reservation, this was viewed as another attempt by a state to extend its laws into Indian Country. The Supreme Court resolved the issue in a manner similar to the way in which it handled the *Moe* decision. The Court upheld the validity of the state tax on both the white purchasers and the non-tribal Indians (*Washington v. Confederated Tribes of the Colville Indian Reservation*, 100 S.Ct. 2069 (1980)). Unfortunately, Justice Byron R. White, who delivered the opinion, did not spell out the tests incisively enough to be used in deciding issues such as these. A careful reading of the opinion, however, reveals that both the *McClanahan* test and the *Williams* doctrine are used. White noted that "the federal statutes cited to us, even when given the broadest reading to which they are fairly susceptible, cannot be said to pre-empt Washington's sales and cigarette taxes" (at 2082). This statement is clearly an application of the *McClanahan* pre-emption test. Later in the opinion White also alludes to the Williams doctrine: "Washington does not infringe the right of reservation Indians to 'make their own laws and be ruled by them'" (at 2083).

The Court in the *Colville Indian* case thus permitted the state of Washington to extend its civil law onto the reservation. But it is important to note that the extension of state jurisdiction is extremely limited. The thrust of the statute was designed to reach (*a*) non-Indians and (*b*) Indians who were not members of the Colville tribe. Indeed, the only burden the Colville tribe had to assume was in the collection of the state tax and this was felt to be a minimal imposition on the tribe. And while the Colville traders did argue that they were being denied a competitive marketing advantage by having to collect the state tax from nontribal consumers, the Court refused to accept this argument. The denial of an artificial competitive market advantage was viewed as not contravening the right of the reservation Indians to make their own laws and to be ruled by them.

Indian tribes will properly conclude that the *Colville* case is important in that it permits the incursion of a state taxing authority into Indian Country. Phrased in terms of preserving tribal sovereignty, the decision is not fatal because it clarifies the objective of the state law dealing with non-Indians and nontribal members; the sanctity of the reservation is preserved for tribal members. But *Colville* drastically narrows the scope and usefulness of the tribal taxing power as an economic tool that is useful to tribal members and Indian property. States, after all, can attract business from other states by offering tax advantages and they create tax shelters that obviously injure other states when businesses move to obtain these benefits. *Colville* in effect limits the rights of tribes to use their sovereign taxing powers and tax immunities to do much the same thing. Not only is the loss of a competitive market advantage economically injurious, but it also works directly against the federal policy of providing a means for Indians to become self-sustaining.

There is no doubt that the flow of Supreme Court decisions has been away from the firm stance of immunity that *Worcester v.*

Georgia and *The Kansas Indians* afforded Indian tribes. The trend of decisions, however, may be a reflection of the changing relationship between Indian reservations and white communities. Tribes are not becoming more isolated from white society; rather, their activities are becoming more interconnected with it. As the contact between Indians and whites increases, particularly in the economic field where competition may be present, the more states are going to attempt to extend their laws and jurisdiction into the affairs of the reservations. The decisions of the Supreme Court are a mirror of these changing conditions. In responding to the intricacies of this closer Indian-state contact, there is every indication that the Court will continue to preserve the sanctity of Indian affairs on the reservation from state encroachment in most respects.

THE INDIAN-STATE CONFLICT OF LAWS

Attempts by the states to impress their laws and jurisdiction into Indian Country are not the only civil controversies confronting Indian tribes and state officials. Legal disputes frequently give rise to a question as to which legal entity has jurisdiction over a given problem, the tribal court or the state court. Both sovereigns may have laws that seem to suggest that each is endowed with the authority to hear the case. Often one of the litigants will attempt to invoke the jurisdiction of the state court while the other litigant will claim that the jurisdiction rightfully belongs to the tribal court. This type of issue gives rise to a classic "conflict of laws" situation. It provokes a legal controversy over which court system has the power to hear and determine the case.

A court's authority to hear and determine a case is usually predicated upon its jurisdiction over (a) the subject matter of the dispute or (b) the parties involved in the dispute (personal jurisdiction). If, for instance, an accident occurs within a state, the state court may assume jurisdiction since the subject matter of the dispute (the accident) occurred within the confines of the state's borders. Personal jurisdiction is invoked when the parties, as opposed to the subject matter, fall under the authority of the court. If two opposing litigants are domiciled within the state, that is, personally and geographically living within its borders, then the state court may assume jurisdiction over their persons so as to entertain jurisdiction. Unfortunately, many of the problems of tribal court civil jurisdiction are not this easily resolved.

As with other significant legal issues, the case of *Williams v.*

Lee, 358 U.S. 217 (1958), assumes an important role in resolving these tribal-state conflicts. The underlying philosophy of *Williams* is designed to protect tribal interests from state intrusions. Absent congressional intent to the contrary, states may not extend their laws into Indian Country if the state laws would infringe upon tribal self-government. Hence, one must begin with the general notion that any conflict between a state civil law and a tribal law regarding reservation affairs is to be resolved in favor of the Indian tribe. But this is only the beginning of a complicated network of jurisdictional conflicts, and while *Williams* constitutes the general guideline for understanding these conflicts, it cannot be universally applied. If *Williams v. Lee* completely covered the situation, tribal courts would logically assume jurisdiction over almost all incidents and legal problems that occurred on Indian reservations. In the parlance of the legal profession, tribal courts would assume subject matter jurisdiction over all incidents occurring in Indian Country. But this is not the case.

With but one exception, tribal courts limit their civil jurisdiction to two areas of concern:

1. When the *defendant* is a member of the tribe or falls within its jurisdiction.
2. When the dispute is between a tribal member and non-member and the issue is brought before the tribal court by stipulation of both parties. (Canby, pp. 220–221)

The first of these two categories obviously is the more important, for tribal court jurisdiction in civil cases is invoked only when the *defendant* is a member of the tribe. Hence, if an accident occurs on the reservation, assuming no stipulation by the parties, the following jurisdictional situations can arise:

1. If both the plaintiff and the defendant are tribal members, the tribal court has jurisdiction.
2. If the plaintiff is a non-Indian and the defendant is a tribal member, the tribal court has jurisdiction.
3. If the plaintiff is a tribal member and the defendant is a non-Indian, the state court probably has jurisdiction, although this point has not yet reached the Supreme Court for clarification.
4. If the plaintiff is a non-Indian and the defendant is a non-Indian, the state court has jurisdiction.

Surprisingly, Indians are forced to seek civil redress against non-Indians in state courts regardless of the fact that the subject matter or incident involved arose on the reservation.

Requiring non-Indian plaintiffs to sue Indian defendants in tribal court has caused difficulties in the past. In *Schantz v. White Lightning*, 231 N.W.2d 812 (1975), a non-Indian plaintiff attempted to sue an Indian defendant in a state court for injuries sustained in an accident that occurred on the reservation. The injuries were caused by the Indian's negligence. The state court and, later, the federal court both dismissed the complaint, noting that this issue fell under tribal jurisdiction. The problem, however, was that the tribal court's jurisdiction extended only to $300, which would not begin to compensate the plaintiff for his loss. This restriction effectively precluded Schantz from redressing his injury. Nominal limits on tribal court civil jurisdiction as found in *Schantz* are not uncommon and this limitation clearly results in a legal defect adversely affecting an innocent injured party.

This legal quagmire concerning whether tribal or state courts should assume jurisdiction in civil matters could easily be remedied. There is no good reason why tribal courts should not assume jurisdiction over all civil matters arising on the reservations regardless of whether the defendant in a case is an Indian or a non-Indian. When Indians venture off the reservation they subject themselves to the jurisdiction of the state courts. It should logically follow that when non-Indians journey into Indian Country they should also fall under the jurisdiction of the tribal courts if they commit any civil injuries. Congress could easily provide this change in jurisdictional limitations if it so desired. And there is little doubt that the courts would uphold it. Providing tribal courts with civil jurisdiction over civil wrongs committed on the reservations is in complete harmony with the prevailing philosophy of *Williams v. Lee* as well as with the contemporary notion of Indian self-determination.

The concept of tribal self-government as emphasized in *Williams v. Lee* has been especially important when courts are faced with issues closely tied to Indian customs and traditions. Family problems, such as child custody and divorce, are but two civil issues that have been the subject of a number of tribal-state court conflicts. More often than not, it is the contesting parties that raise the conflict of laws issue. One party will seek a divorce by invoking the jurisdiction of a state court while the other litigant will attempt to have the matter litigated in tribal court. It has been held that a marriage contract entered into by two tribal members, both of whom are domiciled on their own reservation, must be governed by tribal law (*Whyte v. District Court*, 140 Colo. 334, 346 P.2d 1012 (1959)).

To allow states to infringe upon Indian customs dealing with marriage and divorce on the reservation would clearly undermine

the authority of the tribal government. Tribal courts are given jurisdiction over these matters precisely to make certain that Indian customs and traditions will be considered in any litigation. The jurisdiction of a court, however, is often determined by the "domicile"
(the established and permanent home) of the litigating parties. If,
therefore, both parties in a divorce proceeding are domiciled in the
state and not living on the reservation, a state court may accept jurisdiction of the case (*Bad Horse v. Bad Horse*, 163 Mont. 445, 517
P.2d 893 (1974)). This jurisdiction was held to be true in spite of the
fact that one of the parties in *Bad Horse* had returned to the reservation and attempted to divest the state court of jurisdiction. American Indians are citizens of the state in which they dwell as well as
tribal members and as state citizens they are entitled to sue in the
state courts.

Prior to the passage of the Indian Child Welfare Act of 1978, the
courts used the *Williams v. Lee* test to resolve jurisdictional disputes in child custody cases. Generally, if a child was domiciled on a
reservation, tribal court jurisdiction prevailed. Any attempt by a
state court to assume jurisdiction of the case would have been an
infringement on the tribal powers of self-government (*Fisher v. District Court*, 424 U.S. 382 (1976)). The question of domicile, however,
was more difficult to resolve in child custody cases. In normal conflict of laws cases, domicile is determined in a variety of ways, such
as simply identifying the place where the child is presently residing.
But certain Indian tribes determine a child's domicile as being the
domicile of the child's mother regardless of where the child is presently living. A Maryland court held this way in *Wakefield v. Little
Light*, 276 Md. 333, 347 A.2d 228 (1975), thereby resolving a jurisdictional dispute in favor of a tribal court.

Since there was a significant number of complaints regarding
the activities of state agencies, child adoption programs, and the jurisdictional disputes between competing parents and relatives, Congress finally established some basic ground rules in 1978 when it
passed the Indian Child Welfare Act (P.L. 95-608, 92 Stat. 3069). The
act established minimum federal standards for the removal of Indian
children from their families and the placement of such children
in foster or adoptive homes. The emphasis in the act was making
certain that the cultural values of the tribe were not denied the
orphaned Indian child and, recognizing the continuing nature of
tribal life, ensuring that the tribal government had the legal means
of protecting its minor members.

Congress simply codified the disparate court decisions that had
begun to form the body of Indian child welfare law and provided cer-

tain jurisdictional safeguards for tribal governments that had a desire to become involved in the placement of Indian children. In Title I—Child Custody Proceedings—tribal courts were given considerable leeway in participating in adoption or foster home placement proceedings. In those instances where an Indian child is a ward of the tribal court, the Indian tribe retains exclusive jurisdiction, notwithstanding the present residence or domicile of the child. In state court proceedings for foster care placement or termination of parental rights to an Indian child not domiciled or residing with the reservation, the state court, in the absence of good cause prohibiting it, must transfer its proceedings to the jurisdiction of the tribe. The law gives the Indian custodian and the Indian child's tribe the right to intervene at any point in the proceedings of adoption or foster home placement. Full faith and credit must be given to the judicial proceedings of any Indian tribe applicable to Indian child custody proceedings, thereby elevating the tribal court to equal status with local and state courts in this field.

The statute also establishes an order of preference for the adoption of Indian children, listing a member of the child's extended family first, other members of the Indian child's tribe second, and other Indian families third in preference ahead of non-Indian parties who might wish to adopt the child. This specific provision is understood as the congressional means of supporting and enhancing the Indian family. Presumably, it is the business of the tribal court, the tribal social welfare office or committee, or some other tribally created agency to provide either the state or the tribal court with names of people who would fit into these categories.

The Indian Child Welfare Act is too recent to judge its effectiveness. Much of the initial concern of the tribes was in determining the proper time in which to seek to intervene in state court proceedings. Although tribal courts were given the right to intervene at any time, many people, recognizing the delicate nature of human relationships, felt that more specific instructions should be given regarding intervention. Tribal governments also faced the question of creating their own set of responsible officials who could appear in state court proceedings as representatives of the larger tribal community and both observe and participate in the matter. Although the act appears to give guidance in many areas that had previously been quite nebulous, tribal governments are still discovering that the act has many flaws in it. Some tribes have had difficulty establishing the proper chain of relationships to prove that individual children are members of their tribe and not another tribe in cases of multiple tribal ancestry. And a great deal of reliance must be placed on federal records, which are not always accurate in reflecting the extended Indian family and its complex set of relationships and responsibilities.

The intricacies of tribal-state conflicts of law are just too vast and technical to be covered adequately here. There does remain, however, one last civil jurisdictional issue that is sufficiently important to command attention. This issue relates to the problem of "service of process." Service of process is the formal delivering to a person a notice that he or she is being summoned to court either to be sued or to appear as a witness. If, for example, an Indian has breached a contract that he or she entered into while off the reservation, may the state court obtain jurisdiction over the Indian by serving process on him or her while he or she is on the reservation? To permit this service would allow the state to extend its civil jurisdiction into Indian Country.

Traditionally, courts have held that states could not serve process on an Indian while he or she was on the reservation. These holdings, however, were not without their problems. To insulate the Indians from process on the reservation resulted in the protection of an Indian who had committed a legal wrong off the reservation and placed him or her beyond the reach of the state law as long as he or she remained on the reservation. This immunity from process meant that the innocent party who allegedly had been injured by the Indian was divested of any effective remedy. The innocent party might attempt to bring a cause of action in the tribal court, but if the tribal law restricted civil judgments to no more than $300 or some other nominal figure, this limitation effectively precluded any kind of remedy for a serious injury. The injustice of this situation is evident.

In view of these difficulties, a few courts have reversed the direction of the service of process principle and have permitted state authorities to serve Indians on the reservation. In *State Securities v. Anderson*, 84 N. Mex. 629, 506 P.2d 786 (1973), the court concluded that service of process on an Indian residing on a reservation does not infringe upon the right of self-government of the tribe. And, furthermore, to permit service of process would not displace tribal jurisdiction; it would only make state and tribal jurisdiction concurrent in this one area of concern.

The courts are still divided over the validity of extending service of process on the reservation. In 1976, for example, the state of Arizona reached precisely the opposite conclusion from the decision in *State Securities*. In perpetuating the protective shield for alleged Indian offenders, the Arizona court heavily emphasized the concept of internal Indian sovereignty in disallowing the sheriff of Pima

County to serve process on an Indian residing on the Papago Reservation (*Francisco v. State*, 113 Ariz. 427, 556 P.2d 1 (1976)). A Montana state court, however, took the service of process idea in the *State Securities* case a step further. The court not only permitted the state to serve process on an Indian on the reservation but also allowed the state to execute judgment against the Indian by garnishing the wages that he earned on the reservation (*Little Horn State Bank v. Stops*, 555 P.2d 211 (1976)). The rationalization for justifying the execution of judgment was that it in no way infringed upon the tribe's right to self-government. When this case was appealed to the United States Supreme Court, it declined to hear the case, thereby leaving the Montana state court decision standing (cert. denied 431 U.S. 924, 1977).

William Canby, in a careful study of these problems, conceded that service of process by itself probably does not interfere with tribal self-government (Canby, p. 225). But to extend the service of process notion further so as to justify execution of judgment would appear, according to Canby, to be a considerable intrusion into reservation affairs. To resolve the problem, he proposed that the state court rely upon "long-arm statutes" as a device to reach alleged Indian offenders on the reservation. A long-arm statute is a method that would only serve to give the Indian defendant notice of the proceeding against him or her. It would not confer any other civil jurisdiction on the states. In essence, the use of the long-arm statutes would limit the extension of state civil jurisdiction to service of process only. While *State Securities* would remain law, its extension in *Little Horn State Bank* to include execution of judgments would not be permitted. In this way, Indians who have injured nonreservation people would not be protected from state trials simply because they flee to the reservation. Yet the integrity of tribal self-government would still be preserved by limiting the state intrusion to service of process only.

The problems attendant to the civil system of justice on the reservation are extensive. As in so many other areas of the law, the basic issues continue to revolve around the Indian attempts to maintain a large fund of tribal autonomy while at the same time acknowledging and dealing with the problems brought about by the Indian–non-Indian interaction. Since contact with the white community is bound to increase, not decrease, in the future the courts will undoubtedly continue to play an important role in the attempt to resolve these issues.

9. Public Policy and the Legal Rights of Indians

The primary emphasis of this book has been the judicial system, its roots in both the tribal traditions and Anglo-American law, and its present configuration in Indian Country. We have not emphasized substantive public policy or legislative expressions of policy dealing with Indians because that subject requires extensive probing into historical movements and informal political processes, which are somewhat removed from the normal operation of the judicial process itself. There are, however, certain public policy issues that are so closely related to the judicial process that it is difficult to divorce the two areas and pretend that changes in the political perception of society do not affect every aspect of Indian life and political institutions. Issues that arise in the larger society, even though they are unrelated to Indians both geographically and culturally, inevitably produce changes in the way Indians see themselves and in the way they conduct their affairs.

The emphasis on legal procedure, for instance, which we have seen in the last two decades, conjures up notions of whether or not the judicial system is providing criminal defendants with the fundamental prerequisites of due process of law. How much protection should the accused enjoy in comparison with the "law-abiding" member of society? Methods involved in the recruitment of judges can be associated with questions concerning the qualifications of those people who would select the judges. Inquiries as to whether noncitizens can bring suits in federal and state courts, for example, and whether indigent persons should have access to free legal services are substantive public policy questions that cannot be resolved by a few persons strategically located but must be the product of lengthy public debate and concern before they can muster sufficient support to become an accepted part of the judicial process. Underlying the Indian judicial system is a fundamental public policy question that dominates all federal concerns about Indians: how long will Indians maintain, want to maintain, and be able to maintain separate institutions? Virtually every policy question that affects other Americans finally also affects American Indians and influences the manner in which Indians understand and confront the question of continued separate political and social existence.

The last chapter of this study is therefore devoted to an examination of several of these public policy issues. We have chosen to examine only those issues that either are intimately related to the Indian process of justice or are fundamental to the political and social well-being of American Indians. Our first area of exploration will focus on the civil liberties of American Indians. Included in this survey are the problems of citizenship, voting, and the rights of the criminally accused. Then we will examine the legal difficulties confronting Indians in the area of religious freedom because religion plays a dominant and critical role in all Indian tribal life. Finally, the study will conclude with an analysis of Indian access to basic government services, in particular the educational and social service programs from the federal government. While there are a myriad of other policy issues involving natural resources that are especially important to American Indians, these topics must await a future analysis.

THE CIVIL LIBERTIES OF AMERICAN INDIANS

American Citizenship

The American political system affords a large variety of rights to its inhabitants irrespective of whether or not they are citizens. Indeed, many constitutional guarantees are extended expressly to "persons" living within the United States borders. Citizenship is not a prerequisite for the enjoyment of these privileges. Immigrants, citizens of other countries temporarily living in the United States, and foreign tourists all have basic rights of law under our Constitution that protect them from wholly arbitrary actions by law enforcement agencies and courts. But there are opportunities that are restricted only to those people possessing American citizenship. The holding of public office, for example, and the right to participate in elections require citizenship as a prerequisite, and some social welfare programs are similarly restricted. Thus, while noncitizens are provided with a fund of political and legal rights, the full panoply of guarantees is extended only to those persons who are United States citizens.

Today all American Indians are regarded as citizens of the

United States. Some traditional Indians do not regard themselves as American citizens, preferring to view themselves as citizens only of their own tribe. But the federal government, extending its claim on the basis of statutes and treaties, insists that all Indians born within the continental United States are its citizens. During the embryonic years of American national existence, when Indian tribes had an option to give their support to either Great Britain or the United States, Indians were not viewed as potential citizens. Rather, people conceived of them as members of small nations who would forever remain outside the formal political institutions of the United States. Exactly what legal status this exclusion would entail did not concern people at that time since it was believed that the interior of the continent could not be inhabited by "civilized" people and that there would always be a wilderness populated by tribes of Indians some distance from the centers of civilization.

There were, of course, Indians in the original thirteen states who had already merged with their local neighbors and were virtually indistinguishable from the general populace. For that reason, accomplished assimilation, the framers of the Constitution inserted phraseology concerning "Indians not taxed" to distinguish Indians already living the "civilized" life from those who adhered to tribal customs and lived with their families in Indian Country. Some of the early treaties provided that Indians, by abandoning their tribal relations and adopting the customs of the whites, could become state citizens, in effect then becoming American citizens as well.

The removal treaties of the 1830s recognized a fundamental fact of Indian existence. The tribes of the Ohio River valley and the Deep South had been intermarrying with whites for at least a century and many prominent families were now predominantly white although continuing to live with their Indian relatives. Many of these families did not relish pulling up stakes and moving to the southern plains and beginning anew. They were often well integrated into the society of their region and viewed their potential loss of political and economic power as a burden too great to carry. Consequently, provisions were made with certain chiefs to allow families to remain within the state or territory where the tribe was originally located on small tracts of land that became theirs in fee simple after removal. The Miami families around Fort Wayne, Indiana, for example, were among the wealthiest and most powerful families in the state. They generally chose to remain in Indiana with smaller tracts of land and allowed the rest of the tribe, predominantly full bloods, to move west. The treaties signed with the Five Civilized Tribes provided that any tribal member who wished to remain in Georgia, Alabama, or Mississippi could take an allotment or a land scrip, which would guarantee recognition of landownership by a federal land office. The tribal member was no longer regarded as a tribal member if he or she took this allotment but was regarded as a state citizen without any federal restrictions whatsoever. Nearly a half-century after the Five Civilized Tribes had moved to Oklahoma, the descendants of those individuals who had remained in the south attempted to share in the tribal treasury of the people in the west. In *The Cherokee Trust Funds*, 117 U.S. 288 (1886), the Supreme Court turned aside this effort, remarking that individuals must be citizens of their tribe in order to enjoy the benefits of its property.

Congressional efforts to naturalize tribes of Indians generally fell short of their announced goal. A few tribes fell victim to this confusing policy and spent most of the nineteenth century trying to determine what their actual status was. The Stockbridge-Munsee, or Brotherton Indians, and the Wyandots seemed to be plagued with congressional efforts to make them citizens. From approximately 1839 until the 1850s, these two groups saw thrust upon them a continuing sequence of congressional statutes designed to make them citizens and they responded as best they could. Eventually the tribes were divided into the "Indian" party and the "citizens" party and lived under two basic sets of regulations that were designed to meet the supposed needs of each party. Today when we survey the list of federally recognized Indian tribes and find a "Citizens Potawatomi" or an "Absentee Shawnee" tribe, we find the remnants of a disastrous congressional policy concerning citizenship that somehow went astray from its original goal.

Many people erroneously thought that Indians automatically qualified for American citizenship following the passage of the Fourteenth Amendment. Section 1 of this amendment stipulates that "all persons born or naturalized in the United States, and subject to the jurisdiction thereof, are citizens of the United States . . ." Since Indians were not specifically excluded, some people saw "all" in the phraseology and concluded that Indians were covered by this amendment. However, the Senate Judiciary Committee, instructed by a resolution of the Senate to inquire into the status of Indians in view of the all-inclusive nature of the amendment, reported in December 1870 that Indians who maintained their tribal relations were not made citizens under the amendment because they still adhered to tribal jurisdiction and therefore could not be said to have been born under the *complete* jurisdiction of the United States. Citizenship was viewed by the committee as a two-way street that required the consent of the Indians involved:

To maintain that the United States intended, by a change of its fundamental law, which was not ratified by these tribes, and to which they were neither requested nor permitted to assent, to annul treaties then existing beween the United States as one party, and the Indian tribes as the other parties respectively, would be to charge upon the United States repudiation of national obligations, repudiation doubly infamous from the fact that the parties whose claims were thus annulled are too weak to enforce their just rights, and were enjoying the voluntarily assumed guardianship and protection of this Government. (Senate Report #268, 41st Cong. 3d Sess. December 14, 1870, ss# 1443, p. 11)

A year later in *McKay v. Campbell*, 16 Fed. Cas. No. 161 (D. Or. 1871), the federal district court in Oregon agreed with the Senate Judiciary Report, holding the tribes to be "distinct and independent political communities, retaining the right of self-government," and therefore subjecting their members to sufficient jurisdiction to place them outside the jurisdiction required by the Constitution to make them natural born citizens under the Fourteenth Amendment.

The major citizenship case dealing with Indians, *Elk v. Wilkins*, 112 U.S. 94 (1884), found that, even though John Elk had abandoned his tribal relations and had moved to Omaha, Nebraska, and lived a "civilized" life, he could not become an American citizen and exercise the voting franchise because his intent to become a citizen required a positive and specific response from the United States before it could affect his status as a citizen. In 1890, as an enticement to members of the Five Civilized Tribes to abandon their tribal relations, Congress passed the Indian Territory Naturalization Act (26 Stat. 81, 99–100), which provided that any member of an Indian tribe in Indian Territory could become an American citizen by applying to a federal court. The individual Indian, under this particular statute, did not lose his or her tribal citizenship or the right to share in tribal assets when they were distributed. This statute, perhaps more than any other piece of legislation passed by Congress, seemed to imply that Indians held dual citizenship or could do so by performing the naturalization ritual in a federal court.

The allotment agreements concluded under the General Allotment Act of 1887, of course, provided for the automatic assumption of citizenship after the conclusion of the twenty-five–year period during which the allotment was held in trust by the secretary of the interior. Since some tribes had their period of trust extended by legislation and executive order, it became difficult to determine who was an Indian and who was an American citizen. This question was critically important because, theoretically, when all federal restrictions were removed from the individual and his or her land, he or she was supposed to be legally equal to other Americans, which included legal consumption of liquor. Since few honest tavern owners wished to challenge the complexity of this situation, citizenship became simply a status in which the trust restrictions on Indian lands were removed. This requirement actually meant that citizenship, which is supposed to be a personal right of the individual, was really a function of the status of whatever real estate the Indian might possess.

During this period citizenship became a ceremonial event, something akin to religious conversion. It symbolized the determination of the individual to cast aside traditions and customs and assume the dress, values, and beliefs of the larger society. One citizenship ceremony involved the man "shooting his last arrow" and taking hold of the handles of a plow to indicate his intent to become a citizen. Such formal occasions dwindled rapidly after the First World War, when the Act of November 6, 1919 (41 Stat. 350), and the Act of July 19, 1919 (41 Stat. 163, 222), gave citizenship to all Indians who had been members of the armed forces during the conflict. On June 2, 1924, all Indians born within the territorial limits of the United States were declared to be citizens (43 Stat. 253). Although but a simple paragraph, the act seemed confusing in its effect since it provided "that the granting of such citizenship shall not in any manner impair or otherwise affect the right of any Indian to tribal or other property" and the preservation of tribal property rights and membership was regarded by later policy-makers as indicative of less than full citizenship. Today when anti-Indian sentiment rages among federal and state officials, they clothe their resentments in the citizenship argument, contending that any semblance of tribal relationships and federal protection is in fact a second-class citizenship that should be abolished as a means of assisting Indians. Several of the termination bills recited this litany, indicating that the only purpose of the legislation was to grant "full" citizenship to Indians— a goal that seemed laudable and liberal.

Citizenship must be carefully distinguished from jurisdictional questions because of the tendency of people to confuse the various laws and regulations that deal with Indians and to view them as handicaps in the search for equal rights. Indians are American citizens. They also possess all the rights of tribal members as outlined in their tribe's constitution and by-laws. They are also recipients of federal services of a special nature that involve holding individual tracts of allotted lands within the reservation boundaries or selected under federal supervision off the reservation in a federal trust status that precludes some forms of state and federal taxation.

Voting Rights

Understanding the legal ramifications of voting is cumbersome if one reads only the Constitution of the United States. A few of its provisions are simply not as clear as they might be. Several basic premises flow from the Constitution, however, that can serve as a foundation to understanding the voting rights of American Indians. First, the Constitution does not grant anyone the right to vote. Rather, its most significant command, the Fifteenth Amendment, simply states that no citizen shall be denied the right to vote because of race, color, or previous condition of servitude. In a nutshell, this phrase means that neither the federal government nor the states may *discriminate* against certain groups by denying them the right to vote for these particular reasons. The second important message emanating from the Constitution is that the states are charged with the primary responsibility for determining the standards of voting eligibility. This delegation of power is found in article I, section 4, which provides that the "times, places, and manner" of holding elections shall be prescribed by the states.

To be eligible to vote in the United States one must be a citizen. Prior to the 1924 Indian Citizenship Act, this requirement obviously posed considerable difficulties to those reservation Indians who had not yet been granted citizenship and to those nonreservation Indians who could not prove they had really abandoned their tribal relations. Since 1924 this proof of eligibility has not been a major problem at either the federal or the state level. Arizona, for a period of nearly twenty years, prohibited Indians from voting by interpreting their federal trust relationship as placing them in the status of "persons under disability." This class of citizens was denied the vote in that southwestern state but the designation generally meant non compos mentis rather than persons with a particular political relationship to the federal government. In 1948 in *Harrison v. Laveen,* 67 Ariz. 337, 196 P.2d 456, the state supreme court reversed itself and Indians gained the franchise permanently.

The Fourteenth Amendment stipulates that national citizenship carries with it state citizenship in the state wherein one resides. Still, this stipulation does not automatically provide Indian citizens with the right to vote. States may establish reasonable standards for voter eligibility. If Indian or other citizens cannot satisfy these standards, they will not be permitted to exercise their franchise. The standards, of course, must be reasonable and not arbitrary or discriminatory. Every state, for instance, may require a certain period of residency within its borders before a person is permitted to register as a voter. The period of residency must be of reasonable duration, say thirty days for a state or local election. A year, even three months, has been held to be too long.

In the past a number of states have gone to great lengths to keep minorities disenfranchised. Black Americans struggled for years attempting to overcome voting obstacles, such as literacy tests, grandfather clauses, poll taxes, and the infamous white primary. The legal victories achieved by blacks have made the path to voting somewhat easier for American Indians although Indian encounters with states reluctant to give them the vote have been both frequent and very costly.

Monroe Price has examined the role of states in their attempts to deny Indians their voting franchise. His analysis suggests five basic arguments that states have used to prevent American Indians from registering and voting (Price, pp. 229–237).

Severance of tribal relations. Prior to 1924 some states, such as Minnesota and North Dakota, required that Indians prove they have assumed a "civilized" way of life by severing their relations with their tribe. In the absence of such proof Indians would not be permitted to participate in the electoral process.

Lack of state power over Indian conduct. This argument is an outgrowth of the old idea that those who do not pay taxes should not be permitted to vote. The rationalization, of course, is frequently extended much beyond the tax exemption issue: it goes to the heart of Indian Country immunity. If a state has no jurisdiction over the reservation on which Indians live, the tribal members should not be able to participate in the selection of public state officials. This philosophy is personified in a Minnesota case, *Opsahl v. Johnson*, 138 Minn. 42, 163 N.W. 988 (1917). Here the court reasoned that "the tribal Indian contributes nothing to the state. His property is not subject to taxation, or to the process of its courts. He bears none of the burdens of civilization, and performs none of the duties of its citizens" (pp. 48–49). Judicial opinions of this ilk always seem to conclude with derogatory innuendos to the effect that until the Indians adopt the "habits and customs of civilization" they should not be permitted the prerogatives enjoyed by "civilized" white people.

Fear of political control shifting to Indian majorities. White communities that have sizable minority populations have attempted in the past to keep those potentially large political groups in their so-called proper places. There has been a persistent fear that, if we give black Americans, Chicanos, or American Indians the right to vote, they will eventually take control of the local government because of their large number of voters. Usually this type of argument is quietly kept out of formal policy statements and opinions since it strikes at the heart of democratic theory. Still, occasionally, these positions are boldly admitted. In *Allen v. Merrell*, 6 Utah 2d 32, 305 P.2d 490 (1956), a Utah court noted that "it is thus plain to be seen that in a county where the Indian population would amount to a substantial proportion of the citizenry, or may even outnumber the other inhabitants, allowing them to vote might place substantial control of the county government . . . [in Indian hands]" (p. 39).

Guardianship. A number of states have general laws that preclude people under guardianship from voting. The justification for this stance is that people under legal guardianship usually are either of tender years or in some way mentally handicapped to the extent that they need assistance in managing their affairs. The state of Arizona attempted to use such a law to disenfranchise Indians. It reasoned that, since Indians were under a federal guardianship, they could not qualify as voters. In 1928, the Arizona Supreme Court accepted this argument as a valid basis for precluding Indians from voting (*Porter v. Hall*, 34 Ariz. 308, 271 P. 411 (1928)). This conspicuously discriminatory opinion remained in force until 1948, when the court finally reversed itself in *Harrison v. Laveen*, 67 Ariz. 337, 196 P.2d 456 (1948). The *Harrison* decision distinguished between different types of guardianship. While a judicially established guardianship may serve as a basis to deny a person the right to vote, this condition is considerably different from the federal guardianship designed to preserve the political and social well-being of American Indians. The court went on to note that the opinion in the *Porter* case was a "tortious [*sic*] construction" of the simple phrase "under guardianship." This blatant attempt by the state of Arizona to deny Indians the right to vote thus was dealt the death blow it should have received some twenty years earlier.

Residency. The customary requirement that a person be a resident of the state in order to qualify for voting also has been used to bar Indian participation at the polls. The state of Utah effectively disenfranchised Indians by insisting that Indians residing on the reservation simply did not qualify as residents of the state (*Allen v. Merrell*, 6 Utah 2d 32, 305 P.2d 490 (1956)). The Utah court engaged in an elaborate discussion of the "separateness" of reservation Indians. Not only did their rights and protection emanate from the federal government but also the Indians had a separate culture, spoke a different language, and were unfamiliar with state governmental processes. This clearly set them aside as being different from the non-Indian residents of the state. Justice J. Allen Crockett, of the Supreme Court of Utah, went on to note that once Indians begin to accept state responsibilities, such as owning land and paying taxes, they may then qualify as residents and participate in state elections. Residency, then, was a function of culture and economics rather than geography.

Allen v. Merrell is not an ancient case. The decision, which was handed down in 1956, is considered to be within contemporary vintage. The *Allen* case was appealed to the United States Supreme Court, which vacated the Utah court decision and remanded the case back for a re-hearing (*Allen v. Merrell*, 353 U.S. 932 (1957)). In the interim, however, the state legislature repealed the Utah statute barring Indians from voting because their residency was on the reservation. Utah was the last state to permit Indians to exercise their voting franchise.

Political establishments continue to devise new ways to perpetuate white political control in areas of heavy Indian population. Current strategies and tactics, however, are more subtle. In South Dakota, an attempt was made to keep Indians disenfranchised by attaching three "unorganized" counties lying entirely within the Indian reservations to adjacent counties. Indians, who comprised the largest number of people within the unorganized counties, had no vote in the adjacent counties, which were controlled by the white power structure. This imaginative disenfranchising mechanism was struck down by the federal court, however, when it held that Indians, having a substantial interest in the affairs of the adjacent counties, must be permitted to participate in their elections (*Little Thunder v. South Dakota*, 518 F.2d 1253 (8th Cir. 1975)).

Today the major problems that formerly frustrated Indians in their attempts to vote have been largely overcome. The dictate of the Fifteenth Amendment that no citizen shall be denied the right to vote on account of race, color, or other condition of servitude is a principle largely respected by both the federal government and the states. Congress of late also has contributed to the expansion of voting rights for minorities. In passing the 1965 Voting Rights Act, Congress set in motion a program by which voting registrars can be sent into states and regions where less than 50 percent of the eligible voting population is registered and where a voting device, such as a literacy test, has been utilized. Included in the 1965 law is a "preclearance" requirement: states falling under the 1965 act must submit any changes in their voting laws to the Department of Justice for approval before the proposed laws can be put into effect. This preclearance requirement has been exceptionally effective in dissuading states from passing laws that would prevent minorities, including Indians, from exercising their voting franchise.

One of the more difficult burdens that American Indians face when voting is the language barrier. As do Spanish-speaking people, many Indians continue to cling to their native tongues. For decades federal, state, and local elections were conducted in English only and this frustrated non-English–speaking minorities and in some instances kept them away from the polls entirely. In 1975, the Voting Rights Act was expanded to cover areas in twenty-four states where Spanish, Asian, Indian, and Alaskan languages and dialects are spoken by large numbers of voters. The 1975 act requires bilingual voting information and ballots so as to facilitate voting for the non-English–speaking minorities.

One final issue relating to Indian voting should be mentioned. This area involves the problems of reapportionment and the electoral requirement of one person, one vote. Reapportionment is not related to the *denial* of one's vote; rather, it deals with the *dilution* of one's vote. If one voting district has three times the number of people in it than another district, the voting power of people in the latter district is only one-third of that enjoyed by the people in the former district. This disparity violates the democratic notion of one person, one vote, and denies the people with a diluted vote equal protection of the laws. The Indian Civil Rights Act of 1968 contains an Equal Protection of Law Clause and thus tribal elections may have to be predicated upon the one person, one vote, criterion.

While the substantial equality dictates of one person, one vote, may well fit into the political thought of a Western democratic nation, it does not always blend well with traditional Indian cultural values. Indeed, one Indian commentator has argued that it is "totally alien to our traditional practices—practices still followed by all but four of the [New Mexico] pueblos" (Montoya, p. 7). Since tribal government is a unique phenomenon in American politics, demanding respect for tribal customs and traditions, the full potential of the Equal Protection Clause of the 1968 act has not been pushed to the extent possible. Still, the issue of malapportionment is a sensitive one that could bring about a vigorous conflict between traditional tribal advocates and those holding modern perceptions of electoral equality.

Rights of the Criminally Accused

While the legal implications of criminal law in Indian Country are examined in detail in Chapter 7, it is important to explore a bit further the rights of American Indians accused of committing crimes. The prosecution of Indian offenders by tribal courts does not assume a major role in the overall criminal justice system. The serious felonies all fall under the Major Crimes Act, which is a federal and not a tribal jurisdictional matter. Only with lesser crimes and misdemeanors does the Indian judicial system enter the picture. Nevertheless, some major problems in the area of criminal law involving equal protection and due process emerge when the federal-state-tribal system is examined and compared.

Since Indians accused of major criminal offenses committed on the reservation are tried in federal courts, these Indian defendants are supposed to be extended all the constitutional protections enjoyed by non-Indian offenders who are also accused of a violation of federal statutes. It is true that the Constitution does not totally apply to Indian Country. But U.S. attorneys who are charged with enforcing federal law are restricted by constitutional limitations and they must follow these dictates in all prosecutions, including those involving Indian defendants under the Major Crimes Act. Thus, the constitutional dictates against unreasonable search and seizure, the privilege against self-incrimination, and the right to counsel are all rights that are guaranteed to Indian defendants in the federal criminal trials. In reality, however, the same concern shown for non-Indians living in towns and cities is not demonstrated in the pretrial investigations and preparations. Illegal searches and seizures do occur on Indian reservations. People do not understand their rights and frequently, in an effort to show their innocence, voluntarily surrender evidence that is later used to their detriment. Living in isolation, few accused individuals can prove that they were not given their rights or that evidence was obtained illegally.

Indian offenders, under the Major Crimes Act, as amended, are tried in the same courts and in the same manner as defendants in federal enclave and maritime jurisdictions. Strangely, this effort to produce uniformity resulted in raising a significant issue concerning the interpretation of the act. In *Keeble v. United States*, 412 U.S. 205 (1973), the defendant raised the question of whether an Indian committing a felony against another Indian was entitled to be charged with a lesser included offense instruction, which would have been available to a non-Indian defendant in the same circumstances. The Supreme Court held that the statutory requirement that Indians be tried "in the same manner" as non-Indians meant that they would also receive the benefit of the lesser offense instruction. Although it was not clear that a federal court can convict and sentence an Indian on the lesser offense, two lower federal courts have subsequently done so and the Supreme Court has let those convictions stand (*Felicia v. United States*, 495 F.2d 353, cert. den. 419 U.S. 849 (1974); *United States v. John*, 587 F.2d 683, cert. den. 441 U.S. 925 (1979)).

Enforcement of the Major Crimes Act ultimately revolves around the status of the Indian participant, be he or she accused or victim. The federal status therefore appears to the layperson to be racially determined. In *United States v. Antelope*, 430 U.S. 641 (1977), an Indian was accused of a felony murder of a non-Indian in Indian Country. The Major Crimes Act gave federal jurisdiction. Had a non-Indian killed another non-Indian, under *McBratney* the offense would have been tried in state court. The result of this anomaly was that the burden of proof for first degree murder was reduced when the case was heard in federal court. Antelope argued that he thereby became disadvantaged solely because of his race. The Supreme Court rejected that argument, citing *Morton v. Mancari*, 417 U.S. 535 (1974), and its pronouncement that federal laws respecting Indians and Indian tribes are not racially applicable laws but speak rather to the federal government's long-standing relationship with Indian tribes of a political nature. Although the theory seems consistent, the results can hardly be viewed by the layperson as anything more than Antelope was contending—statutes distinguishable by racial characteristics and classifications.

One final area of concern is that of double jeopardy. Because enforcement of the Major Crimes Act by the federal courts produces the result of a fragmentation of jurisdiction in some cases in the criminal law among three different sovereignties, definitions of criminal acts can be radically different. Under normal conditions one would expect that one set of facts would give rise to only one act of criminal behavior. Such was the claim in *United States v. Wheeler*, 435 U.S. 313 (1978). In that case Wheeler, a member of the Navajo tribe, pleaded guilty in tribal court to a charge of contributing to the delinquency of a minor. He was subsequently indicted by a federal grand jury for statutory rape based on the same incident. Wheeler moved to dismiss the federal charge on the ground that the tribal charge was really a lesser included offense of statutory rape.

In resolving this question the Supreme Court turned to the source of tribal power and determined that tribes still possessed those aspects of sovereignty to punish offenders against the tribe itself. Since that power was not attributable to any power delegated to the tribe by Congress, the two prosecutions were initiated by two different sovereigns and hence were not regarded as being the same offence. The Court was concerned that, if the double jeopardy claim were upheld, tribal codes might offer a safe haven from criminal prosecutions by outlining lesser offences to which quick guilty pleas might be made. The result of *Wheeler* seems to be the Court's acceptance of the principle that too much law is preferable to too little law.

If an Indian violates a criminal provision of the tribal code, thus not falling under the Major Crimes Act, the tribal court does assume jurisdiction over the case. Under these circumstances, the U.S. Constitution does not apply. As the Supreme Court noted in *Talton v. Mayes*, 163 U.S. 376 (1895), the powers of local self-government as exercised by Indians existed prior to the Constitution and neither were created by nor sprung from the Constitution. Hence, Indians have the power to define their own offenses and prosecute those who violate tribal laws without complying with the dictates of the U.S. Constitution.

While immune from the reaches of the federal Constitution, tribal prosecutions do fall under the auspices of the 1968 Indian Civil Rights Act. This "Indian Bill of Rights" has made applicable most, although not all, of the provisions expressed in the first eight amendments to the U.S. Constitution. Ten of these provisions are directed toward protecting the rights of Indians accused of committing crimes on the reservation. They include protections against or guarantees of

Unreasonable searches and seizures
Speedy and public trial
Confrontation and cross-examination
Right to retained counsel
Cruel and unusual punishment
Double jeopardy
Trial by jury
No excessive bail
Due process of law
Self-incrimination

The Due Process Clause of the 1968 act undoubtedly includes a number of fundamental procedural guarantees as well, although tribal courts have yet to define these specifically. Adequate notice of hearing, impartial judges, laws possessing an ascertainable standard of guilt, and a fair accusatory procedure are all procedural prerequisites designed to assure that an Indian defendant is afforded a fair trial.

Even though the 1968 Indian Civil Rights Act imposed these libertarian guarantees on tribal criminal proceedings, the practical implementation of the act has been more symbolic and looking toward the spirit of the law than a rigid application of the letter of the law. Take, for example, the right to counsel provision. Under federal and state laws, a defendant is afforded the right to counsel whether or not he or she can afford one. Under the Indian Civil Rights Act, an Indian defendant is permitted right to counsel only if he or she can afford to hire an advocate and an attorney. Furthermore, in many tribal court proceedings, the advocate-attorney defense team is expected to participate in the resolution of the problem and not to raise technical procedural points used in federal and state courts to free guilty defendants. The spirit of the law is maintained but the technical battles that characterize non-Indian courts and sometimes lead to a sense of outrage in non-Indian society are usually not present. Rigid application of the constitutional protections in tribal courts might well hamper the ability of the judiciary to function as it has. Tribal courts might well become as complicated as have the lower federal courts with cases waiting for years before they are resolved.

AMERICAN INDIAN RELIGIOUS FREEDOM

Religious freedom has been extremely important in the historical development of our country. Indeed, one of the reasons that many people came to America originally can be attributed to religious intolerance in their home countries. Testimony to the importance of religious freedom to American political thought may be found in the First Amendment to the Constitution, which contains two clauses dealing with religion. The first of these is the Free Exercise Clause, which is designed to permit people to worship as they see fit or to not worship at all. The second clause, referred to as the Establishment Clause, creates a wall of separation between church and state so as to make certain the government is not dominated by the church and religion is not controlled by the state. The Establishment Clause, from a legal standpoint, is largely concerned with problems involving either (*a*) the use of public funds appropriated for religious purposes (such as federal aid to parochial education) or (*b*) religious practices in public institutions (such as reciting a prayer in the public schools). Both of these practices are prohibited by the Establishment Clause, although there have since developed legal devices by which to circumvent the prohibition against federal aid to sectarian schools.

Although the history of religious toleration in the United States is generally positive, it is far from being excellent. Indeed, even during the embryonic years of our nationhood, religious sects believing that they possessed the single truth would not permit competitive congregations to exist. Even more prominent among the problems associated with religious freedom is the frequent intolerance exhibited by those who believe against those who do not. One constantly hears the clarion call that we are a "Christian" nation. While Christianity may play an important role in our political, social, and cultural heritage, from a constitutional perspective we are not a "Christian" nation. We are a nation that constitutionally tolerates all religious traditions, Christian and non-Christian, as well as those who do not hold a belief in a Supreme Being at all.

The dictate of the First Amendment is that Congress shall make no law prohibiting the free exercise of religion. This prohibition is not absolute, however, even though it may be phrased in mandatory language. The First Amendment is designed to protect religious *beliefs*. Beliefs are beyond the reach of the government no matter how unorthodox, but religious *practices* can be regulated by the state. If the government can demonstrate a compelling state interest in the subject matter and relate the objective of the regulation to a "valid secular purpose," it may control the religious practice. The government, for example, may prevent a religious sect from engaging in human sacrifices as part of its religious ritual. The protection of human life is not only a valid secular purpose but also a subject in which the state has a compelling interest. Hence the government may step in and prevent such practices even though a religion may claim that this practice should be protected under the Free Exercise Clause.

Issues involving religious freedom are exceedingly important to American Indians. A number of traditional Indian religious practices are foreign to the thinking of white communities and tribes are constantly being harassed by the political establishments that wish to prevent these so-called alien practices. The ceremonial Sun Dance ritual, the controversial Ghost Dance, the religious use of feathers, and the use of peyote have all been challenged and at one time banned by federal and state officials. Can these religious practices of the Indians find protection under the First Amendment of the Constitution, which guarantees them the same respect and status as the freedoms enjoyed by those of the Judeo-Christian tradition?

There were, to be sure, various acts of discrimination based on religious differences during colonial times that meant a direct infringement and sometimes prohibition on Indian religious practices. Most generally, these prohibitions were aimed at Indian healing practices since the colonists did not know enough about the respective tribal religions to specifically prohibit certain rituals and ceremonies. Until the tribes were placed on reservations, there was no compelling federal need to prohibit traditional religious ceremonies. The national government was content to allow whatever rites and ceremonies the Indians wished provided they did not lead to armed conflict. In the late 1880s and early 1890s, a wave of intolerance seemed to sweep across the west. The Mormons were persecuted for polygamous practices and Utah was denied statehood until the economic power of the Mormon Church was partially broken. Various eschatological and apocalyptic religious movements among the tribes promised a redemption by supernatural means and these disturbances, as they were called, prompted repressive measures by Indian agents who saw them as threats to their authority.

The most profound disturbance, of course, was the Ghost Dance, which spread from Nevada through the Rockies and into the Great Plains in the spring and summer of 1890. Originating with a Paiute dreamer named Wovoka, who predicted the end of the world, the return of the buffalo and deceased relatives, and the restitution of the Indians to primacy on the continent, the Ghost Dance had profound influence among the Sioux, who saw it as a means of surviving the dreadful conditions of starvation on their reservation in South Dakota. By the late fall of 1890 it was apparent that the movement could not be contained. In December, Sitting Bull was assassinated and Chief Big Foot fled with his followers to the Cheyenne River Reservation and then headed south to their rendezvous with destiny at Wounded Knee Creek on the Pine Ridge Reservation in southern South Dakota.

Federal policy dictates a repression of Indian religious practices simply because religion was part of the larger cultural complex that federal officials thought necessary to eliminate in order to assimilate Indians into the larger society. State governments, as a matter of course, had no contact with Indian religious practices because Indians were a federal matter. Suppression of traditional Indian religion by states, therefore, was never an important item and it is difficult to find even a mention of state activity in this area. It was actually not until very recent times that freedom of religion became an issue affecting Indians. And then it was an Indian tribal council that first dealt with the subject.

At the midpoint of the twentieth century, the Navajo Tribal Council became concerned over the use of peyote among its tribal members. Ultimately, the council passed an ordinance making it illegal to introduce, sell, use, or possess peyote in Navajo country. The Native American Church, which uses peyote as an integral part of its religious ceremonies, sought an injunction to prevent the enforcement of the tribal ordinance. The church argued that the ordinance violated the Free Exercise Clause of the First Amendment, which the church felt should apply to the Navajo tribe as well as to the federal and state governments. In *Native American Church v. Navajo Tribal Council,* 272 F.2d 131 (10th Cir. 1959), a federal court rejected this argument. Following historic legal principles, the court held that the U.S. Constitution does not apply to Indian tribes. As "domestic dependent nations," Indian tribes are distinct entities separate from both the federal and state governments. The U.S. Constitution, the court went on to note, is binding on Indian nations only where it expressly mentions Indians. The Free Exercise Clause, therefore, since it does not expressly mention Indian tribes, cannot be used as a protective constitutional cloak immunizing the Native American Church from the Navajo tribal ordinance.

If the Constitution cannot be used to protect Indian religious freedoms on the reservation, how can Indians be guaranteed the right to worship as they see fit? The answer rests with Congress. Congress, through its plenary power, can enact laws that provide individual Indians with protection against tribal government interference. Congress did specifically protect individual religious freedoms in the 1968 Indian Civil Rights Act, which prevents tribal governments from making or enforcing any law prohibiting the free exercise of religion. Thus, while tribal members are not afforded the religious freedom guaranteed by the First Amendment of the Constitution, they can invoke the Free Exercise Clause of the 1968 Indian Civil Rights Act.

The 1968 act does not, however, contain an Establishment Clause because it is regarded as less important for Indians. At one time Congress had enacted a provision that stated that no appropriations could be used for the education of Indian children in sectarian schools (25 U.S.C.A. §278), but this prohibition was repealed in 1968. In its place Congress authorized the use of federal funds to sectarian schools of higher education as well as vocational and technical schools (25 U.S.C.A. §278 (a)—280). Critical in this re-interpretation of the relationship of the federal government to sectarian schools is an emphasis on the purpose of the funding. When the primary purpose and effect of an educational grant neither foster nor hinder religious practices, the court will usually leave it intact.

It must be remembered that the 1968 Indian Civil Rights Act is a restriction on tribal government only. If Indians conduct religious ceremonies off the reservation or in a state where Public Law 280 is in effect (giving the state jurisdiction over Indian Country), the 1968 act does not apply. Under these circumstances, however, Indians may claim the First Amendment as a shield to protect their religious freedoms. The availability of the United States Constitution is exceedingly important since states have the reputation of looking askance at any kind of religious behavior that deviates from the white norms and expectations.

The use of peyote in religious ceremonies is precisely the kind of activity that will energize state officials into action. Indeed, this particular ceremony was the basis for litigation in an important Free Exercise Clause case, *People v. Woody*, 61 Cal. 2d 716, 394 P.2d 813 (1964). A group of Navajos met in a hogan near Needles, California, to perform a religious ceremony that included the use of peyote. They were arrested for violating a California statute that prohibited its use. The Indians, who were all members of the Native American Church, insisted that peyote use was an integral part of their religion and therefore was protected by the Free Exercise Clause of the First Amendment. The Supreme Court of California agreed.

The California court noted that, while peyote was a "hallucinogen" as opposed to a narcotic, the state could still proscribe its use. And, although the First Amendment cannot infringe upon religious belief, immunity afforded religious practice is not extended this deference if the state can demonstrate a compelling state interest that outweighs the defendant's interest in religious freedom. With this background the court then addressed the issue as to whether peyote was an integral part of the Indian religious practice. We have reproduced this part of the opinion at length below so that the reader can gain a feel for the type of culturally removed practice that often is involved in determining the legitimacy of claims of religious freedom.

The plant Lophophora williamsii, a small, spineless cactus, found in the Rio Grande Valley of Texas and northern Mexico, produces peyote, which grows in small buttons on the top of the cactus. Peyote's principal constituent is mescaline. When taken internally by chewing the buttons or drinking a derivative tea, peyote produces several types of hallucinations, depending primarily on the user. In most subjects it causes extraordinary vision marked by bright and kaleidoscopic colors, geometric patterns, or scenes involving humans or animals. In others it engenders hallucinatory symptoms similar to those produced in schizophrenia, dementia praecox, or paranoia. Beyond its hallucinatory effect, peyote renders for most users a heightened sense of comprehension; it fosters a feeling of friendliness toward other persons.

Peyote, as we shall see, plays a central role in the ceremony and practice of the Native American Church, a religious organization of Indians. Although the church claims no official prerequisites to membership, no written membership rolls, and no recorded theology, estimates of its membership range from 30,000 to 250,000, the wide variance deriving from differing definitions of a "member." As the anthropologists have ascertained through conversations with members, the theology of the church combines certain Christian teachings with the belief that peyote embodies the Holy Spirit and that those who partake of peyote enter into direct contact with God.

Peyotism discloses a long history. A reference to the religious use of peyote in Mexico appears in Spanish historical sources as early as 1560. Peyotism spread from Mexico to the United States and Canada; American anthropologists describe it as well established in this country during the latter part of the nineteenth century. Today, Indians of many tribes practice Peyotism. Despite the absence of recorded dogma, the several tribes follow surprisingly similar ritual and theology; the practices of Navajo members in Arizona practically parallel those of adherents in California, Montana, Oklahoma, Wisconsin, and Saskatchewan.

The "meeting," a ceremony marked by the sacramental use of peyote, composes the cornerstone of the peyote religion. The meeting convenes in an enclosure and continues from sundown Saturday to sunrise Sunday. To give thanks for the past good fortune or find guidance for future conduct, a member will "sponsor" a meeting and supply to those who attend both the peyote and the next morning's breakfast. The "sponsor," usually but not always the "leader," takes charge of the meeting; he decides the order of events and the amount of peyote to be consumed. Although the individual leader exercises an absolute control of the meeting, anthropologists report a striking uniformity of its ritual.

A meeting connotes a solemn and special occasion. Whole families attend together, although children and young women participate only by their presence. Adherents don their finest clothing, usually suits for men and fancy dresses for women, but sometimes ceremonial Indian costumes. At the meeting the members pray, sing, and make ritual use of drum, fan, eagle bone, whistle, rattle and prayer cigarette, the symbolic emblems of their faith. The central event, of course, consists of the use of peyote in quantities sufficient to produce an hallucinatory state.

At an early but fixed stage in the ritual the members pass around a ceremonial bag of peyote buttons. Each adult may take four, the customary number, or take none. The participants chew the buttons, usually with some difficulty because of extreme bitterness; later, at a set time in the ceremony any member may ask for more peyote; occasionally a member may take as many as four more buttons. At sunrise on Sunday the ritual ends; after a brief outdoor prayer, the host and his family serve breakfast. Then the members depart. By morning the effects of the peyote disappear; the users suffer no after-effects.

Although peyote serves as a sacramental symbol similar to bread and wine in certain Christian churches, it is more than a sacrament. Peyote constitutes in itself an object of worship; prayers are directed to it much as prayers are devoted to the Holy Ghost. On the other hand, to use peyote for nonreligious purposes is sacreligious. Members of the church regard peyote as a "teacher" because it induces a feeling of brotherhood with other members; indeed, it enables the participant to experience the Diety. Finally, devotees treat peyote as a "protector." Much as a Catholic carries his medallion, an Indian G.I. often wears around his neck a beautifully beaded pouch containing one large peyote button.

On the basis of this discussion, the California Supreme Court concluded that peyote was indeed an integral part of the Indians' religious practice. Furthermore, the court held that the state had failed to establish a compelling state interest that would permit an infringement upon this practice. Allegations by the state that the use of peyote was taking the place of modern medical care, that it was indoctrinating children with an adverse sense of values, and that it tended to lead to the use of more harmful drugs were all dismissed. The evidence indicated just the contrary: Indians did not use peyote in place of medicine; statistics revealed that children never, and teenagers rarely, used the hallucinogen. Furthermore, even the attorney general of the state admitted that peyote was not deleterious to Indian health. Experts, in fact, testified that the moral standards of members of the Native American Church were as high if not higher than Indians outside the church. Lest people erroneously misread the opinion, the use of peyote that is not an integral part of a religious ceremony violates the law and users are subject to prosecution.

People v. Woody is an important case. Not only does it crystallize the fact that American Indians are protected by the Free Exercise Clause of the First Amendment in their off-reservation religious practices but it also brings attention to the importance of tolerance by the white community of religious ceremonies strange to them. Today federal narcotic laws, as well as the laws of nineteen states, have exempted the use of peyote when used as a religious exercise by members of the Native American Church. Church members in other states, however, have been harassed and arrested. Other religious practices continue to run afoul of state laws. Religious sites come under assault from those who wish to put them to recreational or commercial use. Religious objects are destroyed or collected as anthropological treasures. Indians are denied the use of sweat lodge ceremonies or the right to wear their hair in a long traditional manner in some state prisons and school systems. The First Amendment has provided Indians with some protection, but there clearly persists a real threat to the unobstructed Indian exercise of religious freedom.

In an attempt to remedy this problem, Congress passed the American Indian Religious Freedom Act in 1978 (Public Law 95-341). The purpose of the act is to promulgate a federal policy by which to protect and preserve the traditional religious practices of American Indians, including Alaska natives and Hawaiians. Among other things, the policy guarantees access to religious sites, use and possession of sacred objects, and freedom to worship through traditional ceremonial rites. In addition to articulating a general policy promoting and preserving traditional Indian religious practices, the act calls for an examination of current federal policy by the relevant government agencies to determine what appropriate changes should be made in order to implement the spirit of the law.

The agencies were instructed to consult with traditional religious leaders to aid in this respect. In response to this provision, the Native American Rights Fund submitted a proposal to begin an implementation study—the American Indian Religious Freedom Project. The project was funded and NARF, together with the American Indian Law Center in Albuquerque, New Mexico, undertook the review. The research data were gathered by the American Indian Law Center and NARF in conjunction with a fifteen-member Native American Religious Advisory Board, which had broad expertise and Indian contacts throughout the country. The results of the project were submitted to the president and Congress for their consideration.

Religious freedom is an emotional and sensitive issue. Historically and constitutionally, the paths of those who worship in an unorthodox fashion have been strewn with hardship and harassment. When the complexity of a religious issue is compounded by the fact that it involves unfamiliar practices, such as are found within traditional Indian religions, then the burden is heavy indeed. In attempting to protect Indian religious interests, the government is faced with numerous questions that have not previously arisen in conjunction with religious practices.

Indian tribal religions for the most part do not have institutional structures comparable to Christian churches and other organized expressions of religion. There is no canon of belief, no ecclesiastical hierarchy, no creeds and dogmas marking off sacred from secular beliefs. Consequently, there is no formal religious authority by which standards can be measured. People as a rule do not join tribal denominations. One can only presume that a tribal member practices his or her tribe's religion but this religion itself has changed since contact and there is no way of knowing whether a ceremony is still being performed except by cautious inquiry. Even then the hesitancy of Indian people to define what they believe to be truly their own before a nontribal member practically precludes even this method of discovering what the practices are.

A significant number of Indian tribal religions rely upon the performance of ceremonies and rituals in specific locations. A particular mountain, lake, butte, or river may be the center of the tribe's religious history and hence form its identity. Such is the case with the Taos Pueblo and Blue Lake. How does the federal bureaucracy allow for the conduct of some tribal ceremonies without running afoul of the religious establishment clause when a tribe feels it must have exclusive use of a location in a national park or forest in order to practice its religion? Does the federal agency prohibit the use of that location and adjoining places to recreational use? Some critics of the American Indian Religious Freedom Resolution argue that this effort borders on establishment. Is it reasonable, they ask, to allow Indians exclusive use of a location when they might only be present there for a few days a year?

There is also a question of which individuals should be protected by this resolution. The federal government must not distinguish on the basis of race; nevertheless, it is difficult for policymakers and administrators to conceive of non-Indians participating in any meaningful way in a tribal religion. The problem is made more difficult because of the propensity of traditional Indians to "adopt" non-Indians as members of their particular following and to admit them to certain rites and ceremonies. The non-Indians cannot help but conclude that they have been admitted to some degree of participation in the tribal religion. The question is whether they have been admitted to practice to the degree that their practice of a ceremony, absent Indians participating in and directing the ceremony, is protected by law. Can non-Indians, even with the most sincere motives and devotional attitudes, be protected by the American Indian Religious Freedom Resolution if they are discovered with a bag of peyote or with eagle feathers?

This question involves much the same issue as other jurisdictional problems. Is "Indian" a racial or political or even religious term? The Supreme Court, first in *Morton v. Mancari*, 417 U.S. 535

(1974), and later in *Fisher v. District Court,* 424 U.S. 382 (1976), has described the relationship of Indians to the federal government as political rather than racial. Yet, on a practical level this political status always seems to involve racial identity. The federal courts have always been deliberately vague regarding the definition of an Indian when confronted with the question in an intercultural context. In *United States v. Rogers,* 45 U.S. (4 How.) 567 (1846), Rogers, accused of murder, argued that he and his victim, although white men, had become adopted members of the Cherokee Nation and were therefore under Cherokee law and jurisdiction. The Court noted that the statutory term Indian "is confined to those who by the usages and customs of the Indians are belonging to their race. It does not speak of members of a tribe, but of the race generally, of the family of Indians." This definition, of course, is not helpful because it is obvious that the Court has race in mind as the standard. And the Court too easily moves from "usages and customs" to race. If applied to the American Indian Religious Freedom Resolution, this definition would not be helpful.

If Indians believed that the passage of the American Indian Religious Freedom Resolution would clarify their rights to religious freedom and assist them in interpreting to the courts the basis of their beliefs and rituals, they were mistaken. If anything, the resolution has made Indian religious practice the target of further harassment and has failed to provide a shield against intrusions. In *Badoni v. Higginson,* 2d 179 (10th Cir. 1980), a group of Navajo medicine men sought to preserve the Rainbow Bridge area in Utah, which was a sacred shrine of their tribe. They sought exclusive use of the area during the ceremonies and removal of the boating dock used by tourists in the area. The Court of Appeals for the 10th Circuit ruled that to accommodate the religious practices of the Navajo at Rainbow Bridge would itself be a violation of the Establishment Clause of the First Amendment since Rainbow Bridge would then become a government-managed shrine. Thus the unique nature of Indian religious practices is sufficiently distinguishable from the practices of other religious sects as to cause courts to see protection as establishment—a result hardly anticipated by the framers of the American Indian Religious Freedom Resolution.

THE RIGHT TO BASIC GOVERNMENTAL SERVICES

Given the low priority accorded to Indians by the federal government when it comes to allocating the country's financial resources, it is little wonder that American Indians have been perennially described as a neglected minority. Even today the federal government responds more quickly to visible and vocal special interest groups and more populous racial minorities, such as the blacks and Chicanos, than it does to American Indians. At the state level the problems are compounded even more. Historically, the states have bristled over the tax-exempt status of Indian lands. They have taken a rigid stance that, since Indians do not contribute to the tax revenues of the state, they are not entitled to participate in state social welfare programs. Indians have suffered tremendously because of this political posture, particularly Indian children who have need of these local resources and programs. Gaining access to basic governmental services at both the federal and state levels has proved a difficult burden for Indians to overcome. This difficulty can be well illustrated by examining the rights of Indians to basic governmental services in the fields of education and social service programs.

Eligibility for Educational Benefits

The Kennedy Special Subcommittee on Indian Education issued a report in 1969 characterizing Indian education as a national tragedy. In a comprehensive report that followed its clarion call for major reforms in Indian education, the Kennedy Subcommittee documented many of the difficulties faced by American Indians today in achieving some kind of educational parity with other Americans. But even this report, wholly sympathetic to Indian aspirations, failed to provide a philosophical-historical framework in which people could understand *why* Indian education was such a disaster and disgrace. Although emphasizing the cultural differences that exist between Indian people and other groups in American society, the report assumed without further critical reflection that, given the same opportunities of access to educational institutions as the white majority, Indians would adopt the same values and come to achieve the same results. Culture, in this context, was merely the trappings of costume, music, and dance and did not include fundamental differences in perspectives about the world.

Education has been one of the major weapons of forced assimilation since the establishment of the first colonies. Missionaries generally provided the impetus toward developing educational institutions for American Indians since they deeply believed that successful defense of Indian rights and assurance of equality for Indians meant complete absorption into the mainstream of American society. Assuming without any critical reflection that America would be Christian, specifically predominantly their denomination, the early missionaries suffered immense hardships in order to bring the Gospel to the tribes, and the first efforts at teaching the Indians reading and writing were for the purpose of placing in their hands at an early date the Holy Scriptures. The missionary tradition continues today although it has more recently been the fundamentalist sects rather than the mainstream Protestant denominations that have accepted the challenge of educating Indian children to their peculiar view of the world.

With the secularization of education as a responsibility of public institutions, the federal government assumed considerably more responsibility for Indian education. Beginning in the 1880s under former army officer Richard Henry Pratt, the Bureau of Indian Affairs developed an extensive network of off-reservation boarding schools designed to inculcate Indian children with the virtues and values of Western civilization and to eliminate the traces of tribal "barbarism" that their own heritage was thought to represent. As the public school system developed, federal incentives to states to assume responsibility for Indian education increased accordingly. The states quickly complained that tribal lands could not be taxed and that requiring them to provide educational services to Indians was unjust in view of the lack of financial contributions the Indians represented. Beginning in the 1900s and continuing through the 1950s the response of the federal government to state pleas for assistance in providing educational services to Indians took two forms: the federal government provided substantial funding to state school systems to provide for Indian children and it gave thousands of acres of land to the local school systems in return for their promise to provide education to Indians.

School districts traditionally received the sixteenth section of land in a township under the provisions enacted first in the act enabling the territory of Ohio to form a constitution and state government (2 Stat. 175) and then reaffirmed under the succeeding statutes that created territories and allocated lands to new states. With the opening of the large plains reservations, the states began to agitate for school lands within reservation boundaries. The Act of March 2, 1901 (39 Stat. 950), allowed a state to test its rights to school lands without joining the tribe as a party if a secretary of the interior was made a party. With this opening wedge assured, states thereafter plagued the federal congress with demands for various kinds of compensation in return for allowing a token number of Indian children to attend public schools under their jurisdiction. The Act of June 7, 1924 (43 Stat. 536), bolstered the authority of the secretary of the interior to "pay any claims which are ascertained to be proper and just, whether covered by contracts or not, for the tuition of Indian pupils in State public schools." Joint Congressional Resolution of February 12, 1922 (42 Stat. 364), allowed the president to pay tuition of the Montana Indian children in the schools of that state.

Land transfers, such as the Act of March 31, 1908 (35 Stat. 53), which authorized the secretary of the interior to issue a patent for certain lands of the Santee Reservation to school district No. 36 in Know County, Nebraska, soon became an accepted way to underwrite Indian participation in local school districts. After the Second World War, when land was beginning to reach a premium price and consolidated school districts were becoming more prominent, this movement was rapidly increased. Sometimes there was an agreement that the school district would thereafter provide free tuition to Indian students but more likely the legislation simply quickly and quietly transferred the Indian and federal school lands to local school systems.

The Snyder Act of 1921 (42 Stat. 208) gave the secretary of the interior general authority to expend federal monies for Indian "benefit, care, and assistance," and a considerable amount of this money was spent in contracts for local school districts to entice them to provide education to Indians. The idea caught on and in 1934 the Johnson-O'Malley Act (48 Stat. 596) expanded the Snyder Act authority. During the 1950s two additional statutes, P.L. 81-815 and P.L. 81-874, the basic federal laws that provide almost all federal assistance to public school systems today, made the education of Indian children a special category of assistance to state school systems.

Indian education, therefore, has been amply funded by the federal government in a variety of transfer payments to states for Indian education. For the most part, state school districts have welcomed the federal funds but not the Indian students. Discrimination, in spite of direct federal allocations to the states, was always a major feature of state-controlled education for Indians. A California statute, for example, provided for the education of Indian children as follows: "The governing body of the school district shall have the power to exclude children of filthy or vicious habits, or children suffering from contagious or infectious diseases, and also to establish separate schools for Indian children and for children of Chinese, Japanese or Mongolian parentage. When such schools are established, Indian children or children of Chinese, Japanese, or Mongolian parentage must not be admitted into any other school." In 1924, however, the constitutionality of the California statute was challenged in *Piper v. Big Pine School District*, 193 Cal. 664, 226 P. 926 (1924).

Alice Piper, an Indian child of fifteen living on a reservation, was excluded from an all-white school as a consequence of the California separation-of-the-races statute. Although there was a BIA Indian school operating within the district, Alice Piper wanted to attend an all-white school. She was denied admittance solely because she was a person of Indian blood. The California Supreme Court struck down the state law as being invalid. While the court focused its attention largely on the principle that all California children were entitled to an education under both state constitutional and statutory provisions, it also tied these state enactments with the Equal Protection Clause of the United States Constitution. The Constitution precluded states from denying persons equal protection of the laws. The court went on to reject the state argument that since Indians did not pay taxes this placed an undue economic burden on the state. Even if this were true, the court noted, this could not serve as a basis for denying Indian children resident in the state an equal opportunity to an education simply because they were Indian. The economic burden question was one to be submitted to the state legislature for redress.

The *Piper* case is viewed as the legal authority for guaranteeing Indian children the right to attend state public schools even though it should have been obvious, with the enormous number of specific statutes that required the respective states to provide public education for Indians, that it was a state responsibility that had been assumed when states accepted federal funds and lands. Today about 80 percent of all Indian children attend public schools. The BIA boarding schools continue in operation although recently a number have been reduced in operation or closed. These boarding schools are now largely predelinquent holding pens rather than educational institutions. Tribes have assumed a part of the bureau's old educational function by contracting the operation of schools on the reservations, leaving primarily students who live in very isolated places (the Navajo Reservation and Alaskan villages) and problem children.

While access to a public education is a settled issue today, there remain a number of problems confronting Indian children and their quest to receive an adequate educational experience. The language problem posed to many Indian children severely restricts their educational opportunities. Money for bilingual programs or even programs designed to teach English as a second language is not plentiful and receives low budgetary priorities. Additionally, non-Indian teachers frequently fail to grasp the cultural differences dividing Indians and non-Indians. Textbook materials also hinder educational development. Indians have been portrayed badly in many texts or, as is more frequently the case, completely ignored. Although American Indians have a right to this most basic service of our democracy, full realization is yet many decades in the future.

Eligibility for Social Service Benefits

When Chief Justice John Marshall in the *Cherokee Nation Cases* referred to Indian nations as "domestic dependent nations," he was providing a preview of at least one Indian problem for years to come. Stripped of their land, their buffalo and salmon, and often their ability to govern themselves, Indian tribes became *dependent* upon the federal government in many ways. Food and clothing alone constituted the most fundamental of many of their needs. As described by one commentator: "Old, crippled, almost helpless Indians are required to come to the agency office in all sorts of weather to get their supplies. On several reservations the survey staff saw poorly clad, old people, with feet soaked by long walks through snow and slush, huddled in the agency office waiting for the arrival of the superintendent or other officer who could give them an order for rations to keep them from actual starvation" (as quoted in Wolf, p. 607).

The federal government was thus forced to embark on a program of providing some form of welfare programs for its Indian "wards." Unfortunately, the efforts of federal assistance agencies were not always as altruistic as they might have been. Food, clothing, and other means of subsistence were often used as political tools by which to promote a particular governmental policy. While these efforts to control individuals may not have been as extreme as those of Lord Jeffrey Amherst, the British commander who suggested sending the Indians blankets infested with small pox (from which comes the old Amherst College song proclaiming the fact that he "placed a pox, in their sox, in the days of yore"), federal control over these services was all too often political.

Indians living on reservations are eligible for a wide variety of federal social service programs designed specifically for Indians. The Indian Health Service, for instance, has established medical facilities and services on a number of reservations and has contract services at some major urban hospitals. Federal programs also have been developed to support job training programs, public housing, and agricultural efforts. Non-Indians, except in some special cases, are not eligible to participate in these programs. While these Indian programs are dispersed throughout a number of different governmental agencies, the BIA has in the past assumed supervision of many of them and still plays a prominent role in this capacity today.

Most of the specially designed Indian social services fall within the category of "general assistance" programs. This usually means that one qualifies for benefits only if there is no other public assistance available. Welfare workers are required to use the state's budgetary plan in determining the extent of welfare benefits and thus these federal benefits vary from reservation to reservation despite the fact that the funds involved come from the federal government.

In addition to those special Indian programs administered by the federal government, American Indians may also qualify for welfare assistance under general federal programs. The food stamp program, for instance, is one of the newest and perhaps the most effective of the general federal assistance programs. Eligibility for food stamps, of course, is not limited to Indians but is offered to all needy persons who qualify regardless of skin color or race. At the federal level of government, then, Indians can seek social service assistance both under programs designed specifically for indigent Indians and under general welfare programs extended to all needy persons, Indian and non-Indian alike.

Indian access to state social service programs, like the struggle for educational opportunities, has met political resistance in most states. The old argument that Indians who do not pay taxes should not be eligible for services has been at the forefront of this state resistance. In 1954, a California court addressed itself to this overall question in *Acosta v. San Diego County*, 126 Cal. App. 2d 455, 272 P.2d 92 (1954). A group of needy Indians living on the Pala Indian Reservation applied for emergency relief from San Diego County. The state denied them benefits on the grounds that Indians did not share in the tax burden and thus should not expect to partake in the benefits of state services. The California court disagreed with this contention and held that reservation Indians were entitled to the emergency relief benefits as were the non-Indians of the state.

In justifying its decision, the court spent a good deal of time demonstrating that Indians were in many ways *sui juris* (possessing full social and political rights). They were not, in the technical sense, simply wards of the government. Indians living on reservations served as jurors, were subject to the draft, could sue in their own name. Indians of necessity had to travel beyond their reservation borders and pay certain types of sales and excise taxes. Furthermore, the court noted that the lives of Indian and non-Indian state residents were intimately interwoven in many ways. Highway funds were shared; Indian lands and people were among those counted in accumulating census data on states. Census population figures, of course, not only determine congressional representation for a state but also provide a basis for allocating federal funds. In a concluding thought the court took cognizance of the fact that many non-Indians in the state lived on tax-exempt property belonging to the federal government or religious institutions, yet this had never been used as a basis for withholding public services. All this evidence led to but one conclusion—that Indians living on reservations in California were bona fide citizens and residents of the state. As such they were endowed with the "rights, privileges and immunities equal to those enjoyed by all other citizens and residents of the state."

The issue appears to be well settled. Indians are eligible to participate in state social service programs just as other residents of the state are as long as the Indians satisfy the established "need" requirements. State arguments that Indians should not participate because they do not pay their way are simply ill-conceived and generally demagogic. In the first place, most state social service programs are actually financed either wholly or largely by the federal government. This fact alone makes a mockery of the state argument. More important, economic activity on the reservation produces a great deal of economic benefit to the states in which reservations are located. Indians receive extensive amounts of money from the federal government each year and most of this money is funneled directly into the state's economy. The money goes to grocers, carpenters, contractors, automobile dealers, and the vast array of commercial merchants who serve reservation needs. This uncontested conclusion does not even take into consideration the "multiplier" effect that the expenditure of federal funds has on a local marketing area. Even the courts have recognized that the money contributed by the federal government to Indian programs is substantial in benefiting non-Indian residents of the state as well as reservation Indians. States should be gratified in having reservations in their midst, not hostile to their presence.

While American Indians have had to struggle to gain access to basic governmental services, the struggle has produced needed results. In addition to programs designed specifically for Indians, such as the Indian Health Service, Indians are eligible to participate both in the large variety of federal *and* in state social service programs. The key to this eligibility is that Indians are citizens and residents of the United States and the states wherein they reside and as such are entitled to the full benefits and privileges that are offered to all citizens.

Bibliographic References

American Indian Life. Bulletin no. 12, June 1928.

Annual Report of the Commissioner of Indian Affairs to the Secretary of the Interior [AR-CIA]. Washington, D.C.: Government Printing Office, 1875, 1877, 1884, 1885.

Brown, Joseph Epes. *The Sacred Pipe.* Norman: University of Oklahoma Press, 1953.

Canby, William C., Jr. "Civil Jurisdiction and the Indian Reservation System." 1973 *Utah Law Review* 206 (1973).

Chambers, Reid P. "Discharge of the Federal Trust Responsibility to Enforce Legal Claims of Indian Tribes: Case Studies of Bureaucratic Conflict of Interests." In *A Study of Administrative Conflicts of Interests in the Protection of Indian Natural Resources,* Subcommittee on Administrative Practice and Procedure, Senate Committee on the Judiciary. 91st Cong., 1971.

Cohen, Felix. *Handbook of Federal Indian Law.* Albuquerque: University of New Mexico Press, 1942.

Collier, John. *Memorandum, Hearings on H.R. 7902 before the House Committee on Indian Affairs.* 73rd Cong., 2d Sess., pp. 16–18, 1934.

Combs, Jerald A. *The Jay Treaty: Political Background of the Founding Fathers.* Berkeley: University of California Press, 1970.

Coulter, Robert K. "Federal Law and Indian Tribal Law: The Right to Civil Counsel and the 1968 Indian Bill of Rights." In *Columbia Survey of Human Rights Law,* vol. 3 (1970–71), pp. 49–93. Baltimore: Deford and Co.

Debo, Angie. *The Rise and Fall of the Choctaw Republic.* Norman: University of Oklahoma Press, 1961.

Driver, Harold E. *Indians of North America.* 2d ed. Chicago: University of Chicago Press, 1975.

Getches, David H., Daniel M. Rosenfelt, and Charles F. Wilkinson. *Cases and Materials on Federal Indian Law.* St. Paul: West Publishing Co., 1979.

Grinde, Donald A. Jr. *The Iroquois and the Founding of the American Nation.* San Francisco: American Indian Historian Press, 1977.

Gross, Michael Paul. "Reckoning for Legal Services: A Case-Study of Legal Assistance in Indian Education." 49 *Notre Dame Law Review* 78 (1973).

House Report 473. *Report of the Committee on Indian Affairs of the House of Representatives.* 32d Cong., 1st Sess., vol. 4, May 20, 1834.

House Report 2503. *Report with Respect to the House Resolution Authorizing the Committee on Interior and Insular Affairs to Conduct an Investigation of the Bureau of Indian Affairs.* 82d Cong., 2d Sess., 1952.

Kerr, James R. "Constitutional Rights, Tribal Justice, and the American Indian." 18 *Journal of Public Law* 311 (1969).

Meriam, Lewis. *The Problem of Indian Administration.* Baltimore: Johns Hopkins University Press, 1928.

Montoya, Domingo. *Testimony before the Subcommittee on Constitutional Rights of the Senate Committee of the Judiciary.* 91st Cong., 1st Sess., pp. 6–9, 1969.

National American Indian Court Judges Association. *Indian Courts and the Future,* ed. David Getches. Washington, D.C.: National American Indian Court Judges Association, 1978.

———. "The Indian Judiciary and the Concept of Separation of Powers." In *Justice and the American Indian,* vol. 2. "Federal Prosecution of Crimes Committed on Indian Reservations." In ibid., vol. 5. Washington, D.C.: National American Indian Court Judges Association, 1974.

Native American Rights Fund. *Annual Report, 1979.* Boulder: Native American Rights Fund, 1980.

Olson, James. *Red Cloud and the Sioux Problem.* Lincoln: University of Nebraska Press, 1965.

Otis, D. S. *History of the Allotment Policy, Hearings on H.R. 7902 before the House Committee on Indian Affairs.* 73rd Cong., 2d Sess., pt. 9, pp. 428–489, 1934.

Price, Monroe. *Law and the American Indian: Readings, Notes, and Cases.* New York: Bobbs-Merrill Company, 1973.

———. "Lawyers on the Reservation: Some Implications for the Legal Profession." 1969 *Law and Social Order* 161 (1969).

Rice, W. G. "The Position of the American Indian in the Law of the United States." *Journal of Comparative Legislation and International Law* 3d ser., 16 (February 1934): 78–95.

Russell, Frank. "A Pima Constitution." *Journal of American Folklore* 16 (December 1903): 222–228.

Survey of Conditions of the Indians in the United States. Hearings before a Subcommittee of the Committee on Indian Affairs, United States Senate, Seventy-first Congress, Third Session. Parts 11–13, 1929–1931. Washington, D.C.: Government Printing Office, 1931.

Swan, Robert C. "Indian Legal Service Programs: The Key to Red Power." 12 *Arizona Law Review* 594 (1970).

Taylor, Graham D. *The New Deal and American Indian Tribalism: The Administration of the Indian Reorganization Act, 1934–45.* Lincoln: University of Nebraska Press, 1980.

"Tribal Self-Government and the Indian Reorganization Act of 1934." 70 *Michigan Law Review* 955 (1972).

United States Civil Rights Commission. *1961 Annual Report.* Washington, D.C.: Government Printing Office, 1961.

Vitoria, Francisco de. *Francisci de Victoria De Indis et De Jure Belli Relectiones.* Translated by John Pawley Bate; edited by Ernest Nys. Section 2, 1557. Washington, D.C.: Carnegie Institution, 1917; reprinted, Dobbs Ferry, N.Y.: Oceana Press, 1964.

Wilkinson, Charles F., and Eric R. Biggs. "The Evolution of the Termination Policy." 5 *American Indian Law Review* 139 (1977).

Wolf, Roger. "Needed: A System of Income Maintenance for Indians." 10 *Arizona Law Review* 597 (1968).

Index of Cases

Acosta v. San Diego County, 126 Cal. App. 2d 445, 272 P.2d 92 (1954): 245

Allen v. Merrell, 6 Utah 2d 32, 305 P.2d 490 (1956): 224

Allen v. Merrell, 353 U.S. 932 (1957): 225

Andy, Application of, 40 Wash. 2d 449, 302 P.2d 963 (1956): 75

Arizona ex rel. Merrill v. Turtle, 413 F.2d 683 (9th Cir. 1969): 191

Bad Horse v. Bad Horse, 163 Mont. 445, 517 P.2d 893 (1974): 212

Badoni v. Higginson, 638 F.2d 179 (10th Cir. 1980), cert. den. 49 U.S.L.W. 3931 (1981): 239

Bates v. Clark, 95 U.S. 204 (1877): 67, 68

Beardslee v. United States, 387 F.2d 280 (8th Cir. 1967): 76

Buehl, In Re, 87 Wash. 649, 555 P.2d 1334 (1976): 120

Cherokee Nation v. Georgia, 30 U.S. (5 Pet.) 1 (1831): 4, 29–32, 51, 63, 126

Cherokee Trust Funds, The, 117 U.S. 288 (1886): 219

City of New Town v. United States, 454 F.2d 121 (8th Cir. 1972): 76, 77

Colliflower v. Garland, 324 F.2d 369 (9th Cir. 1965): 127, 131–132

Colwash, In Re, 57 Wash. 2d 196, 356 P.2d 994 (1960): 75

Crichton v. Shelton, 33 I.D. 215 (1891): 71

Crow Dog, Ex Parte, 109 U.S. 556 (1883): 11, 169, 171

DeCoteau v. District County Court, 420 U.S. 425 (1975): 77

Delaware Tribal Business Committee v. Weeks, 430 U.S. 73 (1977): 42

Dodge v. Nakai, 298 F. Supp. 26 (D. Ariz. 1969): 132, 153

Donnelly v. United States, 228 U.S. 243 (1913): 71, 72, 73, 75

Elk v. Wilkins, 112 U.S. 94 (1884): 220

Federal Power Commission v. Tuscarora Indian Nation, 362 U.S. 99 (1960): 21

Felicia v. United States, 495 F.2d 353, cert. den. 419 U.S. 849 (1974): 228

Fisher v. District Court, 424 U.S. 382 (1976): 212, 239

Francisco v. State, 113 Ariz. 427, 556 P.2d 1 (1976): 215

Harrison v. Laveen, 67 Ariz. 337, 196 P.2d 456 (1948): 222, 224

Henry v. United States, 432 F.2d 114 (9th Cir. 1970): 170

Jim v. CIT Financial Services Corporation, 87 N. Mex. 362, 533 P.2d 751 (1975): 120

Johnson v. McIntosh, 21 U.S. (8 Wheat.) 543 (1823): 4, 26, 30

Kansas Indians, The, 5 Wall. 737, 755–756 (1866): 53, 54, 204, 205, 209

Keeble v. United States, 412 U.S. 205 (1973): 172, 227

Little Horn State Bank v. Stops, 555 P.2d 211 (1976): 215

Little Thunder v. South Dakota, 518 F.2d 1253 (8th Cir. 1975): 225

Lone Wolf v. Hitchcock, 187 U.S. 553 (1903): 43–44, 45, 156

McClanahan v. Arizona State Tax Commission, 411 U.S. 164 (1973): 54–55, 77, 204, 205, 206, 208

McKay v. Campbell, 16 Fed. Cas. No. 161 (D. Ore. 1871): 220

Mattz v. Arnett, 412 U.S. 481 (1973): 77

Merrion v. Jicarilla Apache Tribe, 102 S.Ct. 894 (1982): 55

Moe v. Confederated Salish and Kootenai Tribes of the Flathead Indian Reservation, 425 U.S. 463 (1976): 56, 78, 207

Morgan, Ex Parte, 20 F. 298 (D.C.W.D. Ark. 1883): 190–191

Morton v. Mancari, 417 U.S. 535 (1974): 228, 238

Native American Church v. Navajo Tribal Council, 272 F.2d 131 (10th Cir. 1959): 131, 165, 233

Oliphant v. Suquamish Indian Tribe, 435 U.S. 191 (1978): 180, 189, 190

Opsahl v. Johnson, 138 Minn. 42, 163 N.W. 988 (1917): 223

People v. Woody, 61 Cal. 2d 716, 394 P.2d 813 (1964): 234

Perrin v. United States, 232 U.S. 478 (1914): 73

Piper v. Big Pine School District, 193 Cal. 664, 226 P. 926 (1924): 242, 243

Porter v. Hall, 34 Ariz. 308, 271 P. 411 (1928): 224

Pyramid Lake Paiute Tribe of Indians v. Morton, 354 F. Supp. 252 (D.C. 1973): 39

Quick Bear v. Leupp, 210 U.S. 50 (1908): 156

Red Fox v. Red Fox, 23 Ore. App. 393, 542 P.2d 918 (1975): 119

Rosebud Sioux Tribe v. Kneip, 430 U.S. 584 (1977): 77

Santa Clara Pueblo v. Martinez, 436 U.S. 49 (1978): 120, 133–135

Schantz v. White Lightning, 231 N.W.2d 812 (1975): 211

Scholder v. United States, 428 F.2d 1123 (9th Cir. 1970): 106

Seminole Nation of Indians v. United States, 316 U.S. 286 (1942): 38

Seneca Nation of Indians v. Brucker, 262 F.2d 27 (D.C. 1959): 44

Seneca Nation of Indians v. United States, 338 F.2d 55 (2d Cir. 1964): 44

Settler v. Yakima Tribal Council, 419 F.2d 486 (9th Cir. 1969): 132

Seymour v. Superintendent, 368 U.S. 351 (1962): 75–76, 187

State ex rel. Old Elk v. District Court of Big Horn, 552 P.2d 1394 (Mont. 1976); cert. den. 429 U.S. 1030 (1976): 191

State Securities v. Anderson, 84 N. Mex. 629, 506 P.2d 786 (1973): 214, 215

Talton v. Mayes, 163 U.S. 376 (1895): 127, 131, 165, 229

Udall v. Littell, 366 F.2d 668 (D.C. Cir. 1968): 154
United States v. Antelope, 430 U.S. 641 (1977): 228
United States v. Clapox, 35 Fed. 575 (D.C. Ore. 1888): 115
United States v. Forty-eight Pounds of Rising Star Tea, 38 F. 400 (C.C.N.D. Cal. 1889): 71
United States v. John, 587 F.2d 683, cert. den. 441 U.S. 925 (1979): 228
United States v. Joseph, 94 U.S. 614 (1876): 72, 113
United States v. Kagama, 118 U.S. 375 (1886): 41, 42, 171
United States v. Lucero, 1 N.M. 422 (1869): 139
United States v. McBratney, 104 U.S. 621 (1881): 68, 181–182, 228
United States v. McGowan, 302 U.S. 535 (1938): 74
United States v. Marcyes, 557 F.2d 1361 (9th Cir. 1977): 174
United States v. Mazurie, 419 U.S. 544 (1975): 55, 190
United States v. Muskrat, 219 U.S. 346 (1911): 43
United States v. Pelican, 232 U.S. 442 (1914): 73, 75
United States v. Ramsey, 271 U.S. 467 (1926): 73
United States v. Rogers, 45 U.S. (4 How.) 567 (1846): 239

United States v. Sandoval, 231 U.S. 28 (1913): 72, 73, 75
United States v. Sioux Nation of Indians, 100 S.Ct. 2716 (1980): 45
United States v. Washington, 384 F. Supp. 312 (W.D. Wash. 1974): 47
United States v. Wheeler, 435 U.S. 313 (1978): 228–229
United States v. Winans, 198 U.S. 371 (1905): 49
United States v. Winnebago Tribe of Nebraska, 542 F.2d 1002 (8th Cir. 1976): 44

Wakefield v. Little Light, 276 Md. 333, 347 A.2d 228 (1975): 212
Washington v. Confederated Tribes of the Colville Indian Reservation, 100 S.Ct. 2069 (1980): 56, 207–208
White Mountain Apache Tribe v. Bracker, 100 S.Ct. 2578 (1980): 206
Whyte v. District Court, 140 Colo. 334, 346 P.2d 1012 (1959): 211
Williams v. Lee, 358 U.S. 217 (1959): 54, 204, 205, 206, 208, 209–210, 211, 212
Williams v. United States, 327 U.S. 711 (1946): 174
Winters v. United States, 207 U.S. 564 (1908): 49–50
Worcester v. Georgia, 31 U.S. (6 Pet.) 515 (1832): 4, 32–33, 51, 54, 204, 205, 208

Index of Topics

Abourezk Commission, 23, 24
Absentee Shawnee tribe, 219
Advocates. *See* Indian advocates
Allotment, 8–12, 15
American Bar Association, 143
American Civil Liberties Union
  (ACLU), 155, 158, 160
American Indian Defense Associa-
  tion, 12, 13
American Indian Law Center, 237
American Indian Movement, 159
American Indian Policy Review
  Commission, 23, 24
American Indian Religious Freedom
  Act, 237–239
American Revolution, 59–60
Amherst, Jeffrey, 244
Area Redevelopment Administra-
  tion, 21
Arickara Indians, 100
Arthur, Chester A., 8, 9
Articles of Confederation, 26
Assimilation, 8, 10–11, 116
Assimilative Crimes Act, 173–174,
  177, 179, 180, 181
Atotarho, 88
Attorneys, 139
  federal Indian law, 140–142
  Indian attorneys, 144–145
  Legal Services attorneys,
    151–153, 157, 158
  secretarial approval, 153–155
  specializing in Indian affairs, 142
  tribal court proceedings, 148–151

U.S. Attorney's Office, 145–148,
  183–184, 186, 192, 227

"Backdrop" doctrine, 54, 55, 56, 77,
  205–207
Bad Wound, 96
Bail, 130, 229
Baldwin, Henry, 30, 31
Banks, Dennis, 147, 186
Big Foot, Chief, 323
Biggs, Eric, 20
Bill of Rights, 126–130, 175
Black, Hugo, 74
Black Americans, 223
Black Elk, 115
Blackfeet Indians, 94
Blue Lake, 238
Boarding schools. *See* Indian Board-
  ing schools
Brant, Joseph, 60
Brotherton Indians, 219
Brown, Joseph Epes, 115
Bureau of Indian Affairs (BIA), 23,
  99, 100, 104, 105, 159
  boarding schools, 241, 243
  health services, 19
  Indian Reorganization Act, 14
  Law and Order Branch, 185
  law enforcement, 182, 183,
    184–185
  rule-making power, 38
  social services, 244
  termination policy, 102
  tribal complaints, 13

tribal courts, 113–116, 125, 154
tribal government, 104
War Department, 36
Bureau of Land Management,
    106–107
Bureau of Reclamation, 106
Burke Act, 10

California Indian Legal Services,
    156
Canby, William, 215
Carnegie Corporation, 158
Carter, Jimmy, 35, 186
Cayuga Indians, 88
CFR courts. *See* Court of Indian
    Offenses
Chamber, Reid, 107
Checkerboard lands, 70
Cherokee Indians, 6, 7, 27–33, 57,
    59, 90, 97, 127, 131, 191, 239
Cherokee Nation Cases, 4, 27–33,
    41, 45, 46, 51, 126, 244
Cheyenne Indians, 83, 84, 86
Chickasaw Indians, 90, 91, 97
Child adoption, 196, 212
Child custody, 211, 212, 213
Chinese Exclusion Act, 8
Chinook language, 47–48
Chippewa Indians, 64, 93
Choctaw Indians, 7, 86–87, 90, 91,
    97
Christian missionaries, 7, 240–241
Citizenship, 10, 11, 217–222, 246
Citizens Potawatomi tribe, 219
Civil law, 193
    conflict of laws, 209–215
    domestic law, 196–197
    jurisdiction, 210–213, 214
    system in operation, 198–203
    traditional Indian law, 194–198
    tribal customs, 194–195
Civil liberties, 217–230. *See also*
    Indian Civil Rights Act of 1968
    citizenship, 217–222, 246
    criminal rights, 226–230
    voting rights, 222–226
Cohen, Felix S., ix–x, xii, 2, 5–6,
    99

Coke Act, 9
Collier, John, 13, 14, 16, 99
Colliflower, Madeline, 131
Colville Indians, 20, 100–101, 207,
    208
Comity, 119
Commerce Clause, 26, 34, 39, 41
Confrontation and cross-examina-
    tion, 129, 130, 229
Congressional powers, 34, 39–45
Conquering Bear, 48
Constitutions, 82, 87, 98–99, 101,
    116
Corn Tassel, 28
Corps of Engineers, 44
Coulter, Robert, 116–118
Counsel, right to, 129, 130, 227,
    229, 230
Court of Indian Offenses (CFR), 95,
    96, 99, 113–116, 118
Crazy Horse, 168
Creek Confederacy, 85–87, 91
Creek Indians, 27, 59, 83, 85–87,
    90, 91, 97
Criminal law, 161
    Assimilative Crimes Act, 173–
        174, 177, 179, 180, 181
    cross-deputization, 187–188
    extradition, 188, 190, 192
    federal statutes, 162–182
    fresh pursuit, 187–188, 192
    General Crimes Act, 166–168,
        174, 177, 179, 180, 181
    implied consent, 189, 192
    jurisdiction, 178–182
    lesser included offenses doctrine,
        172, 227–228
    Major Crimes Act, 11, 41, 92,
        116, 145, 168–173, 177, 179,
        180, 227–229
Crockett, J. Allen, 225
Cross-deputization, 187–188
Crow Dog, 11, 168–170
Cruel and unusual punishment,
    129, 130, 229

Dancing Bear Creek, Treaty of, 7
Dawes, Henry, 9

Dawes Act. *See* General Allotment Act
Declaration of Independence, 81
Dekanawideh, 88
Delaware Indians, 3, 36, 37
Democratic Party, 17
Dinebeiin a Nahiilna be Agaditahe, 152. *See also* DNA
Discovery and conquest, theory of, 2–6
Divorce, 118, 196, 197, 211, 212
DNA, 132, 152–153, 158
Domestic dependent nations, 30, 33, 198, 204, 233, 244
Domestic law, 196–197
Domicile, 212
Doomsday Book, 17
Double jeopardy, 129, 228, 229
Driver, Harold, 83
Due Process Clause, 129, 130, 229
Duvall, Gabriel, 31

Eaton, John H., 29
Economic Opportunity Act, 22
Education, 19, 22, 231, 233, 240–244. *See also* Indian boarding schools
Eisenhower, Dwight D., 35, 36, 102, 103
Equal Protection Clause, 129, 130, 226, 243
Ervin, Sam, 127–128
Establishment Clause, 130, 230, 233, 239
Execution of judgment, 215
Extradition, 188, 190, 192

Federal Bureau of Investigation (FBI), 183, 184, 185–186, 192
Federal preemption, 54, 205–208
Fiduciary duty, 33
Fifteenth Amendment, 222, 225
First Amendment, 129, 230, 231, 232
Fishing rights, 47–49
Five Civilized Tribes, 42, 66, 73, 86, 90, 91, 92, 126, 140, 218, 219, 220

Five Nations, 88
Food stamps, 245
Fourteenth Amendment, 129, 219, 220, 222
Fourth International Russell Tribunal, 159
Ford Foundation, 156
Fort Berthold Reservation, 76, 100
Fort Laramie, Treaty of, 48
Franklin, Benjamin, 82
Free Exercise Clause, 129, 230, 231, 232, 233, 234
French and Indian War, 59
Fresh pursuit, 187–188, 192
Full Faith and Credit, 119–120, 213

Gayaneshagowa, 82. *See also* Great Binding Law of the Five Nations
General Allotment Act, 9, 10, 69, 72, 73, 92, 220–221
General assistance programs, 245
General Crimes Act, 166–168, 174, 177, 179, 180, 181
Ghent, Treaty of, 63
Ghost dance, 231, 232
Gilmer, George G., 28, 29
Governmental services, 239
education, 240–244
social services, 244–246
Grand jury, 127, 130
Grand Ronde Reservation, 18
Grant, Ulysses S., 36
Great Binding Law of the Five Nations, 82, 87, 88
Great Society, 22, 143
Greenberg, Jack, 156
Greenville, Treaty of, 61
Gros Ventre Indians, 100
Gross, Michael, 158
Guardianship theory, 37–38, 40, 41–42, 171, 224

Habeas corpus, writ of, 130, 132
Harrison, William Henry, 17
Hayes-Tilden affair, 8
Hiawatha, 88
Hitchcock, Ethan A., 43

Hoover Commission, 16
Hopewell, Treaty of, 61
Hopi Indians, 83
House Concurrent Resolution 108, 18, 19, 20
House of Kings, 90
House of Warriors, 90

Ickes, Harold, 99
Imala labotskalgi, 86
Imala lakalgi, 86
Impact aid programs, 19
Implied consent, 189, 192
Indian advocates, 149
Indian agents, 96, 97–98
Indian Bill of Rights. *See* Indian Civil Rights Act of 1968
Indian boarding schools, 11, 12, 74, 241, 243
Indian chiefs, 83, 87, 97, 98
Indian Child Welfare Act, xii, 212, 213
Indian citizenship, 10, 11, 217–222, 246
Indian Citizenship Act of 1924, 221, 222
Indian Civil Rights Act of 1968 (ICRA), xii, 22, 53, 126–130, 132–134, 171, 174–175, 177, 181, 226, 229–230, 233
    provisions, 128–130
    tribal courts, 125–130
Indian Claims Commission, 6, 147
Indian Claims Commission Act, 142
Indian Commerce Clause, 41
Indian council. *See* Tribal council
Indian Country, 58
    Act of January 17, 1800, 62–63
    Act of March 3, 1817, 63–64
    criminal jurisdiction, 65–66, 75
    defined by courts, 71
    executive order reservations, 71
    General Allotment Act, 69, 72
    Indian Reorganization Act of 1934, 74
    Interior, Department of, 70, 74
    Public Law 280, 75–76

Trade and Intercourse Act of 1790, 61–62
Trade and Intercourse Act of 1834, 65–67, 71
Indian courts. *See* Tribal courts
Indian Education Act of 1972, 22. *See also* Education
Indian government. *See* Tribal government
Indian Health Service, 19, 133, 244, 246
Indian Intercourse Act of 1790, 165
Indian judges. *See* Tribal judges
Indian Law Resource Center, 159
Indian Law Support Center, 123, 149, 157
Indian police. *See* Tribal police
Indian Removal Act of 1830, 7, 28, 64–65, 91
Indian Reorganization Act of 1934 (IRA), 14–15, 24, 74, 92, 99–102, 115, 116, 131
Indian Rights Association, 156
Indian Self-Determination and Education Assistance Act of 1975, 23
Indian Service. *See* Bureau of Indian Affairs
Indians of Nevada, 74
Indian sovereignty. *See* Tribal sovereignty
Indian Territory Naturalization Act, 220
Indian title, 4, 26–27
Indian Tribal Councils Bill, 99
Institute of Government Research, 12
Interest groups, 155–160
Interior, Department of, 13, 14, 35, 70, 74, 183
Interior, secretary of, 153–155
Iowa Indians, 64
Iroquois Confederacy, 35, 58, 59, 82, 87, 88, 97
Iroquois Indians, 162, 164

Jackson, Andrew, 4, 6–7, 28, 33, 34
Jackson, Helen Hunt, 12

Jackson, Henry M., 20
Jefferson, Thomas, 6
Johnson, Lyndon B., 20, 22, 34
Johnson, William, 30, 31, 51
Johnson-O'Malley Act, 242
Joseph, Chief, 97
Judicial recruitment, 120–122
Jurisdiction, 209–210, 211–213, 214
Jury trial, 129, 130, 229
Justice, Department of, 35, 145, 146–148, 225

Kennedy, Edward, 22, 240
Kennedy, John F., 20
Klamath Indians, 18, 21, 77, 99

Lancaster, Treaty of, 58–59, 163
Law enforcement, 124–125, 182–192
Law Enforcement Assistance Administration (LEAA), 123
Legal guardianship, 224
Legal Services attorneys, 151–153, 157, 158
Legal Services Corporation, 123, 146, 156
Lesser included offenses doctrine, 172, 227–228
Locke, John, 81
Long-arm statutes, 215

McLean, John, 30,31
Major Crimes Act, 11, 41, 92, 116, 145, 168–173, 177, 179, 180, 227–229
Mandan Indians, 100
Manuelito, 114
Margold, Nathan, 13, 99
Marriage, 196
Marshall, John, 36, 125
  Cherokee Nation Cases, 4, 27–33, 45, 46, 51
  domestic dependent nations doctrine, 4, 30
  Indian title, 4, 26–27
  Johnson v. McIntosh, 26
Marshall, Thurgood, 134–135

Martinez, Julia, 133, 134
Mashpee Indians, 90
Means, Russell, 147, 186
Menominee Indians, 18, 64
Meriam, Lewis, 12
Meriam Report, 12, 13, 14, 99
Miami Confederacy, 61, 90
Miami Indians, 53, 218
Micco, 85, 86, 90
Micco apotka, 86
Miller, Samuel E., 41, 67
Mitchell, Theodore, 132, 153
Mohawk Indians, 60, 88, 159
Montesquieu, Charles de, 81
Morgan, Frank, 191
Mormon Church, 232
Myer, Dillon, 17

National American Indian Court Judges Association, 89, 108, 118, 123, 136, 182, 186, 188, 189, 191
National Association for the Advancement of Colored People (NAACP), 155, 156, 158, 160
National Congress of American Indians, 156
National Council of Churches, 16
National Indian Law Library, 158
National Lawyers Guild, 156
Native American Church, 232–233, 234–237
Native American Religious Advisory Board, 237
Native American Rights Fund (NARF), 105, 123, 149, 156, 237
Navajo Indians, 15, 54, 77, 121, 131–132, 144, 151–152, 158, 191, 232–234, 239
New Deal, 92, 99
New Echota, Treaty of, 33
New Frontier, 103
Nixon, Richard, 20, 22, 39
Non-Intercourse Act of 1790, 40–41

Office of Economic Opportunity, 143, 151

Office of Management and Budget, 35
Oglala Sioux Indians, 96, 117
Omaha Indians, 8
Oneida Indians, 88
One person, one vote, 226
Onondaga Indians, 88
Osage Indians, 73, 95
Ottowa Indians, 64
Ouray, Chief, 97

Paiute Indians, 18, 39, 82
Pala Indians, 106
Papago Indians, 153
Paris, Treaty of, 60
Parker, Quanah, 197
Parochial schools, 231
Peacemakers' Court, 113
"Persons under disability," 222
Peyote, 231, 232, 234–236
Phoenix Indian School, 74
Pima Indians, 98
Pottawatomi Indians, 64
Pratt, Richard Henry, 241
Preclearance, 225–226
Preemption. *See* Federal
    preemption
Presidential powers, 34–39, 40
    executive orders, 37
    treaty-making, 35–37
Price, Monroe, 223
Public Law 280, 18, 22, 53, 75–76,
    175–177, 178, 179, 203, 233
Pueblo Indians, 72, 83, 113, 128,
    133

Quakers, 155, 156
Quechan Indians, 107

Racial classifications, 228,
    238–239, 242
Rainbow Bridge, 239
Reagan, Ronald, xii, 24, 35
Reapportionment, 226
Red Cloud, 96, 97, 168
Red Lake Chippewa Band, 92–93
Register, George, 76
Rehnquist, William, 180, 181

Religious ceremonies, 231–239
Religious freedom, 230–239
Removal and relocation, 6–8
Reno Indian Colony, 74
Republican Party, 17
Reserved rights doctrine, 48, 49–50
Residency, 223, 224
Rincon Indians, 106
Rodiyaners, 88
Roosevelt, Franklin D., 13, 37, 99
Rosebud Sioux Indians, 76, 151

St. Clair, Arthur, 61
Salish and Kootenai Indians of
    Flathead Reservation, 100
Salt River Pima-Maricopa Indians,
    189
Santee Indians, 242
Search and seizure, unreasonable,
    129, 227, 229
Seaton, Fred, 20
Self-determination, 21–24
Self-Determination and Education
    Assistance Act of 1975,
    103–105
Self-incrimination, privilege
    against, 129, 227, 229
Seminole Indians, 5, 38, 90, 91, 190
Seneca Indians, 20, 88
Sentencing, 111–112
Sequoyah, 28
Service of process, 214–215
Shawnee Indians, 53
Shoshone Indians, 82
Siletz Reservation, 18
Sioux Indians, 43, 44, 45, 48, 82,
    115, 168
Sitting Bull, 168, 232
Six Nations, 88, 89, 159, 164–165
Sloan, Thomas, 140
Snyder Act, 242
Social services, 196, 244–246
Social welfare, 196
Solicitor (Interior), 106, 148
Solicitor General's Office, 146
Sovereign immunity, 203–209,
    214–215, 223
Spain, 2–3

Spotted Tail, Chief, 11, 168
State encroachment, 203–209
State taxation, 205–208
Stockbridge-Munsee Indians, 219
Story, Joseph, 31
Sun dance ritual, 231
Supreme Court, 34, 45–57

Taos Pueblo Indians, 39, 238
Tastanagalgi, 86
Tax exemption, 223, 225, 240, 245,
    246
Termination policy, 15–21,
    102–103
Thlocco, 86, 90
Thompson, Smith, 31, 126
Three Affiliated Tribes of Fort
    Berthold, 76, 100
Trade and Intercourse Act of 1790,
    61–62
Trade and Intercourse Act of 1834,
    65–67, 71, 166
Trail of Tears, 7, 33
Treaty abrogation, 43–44
Treaty-making, 2–4, 35–37
Trial, speedy and public, 129, 130,
    229
Tribal council, xi, 94, 96
Tribal courts, 110, 149
    attorneys, role of, 148
    civil jurisdiction, 210–211
    Court of Indian Offenses, 95, 96,
        99, 113–116, 118
    federal review of decisions,
        131–136
    Indian advocates, 149
    modern tribal courts, 116–120
    strengths, 136–137
    traditional courts, 111–112
    weaknesses, 137–138
Tribal government, xi, 80
    categories, 108–109
    Cheyenne model, 83–84
    continuing problems, 107–108
    Creek model, 85–86
    Indian Reorganization Act, 99
    Iroquois model, 88–89
    modern, 99–105

power to tax, 55–57
precontact days, 81
theocratic form, 83
traditional, 82–89
transitional, 89–99
Tribal judges, 120–125, 150
    decision-making, 122
    problems confronting, 123–125
    qualifications, 121–123
    recruitment, 121
    role, 118–119
    traditional, 112–113
Tribal police, 114, 184
Tribal self-government. *See* tribal
    sovereignty
Tribal sovereignty, x, 3, 53–57, 168,
    204–208, 209, 214–215. *See
    also* "Backdrop" doctrine; Fed-
    eral preemption; Williams
    doctrine

Uniform Criminal Extradition Act,
    190
United Nations, 159
U.S. Attorney's Office, 145–148,
    183–184, 186, 192, 227
Ute Mountain Ute Indians, 5

Vitoria, Francisco de, 3, 4
Voting rights, 222–226
Voting Rights Act of 1965, 225–226
Voting Rights Act of 1975, 226

Wampanoag Indians, 90
War, Department of, 40
Warm Springs Indians, 39
War of 1812, 63
Warren, Earl, 126
Washington, George, 35
Watkins, Arthur V., 18
Wayne, Anthony, 61
Weas Indians, 53
Wheeler-Howard Act. *See* Indian
    Reorganization Act of 1934
White, Byron R., 207
White, Edward D., 44
White Mountain Apache Indians,
    206

White Roots of Peace, 87
Wilkinson, Charles F., 20
Williams doctrine, 54, 204–206, 208–212
Winnebago Indians, 46, 64
Worcester, Samuel, 29, 33, 156
Work, Hubert, 12
Wounded Knee, 54, 147, 185, 232
Wovoka, 232
Wyandot Indians, 164, 219

Yakima Indians, 39, 48–49, 75
Yankton Sioux Indians, 73, 95, 96

Zimmerman, William, 16
Zuni Plan, 104
Zuni Pueblo Indians, 104